Frommer's®

PORTABLE
New Orleans

7th Edition

by Mary Herczog

SO-AZS-752

Here's what critics say about Frommer's:

"Amazingly easy to use. Very portable, very complete."

—*Booklist*

"Detailed, accurate, and easy-to-read information for all price ranges."

—*Glamour Magazine*

WILEY
Wiley Publishing, Inc.

Published by:

WILEY PUBLISHING, INC.
111 River St.
Hoboken, NJ 07030-5744

ISBN-13: 978-0-471-74890-8
ISBN-10: 0-471-74890-0

Editor: Cate Latting
Production Editor: Eric T. Schroeder
Photo Editor: Richard Fox
Cartographer: Andrew Murphy
Production by Wiley Indianapolis Composition Services

For information on our other products and services or to obtain technical support, please contact our Customer Care Department within the U.S. at 800/762-2974, outside the U.S. at 317/572-3993 or fax 317/572-4002.

Wiley also publishes its books in a variety of electronic formats. Some content that appears in print may not be available in electronic formats.

Manufactured in the United States of America

5   4   3   2   1

Contents

List of Maps

ACKNOWLEDGMENTS

My deep appreciation and enormous thanks to Cate Latting and to Frommer's for their thoughtful solutions and help during this difficult and complicated time. Thank you to Jill, Charles, Rob, Helene, and Michael for aid and sustenance. If the house could speak, it would say thank you for high ground and Henry Hahn. Thank you to the Fat Pack (Diana, Robin, Chuck, Wesly, Nettie, Dave, John, Fiona) for spiritual and caloric support. Be it during feast or flood, the North Rendon All-Stars are perfect. There is no one would I rather rip out sodden drywall with than Steve Hochman.

ABOUT THE AUTHOR

Some of **Mary Herczog**'s work, many of her dearest friends, and all of her heart is in New Orleans. She is honored to be the long-time author of *Frommer's New Orleans*. Her other titles include *Frommer's Las Vegas, Los Angeles for Dummies, Las Vegas for Dummies, and California for Dummies.* When she's not writing for Frommer's she works in the film industry. She and her husband co-own a house with some friends in Bayou St. John, and now they know something about mold eradication and roof repair.

AN INVITATION TO THE READER

In researching this book, we discovered many wonderful places—hotels, restaurants, shops, and more. We're sure you'll find others. Please tell us about them, so we can share the information with your fellow travelers in upcoming editions. If you were disappointed with a recommendation, we'd love to know that, too. Please write to:

Frommer's Portable New Orleans, 7th Edition

Wiley Publishing, Inc. • 111 River St. • Hoboken, NJ 07030-5744

AN ADDITIONAL NOTE

FROMMER'S STAR RATINGS, ICONS & ABBREVIATIONS

Every hotel, restaurant, and attraction listing in this guide has been ranked for quality, value, service, amenities, and special features using a **star-rating system.** In country, state, and regional guides, we also rate towns and regions to help you narrow down your choices and budget your time accordingly. Hotels and restaurants are rated on a scale of zero (recommended) to three stars (exceptional). Attractions, shopping, nightlife, towns, and regions are rated according to the following scale: zero stars (recommended), one star (highly recommended), two stars (very highly recommended), and three stars (must-see).

In addition to the star-rating system, we also use **seven feature icons** that point you to the great deals, in-the-know advice, and unique experiences that separate travelers from tourists. Throughout the book, look for:

Finds	Special finds—those places only insiders know about
Fun Fact	Fun facts—details that make travelers more informed and their trips more fun
Kids	Best bets for kids and advice for the whole family
Moments	Special moments—those experiences that memories are made of
Overrated	Places or experiences not worth your time or money
Tips	Insider tips—great ways to save time and money
Value	Great values—where to get the best deals

The following **abbreviations** are used for credit cards:

AE	American Express	DISC	Discover	V	Visa
DC	Diners Club	MC	MasterCard		

FROMMERS.COM

Now that you have the guidebook to a great trip, visit our website at **www.frommers.com** for travel information on more than 3,000 destinations. With features updated regularly, we give you instant access to the most current trip-planning information available. At Frommers.com, you'll also find the best prices on airfares, accommodations, and car rentals—and you can even book travel online through our travel booking partners. At Frommers.com, you'll also find the following:

- Online updates to our most popular guidebooks
- Vacation sweepstakes and contest giveaways
- Newsletter highlighting the hottest travel trends
- Online travel message boards with featured travel discussions

Introduction

One of the pleasures of New Orleans used to be that the city changed very slowly, if at all. This was a city that objected strenuously when a certain decades-old restaurant dared to switch from hand-chipped ice to machine made. This was a city where 10 years could go by between your visits, but your favorite bookstore would still be in business when you came back, and your favorite bookseller would still be behind the counter, possibly with a volume he had been holding for you against the day you finally returned.

But on August 29, 2005, New Orleans changed forever. In the wake of Hurricane Katrina, which was not quite as strong as nor the direct hit originally predicted, at least three of the levees designed to keep the below-sea-level city safe from the waters of Lake Pontchartrain either broke or were breeched. Eighty percent of one of the most historic and culturally rich cities in America was underwater. The water remained for weeks, months in certain places, and by the time it was gone, the landscape of New Orleans was permanently altered.

Throughout that time, and as the floodwater was pumped out, there were impossible images. Like those of the ravaged Lower 9th Ward, where house after house was reduced to piles of random lumber, unrecognizable as anything much less someone's home; or others of houses, once lined up in an orderly row, now smashed at various angles into each other, sometimes, incredibly, sitting on top of each other. Vacant lots had materialized where homes had literally been blown away. Sometimes, concrete pilings were left behind, making the lot look like a cemetery, which it was, in a sense. Sometimes just the front steps were left, leading to nowhere, a metaphor that doesn't bear explication. Across town, in Lakeview, homes appeared fine from the outside, but inside, furniture lay about in careless heaps, like the contents of a snow globe shaken by a giant, the consequence of floating in 10 feet or more of water for weeks on end. Everything, from stuffed toys to pianos to pictures on the wall was and is covered in thick fuzzy mold—family homes, rotten to the core. And adding to the brokenness of it all was the color—verdant, tropical New Orleans turned brown, gray, and dusty. The vegetation itself had drowned.

It takes a long time to come back from something like this. But New Orleans was given two gifts. The first was that the narrow band of land that did not flood at all included the most historic and best-loved areas, the French Quarter and the part of Uptown that included the Garden District. New Orleans is considerably more than those much-photographed neighborhoods, make no mistake, but what the average visitor imagines when he or she thinks of New Orleans remains much as it ever did.

The second is the spirit of the people of New Orleans. Within weeks of the catastrophe, intrepid remaining citizens threw a jazz funeral, complete with an exalting, rejuvenating second line, for the disaster and its victims. Then they got their hands down in the muck, and began to clean. Restaurants and clubs reopened even when it meant grilling on the sidewalk and keeping the beer cold with a generator. Plans were made for Mardi Gras, and pleas were made for the return of Jazz Fest, because this is a city that loves its parties, and what's a party for except to celebrate life and survival? And sure enough, Mardi Gras parades rolled, and many contained floats openly mocking the terrible thing that had happened just 6 months before, a thumbing of the nose at events that may have left the city broken, but not bowed.

Today, recovery is ongoing, and the process goes slowly. All manner of important things are, maddeningly, no closer to being resolved than in the early days after the storm, while the fate of many citizens and establishments remains in question. Which prompts a question of your own, probably: Should you go?

Oh, yes.

Go, because everything in life is fragile and precarious, and we can take nothing for granted, and some day, it really will all be gone. Go, because it's not gone, not at all. Go, because the things you wanted—the beautiful architecture, the majestic oaks, the river wind, the quality of light that gives even the most mundane just a little bit magic—all remain. Go, because people are there, and as long as they are, there will be music, and food, and it will be some of the best of your life. Go, because perhaps you've wanted to help in any way you can, and now the best way you can is to help a historic city regain its economic feet. Go, because every brick in the French Quarter has a story to tell, and so does the damaged ground of the 9th Ward, and you should bear witness. Go, because there is much to celebrate, and this is still the best place there is to do so.

"I want to be in that number," goes the song. I do indeed. I hope you do, too.

Planning Your Trip to New Orleans

This chapter will give you the information to make informed plans about your New Orleans trip and help point you toward some additional resources.

1 Visitor Information

New Orleans is a city in flux and is likely to remain that way for a long time. In theory, everything will only get better as time passes, but in reality, all manner of things can change, especially if the economy does not improve. Accordingly, for the most recent information, be it restaurant status, museum operating hours, new and accurate phone numbers, and pretty much just about anything you can think of, it's worth making phone calls or sending e-mails asking relevant questions in advance of your trip.

Even a seasoned traveler should consider writing or calling ahead to the **New Orleans Metropolitan Convention and Visitors Bureau,** 2020 St. Charles Ave., New Orleans, LA 70130 (© **800/ 672-6124** or 504/566-5011; **www.neworleanscvb.com**). The staff is extremely friendly and helpful, and you should be able to get any information you can't find in this book from them. Their site offers an "Open for Business" link that lists many local businesses, including hotels, restaurants, attractions, and more, and gives a post-storm status for each. For each establishment, click on "More Information" and then "Rebuilding Status" to learn about the damage (or lack thereof) and what, if anything, remains to be done and when the business in question will reopen, if it has not already.

For further information, **www.nola.com**, a terrific resource linked to the online edition of the *Times-Picayune* (which operates it, though it is more than just the newspaper), includes restaurant listings, entertainment guides, much Katrina dialogue, the 24-hour Bourbocam (trained on the action of New Orleans's most active street), and more. Also, local food writer Tom Fitzmorris is keeping an exhaustive list of reopened restaurants at www.nomenu.com/ RestaurantsOpen.html.

Another source of information is the **New Orleans Multicultural Tourism Network,** 2020 St. Charles Ave., New Orleans, LA 70130 (© **800/725-5652** or 504/523-5652; www.soulofneworleans. com); you may be particularly interested in their self-directed tours of African-American landmarks.

2 Money

Not surprisingly, prices are flopping every which way these days as local businesses try to get themselves righted again. Even once things stabilize, expect prices for accommodations to skyrocket during major events and festivals (see "Planning a Visit for Mardi Gras or Jazz Fest," later in this chapter). New Orleans generally is quite popular in the fall during what was the convention season, as it ideally will become again. The heat and humidity of the summer months (July–Aug) keep tourism in the city to its yearly low, so if the weather doesn't bother you, you can find some incredible hotel bargains, though even at other times these days, if a hotel is feeling a paucity of tourists, you can get some good deals.

ATMs   Almost all New Orleans ATMs are linked to a national network that most likely includes your bank at home. **Cirrus** (© **800/ 424-7787;** www.mastercard.com) and **PLUS** (© **800/843-7587;** www.visa.com) are the two most popular networks.

Some centrally located ATMs in New Orleans are at the **First National Bank of Commerce,** 240 Royal St.; **Hibernia National Bank,** 701 Poydras St.; and **Whitney National Bank,** 228 St. Charles Ave. There are now ATMs all over the French Quarter, a big change from some years ago when there was just one.

Expect to pay a $3 or more service charge each time you withdraw money from an ATM in addition to what your home bank charges.

3 When to Go

This used to be a pretty easy answer to give; we'd say, with the possible exception of July and August (unless you happen to thrive on heat and humidity), just about any time is the right time to go to New Orleans. Now? We still say that—if we haven't made it clear by now, the city needs you, so go, already—though we add a whole lot of qualifiers having to do with ongoing problems regarding basic infrastructure issues, many of which should be resolved by the time you read this.

But let's pretend the main problems are behind the city, even if years of reconstruction are ahead of it, and the old guidelines are back in place. Mardi Gras is, of course, the time of year when it's hardest to get a hotel room, but it can also be difficult during the various music festivals throughout the year, especially during Jazz Fest (see "Planning a Visit for Mardi Gras or Jazz Fest," later in this chapter). It's important to know what's going on when; the city's landscape can change dramatically depending on what festival or convention is happening, and prices can also reflect that. The best time of year, in our opinion, is December, before and during Christmas. The town is gussied up with decorations, there are all kinds of seasonal special events, the weather is nice—but for some reason, tourists become scarce. Hotels, eager to lure any business, lower their rates dramatically, and most restaurants are so empty that you can walk in just about anywhere without a reservation. Take advantage of it.

THE WEATHER

The average mean temperature in New Orleans is an inviting 70°F (21°C), but it can drop or rise considerably in a single day. (We've experienced 40°F/4°C and rain one day, 80°F/27°C and humidity the next.) Conditions depend primarily on two things: whether it rains and whether there is direct sunlight or cloud cover. Rain can provide slight and temporary relief on a hot day; for the most part, it hits in sudden (and sometimes dramatically heavy) showers, which disappear as quickly as they arrived. Anytime the sun shines unimpeded, it gets much warmer. The region's high humidity can make even mild warms and colds feel intense. Still, the city's semitropical climate is part of its appeal—a slight bit of moistness makes the air come sensually alive.

It will be pleasant at almost any time of year except July and August, which can be exceptionally hot and muggy (though not necessarily; you might well have perfectly lovely, balmy weather). If you do come during those months, you'll quickly learn to follow the natives' example, staying out of the noonday sun and ducking from one air-conditioned building to another. Winter is very mild by American standards but is punctuated by an occasional cold snap, when the mercury can drop below the freezing point.

In the dead of summer, T-shirts and shorts are absolutely acceptable everywhere except the finest restaurants. In the spring and fall, something a little warmer is in order; in the winter, you should plan to carry a lightweight coat or jacket. Umbrellas and cheap rain jackets are available everywhere for those tourists who inevitably get caught in a sudden, unexpected downpour.

And in case you were wondering, hurricane season is from June 1 to November 1.

New Orleans Average Temperatures & Rainfall

	Jan	Feb	Mar	Apr	May	June	July	Aug	Sept	Oct	Nov	Dec
High (°F)	61	64	71	78	84	89	90	90	87	80	71	64
High (°C)	16	18	22	26	29	32	32	32	31	27	22	18
Low (°F)	44	47	54	60	67	73	74	74	71	61	54	47
Low (°C)	7	8	12	16	19	23	23	23	22	16	12	8
Days of Rainfall	10	9	9	7	8	10	15	13	10	5	7	10

NEW ORLEANS CALENDAR OF EVENTS

For more information on **Mardi Gras, Jazz Fest,** and other major area events, see below. For general information, contact the **New Orleans Metropolitan Convention and Visitors Bureau,** 2020 St. Charles Ave., New Orleans, LA 70130 (© **800/672-6124** or 504/566-5011; www.neworleanscvb.com).

January

Nokia Sugar Bowl Classic. First held in 1934, this is New Orleans's oldest yearly sporting occasion, and it will return to the city in 2007, after a massive renovation of the Superdome. The football game is the main event, but there are also tennis, swimming, basketball, sailing, running, and flag-football competitions. Fans tend to be really loud, really boisterous, and everywhere during the festivities. For information, contact Nokia Sugar Bowl, 1500 Sugar Bowl Dr., New Orleans, LA 70112 (© **404/221-2445;** www.nokiasugarbowl.com). January 2.

February

Lundi Gras. An old tradition that has been revived in the last decade or so. Celebrations take place at Spanish Plaza. It's free, it's outdoors, and it features music (including a jazz competition) and the arrival of Rex at 6pm, marking the beginning of Mardi Gras. For more information, contact New Orleans Riverwalk Marketplace, 1 Poydras St., New Orleans, LA 70130 (© **504/522-1555**). Monday before Mardi Gras (Feb 19, 2007).

Mardi Gras. The culmination of the 2-month-long carnival season, Mardi Gras is the big annual blowout, a citywide party that takes place on Fat Tuesday (the last day before Lent in the Christian calendar). The entire city stops working (sometimes days in advance!) and starts partying in the early morning, and the streets are taken over by some overwhelming parades—which, these days, go through the Central Business District (CBD) instead of the French Quarter. Day before Ash Wednesday (in 2007, it'll be Feb 20). See later in this chapter for more details.

March

St. Patrick's Day Parades. There are two: One takes place in the French Quarter beginning at Molly's at the Market (1107 Decatur St.), and the other goes through the Irish Channel neighborhood following a route that begins at Jackson Avenue and Magazine Street, goes over to St. Charles Avenue, turns uptown to Louisiana Avenue, and returns to Jackson Avenue. The parades have the flavor of Mardi Gras, but instead of beads, watchers are pelted with cabbages, carrots, and other veggies. For information on the French Quarter parade, call **Molly's at the Market** (© **504/525-5169**). The Irish Channel parade takes place in early March.

Black Heritage Festival. Honors the various African-American cultural contributions to New Orleans. Write or call the Black Heritage Foundation, 4535 S. Prieur St., New Orleans, LA 70125 (© **504/827-0112**) for more info. March 15 to March 16.

St. Joseph's Day Parade. In addition to the parade, which takes place March 19, you may want to visit the altar devoted to St. Joseph at the American Italian Museum and Library, 537 S. Peters St. For more information, call © **504/522-7294.** March 17 to March 19.

Super Sunday. This is the annual Mardi Gras Indians showdown, which takes place on the Sunday following St. Joseph's Day.

Tennessee Williams New Orleans Literary Festival. A 5-day series celebrating New Orleans's rich literary heritage, it includes theatrical performances, readings, discussion panels, master classes, musical events, and literary walking tours dedicated to the playwright. By the way, the focus is not confined to Tennessee Williams. Events take place at venues throughout the city. For info, call © **504/581-1144** or go to **www.tennesseewilliams. net**. Late March.

Spring Fiesta. The fiesta, which begins with the crowning of the Spring Fiesta queen, is more than half a century old and takes place throughout the city—from the Garden District to the French Quarter to Uptown and beyond. Historical and architectural tours of many of the city's private homes, courtyards, and plantation homes are offered in conjunction with the 5-day event. For the schedule, call the Spring Fiesta Association (© **504/581-1367**) or go to **www.springfiesta.com**. Last two weekends in March or early April.

April

The French Quarter Festival. For hard-core jazz fans, this is rapidly becoming an alternative to Jazz Fest, where actual jazz is becoming less and less prominent. It kicks off with a parade down Bourbon Street. Among other things, you can join people dancing in the streets, learn the history of jazz, visit historic homes, and take a ride on a riverboat. Many local restaurants set up booths in Jackson Square, so the eating is exceptionally good. Events are held all over the French Quarter. Call or write French Quarter Festivals, 400 N. Peters St., Suite 205, New Orleans, LA 70130 (© **504/522-5730**; www.frenchquarterfestivals.org). Second to last weekend in April.

The New Orleans Jazz & Heritage Festival (Jazz Fest). A 10-day event that draws musicians, music fans, cooks, and craftspeople to celebrate music and life, Jazz Fest rivals Mardi Gras in popularity. Lodgings in the city tend to sell out up to a year ahead, so book early. Events take place at the Fair Grounds Race Course and various venues throughout the city. For information, call or write the **New Orleans Jazz and Heritage Festival,** 1205 N. Rampart St., New Orleans, LA 70116 (© **504/522-4786**; www.nojazzfest.com). Usually held the last weekend in April and first weekend in May. Look for more information below.

The Crescent City Classic. This 10km (6-mile) road race, from Jackson Square to Audubon Park, brings an international field of top runners to the city. For more info, call or write the Classic, P.O. Box 13587, New Orleans, LA 70185 (© **504/861-8686**; www.ccc10k.com). Saturday before Easter.

May

Greek Festival. Three days of Greek folk dancing, specialty foods, crafts, and music at the Holy Trinity Cathedral's Hellenic Cultural Center. For more information, call or write Holy Trinity Cathedral, 1200 Robert E. Lee Blvd., New Orleans, LA 70122 (© **504/282-0259**; www.greekfestnola.com). Last weekend of May.

June

International Arts Festival. This 3-day gathering of calypso, reggae, and soca (a blend of soul and calypso) musicians is held in City Park and includes a heady helping of ethnic foods and arts and crafts. For more information, call or write Ernest Kelly,

P.O. Box 6156, New Orleans, LA 70174 (© **888/767-1317** or 504/367-1313). Second week of June.

July

Go Fourth on the River. The annual Fourth of July celebration begins in the morning at the riverfront and continues into the night, culminating into a spectacular fireworks display. For more information, go to **www.go4thontheriver.com**. July 4th.

September

Southern Decadence. All over the French Quarter, thousands of folks—drag queens, mostly—follow a secret parade route, making sure to stop into many bars along the way. People travel from far and wide to be a part of the festivities. There is only an informal organization associated with the festival, and it's hard to get anyone on the phone. For information, try the website **www. southerndecadence.com** or contact *Ambush* magazine (© **800/ 876-1484** or 504/522-8047). Labor Day weekend.

Festivals Acadiens. This is a series of happenings that celebrate Cajun music, food, crafts, and culture in and near Lafayette, Louisiana. (Most of the events are in Lafayette.) For more information, contact the **Lafayette Convention & Visitors Commission,** P.O. Box 52066, Lafayette, LA 70505 (© **800/346-1958** in the U.S., 800/543-5340 in Canada, or 337/232-3737; www.lafayettetravel.com). Third week of September.

Swamp Festival. Sponsored by the Audubon Institute, the Swamp Festival features long days of live swamp music performances (lots of good zydeco here) as well as hands-on contact with Louisiana swamp animals. Admission to the festival is free with zoo admission. For information, call or write the Audubon Institute, 6500 Magazine St., New Orleans, LA 70118 (© **504/861-2537;** www.auduboninstitute.org). Last weekend in September and first weekend in October.

October

Art for Arts' Sake. The arts season begins with gallery openings throughout the city. Julia, Magazine, and Royal streets are where the action is. For more information, contact the Contemporary Arts Center, 900 Camp St., New Orleans, LA 70130 (© **504/ 528-3800;** www.cacno.org). Throughout the month.

Louisiana Jazz Awareness Month. The Louisiana Jazz Federation sponsors nightly concerts (some of which are free), television and radio specials, and lectures. For more information and a schedule, contact the Louisiana Music Commission (© **504/ 736-8605;** www.louisianamusic.org). All month.

Gumbo Festival. This festival showcases one of the region's signature dishes and celebrates Cajun culture to boot. It's 3 days of gumbo-related events (including the presentation of the royal court of King and Miss Creole Gumbo) plus many hours of Cajun music. The festival is held in Bridge City, on the outskirts of New Orleans. For more information, contact the Gumbo Festival, P.O. Box 9069, Bridge City, LA 70096 (© **504/436-4712**). October 9 to October 11.

New Orleans Film Festival. Canal Place Cinemas and other theaters throughout the city screen award-winning local and international films and host writers, actors, and directors over the course of a week. Admission prices range from $6.25 to $7.25. For dates, contact the New Orleans Film and Video Society, 843 Carondelet, New Orleans, LA 70130 (© **504/523-3818;** www.neworleansfilmfest.com). Mid-month.

Halloween. Rivaling Mardi Gras in terms of costumes, Halloween is certainly celebrated more grandly here than in any other American city. After all, New Orleans has a way with ghosts. Past events have included Boo-at-the-Zoo (Oct 30 and 31) for children, costume parties (including a Monster Bash at the Ernest N. Morial Convention Center), haunted houses (one of the best is run by the sheriff's department in City Park), the Anne Rice Vampire Lestat Extravaganza, and the Moonlight Witches Run. You can catch the ghoulish action all over the city—many museums get in on the fun with specially designed tours—but the French Quarter, as always, is the center of the Halloween-night universe. October 31.

November

Words & Music: A Literary Feast in New Orleans. A highly ambitious literary and music conference (originated in large part by the folks behind Faulkner House Books) offering 5 days worth of roundtable discussions with eminent authors (with varying connections to the city), original drama, poetry readings, master classes, plus great music and food. For authors seeking guidance and inspiration and for book lovers in general, call © **504/586-1609** or visit their website at **www.wordsandmusic.org** for exact dates. November 2 to November 6, 2006.

December

Christmas New Orleans Style. New Orleans loves to celebrate, so it should be no surprise that it does Christmas really well. The town is decorated to a fare-thee-well, there is an evening of candlelight caroling in Jackson Square, bonfires line the levees along River Road on Christmas Eve (to guide Papa Noel, his sled drawn by alligators, on his gift-delivering way), restaurants offer specially created multicourse Réveillon dinners, and hotels throughout the city offer "Papa Noel" rates. Why? Because despite all the fun and the generally nice (read: not hot and humid) weather, tourism goes *waaay* down at this time of year, and hotels are eager to lure you all in with cheaper rates. For information, contact French Quarter Festivals, 400 N. Peters St., Suite 205, New Orleans, LA 70130 (© **504/522-5730;** www.frenchquarterfestivals.org). All month.

Celebration in the Oaks. Lights and lighted figures, designed to illustrate holiday themes, bedeck sections of City Park. The return of this annual display of winter wonderment, open for driving and walking tours, was a sign of post-Katrina recovery much welcomed by weary residents in need of some holiday cheer in 2005. Driving tours are $12 per family car or van, and walking tours are $5 per person. For information, contact New Orleans City Park, 1 Palm Dr., New Orleans, LA 70124 (© **504/483-9415;** www.neworleanscitypark.com). Late November to early January.

New Year's Eve. The countdown takes place in Jackson Square and is one of the country's biggest and most reliable street parties. In the Southern equivalent of New York's Times Square, revelers watch a lighted ball drop from the top of Jackson Brewery. December 31.

4 Planning a Visit for Mardi Gras or Jazz Fest

MARDI GRAS

There was a great deal of speculation about whether New Orleans should cancel Mardi Gras in 2006, whether it was appropriate to hold the traditional massive celebration at such a somber time. The opposition failed to take into account several things; since it is a holiday separate from any observation of it, one can no more "cancel" Mardi Gras than one can cancel Christmas. Secondly, Mardi Gras celebrations—that is, parades and parties—are all privately funded and operated, so it's not really a city decision. And finally, for a town that tends to throw a party just because it's a day with a "Y" in it, the response to any suggestions that official celebrations should be postponed for a year was "Fine. Then we will load up little red wagons with a bunch of beads, and walk down the streets and do it ourselves."

It didn't come to that after all. Six months to the virtual day after Katrina, Zulu and Rex paraded as usual, along with the other krewes who march earlier. Some parades were a little shorter, but the beads and other throws were even more plentiful. The crowds may not have been as thick as usual (though conversely, Sunday night may have set a record for attendance) but that wasn't unexpected. More to the point, the spirit was immeasurably high, as New Orleanians and lovers of same alike turned out in their most glittery or satirical costumes, screaming for beads, engaging in their traditions, and generally exalting in a moment that not that long before seemed like it would never come again. They had survived, and they were filled with hope that their city would, too.

Forget sensational media reports that tend to focus on the sala-cious action. There is a lot more to Carnival than that, and it remains one of the most exciting times to visit. You can spend sev-eral days admiring and reveling in the traditions and never even ven-ture into the frat-party atmosphere of Bourbon Street.

THE SEASON   The date of Fat Tuesday is different each year, but Carnival season always starts on **Twelfth Night,** January 6, as much as 2 months before Mardi Gras. On that night, the Phunny Phorty Phellows kick off the season with a streetcar ride from Carrollton Avenue to Canal Street and back.

Two or three weeks before Mardi Gras, parades begin chugging through the streets with increasing frequency. There are plenty of par-odies, such as the parade of the **Mystick Krewe of Barkus.** Barkus is, as you might guess, a krewe for pets that parades through the Quar-ter (some of the dogs get quite gussied up) and is a total hoot.

If you want to experience Mardi Gras but don't want to face the full force of craziness, consider coming for the weekend 10 days before Fat Tuesday (the season officially begins the Fri of this week-end). You can count on 10 to 15 parades during the weekend by lesser-known krewes such as Cleopatra, Pontchartrain, Sparta, and Camelot. The crowds are more manageable during this time.

The following weekend there are another 15 parades—the biggies. Everything's bigger: The parades are bigger; the crowds are bigger; the city has succumbed to Carnival fever. After a day of screaming for beads, you'll probably find yourself heading somewhere to get a drink or three. The French Quarter will be the center of late-night revelry; all of the larger bars will be packed. The last parade each day (on both weekends) usually ends around 9:30pm or later.

LUNDI GRAS   In the 19th century, Rex's **King of Carnival** arrived downtown from the Mississippi River on this night, the Monday before Fat Tuesday. Over the years, the day gradually lost its special significance, becoming just another day of parades. In the 1980s, however, Rex revived Lundi Gras, the old tradition of arriving on the Mississippi.

These days, festivities at the riverfront begin in the afternoon with lots of drink and live music leading up to the king's arrival at around 6pm. Down the levee a few hundred feet, at Wolfenberg Park, Zulu has its own Lundi Gras celebration with the king arriving at around 5pm. In 1999, for the first time, King Zulu met up with Rex in an impressive ceremony. That night, the **Krewe of Orpheus** holds their parade. It's one of the biggest and most popular parades, thanks to the generosity of the krewe's throws. It holds fast to old Mardi Gras traditions, including floats designed by master float creator Henri Schindler. For Mardi Gras 2000, venerable Proteus returned to parading, right before Orpheus.

Because Lent begins the following night at midnight, Monday is the final dusk-to-dawn night of Mardi Gras. A good portion of the city forgoes sleep so as not to waste the occasion—which only adds to the craziness.

MARDI GRAS The day begins early, starting with the two biggest parades, **Zulu** and **Rex,** which run back to back. Zulu starts near the Central Business District (CBD) at 8:30am; Rex starts Uptown at 10am. Generally, the best place to watch parades on St. Charles Avenue is between Napoleon and Jackson avenues, where the crowds are somewhat smaller and consist mostly of local families and college students.

It will be early afternoon when Rex spills into the CBD. Nearby at about this time, you can find some of the most elusive New Orleans figures, the **Mardi Gras Indians.** The "tribes" of New Orleans are small communities of African Americans and black Creoles (some of whom have Native American ancestors), mostly from the inner city. Their elaborate (and that's an understatement) beaded and feathered costumes, rivaling Bob Mackie Vegas headdresses in outrageousness and size, are entirely made by hand.

After the parades, the action picks up in the Quarter. En route, you'll see that Mardi Gras is still very much a family tradition, with whole families dressing up in similar costumes. Marvel at how an entire city has shut down so that every citizen can join in the celebrations. Some people don't bother hitting the streets; instead, they hang out on their balconies watching the action below or have barbecues in their courtyards. If you are lucky and seem like the right sort, you might well get invited in.

In the Quarter, the frat-party action is largely confined to Bourbon Street. The more interesting activity is in the lower Quarter and the Frenchmen section of the Faubourg Marigny (just east of the Quarter), where the artists and gay community really know how to celebrate. The costumes are elaborate works of art. Although the people may be (okay, probably *will* be) drunk, they are boisterous and enthusiastic, not (for the most part) obnoxious.

PLANNING A VISIT DURING MARDI GRAS

LODGING   You can't just drop in on Mardi Gras. If you do, you may find yourself sleeping in Jackson Square or on a sidewalk somewhere. Accommodations in the city and the nearby suburbs are booked solid, *so make your plans well ahead and book a room as early as possible.* Many people plan a year or more in advance. Prices are usually much higher during Mardi Gras, and most hotels and guesthouses impose minimum-stay requirements.

CLOTHING   As with anything in New Orleans, you must join in if you want to have the best time. Simply being a spectator is not enough. And that means a **costume** and **mask.** Once you are masked and dressed up, you are automatically part of it all. (Tellingly, the Bourbon St. participants usually do not wear costumes.) As far as costumes go, you need not do anything fancy. If you've come unprepared, several shops in town specialize in Mardi Gras costumes and masks. Or just don an old suit and a cheap Halloween mask.

DINING   If you want to eat at a restaurant during Mardi Gras, make reservations as early as possible. And pay very close attention to **parade routes,** because if there is one between you and your restaurant, you may not be able to cross the street, and you can kiss your dinner goodbye. This might work to your advantage; often restaurants have a high no-show rate during Mardi Gras for this reason, and so a well-timed drop-in may work.

PARKING   Even though the huge crowds everywhere add to the general merriment, they also grind traffic to a halt all over town. So our admonition against renting a car is even stronger during Mardi Gras. *Don't drive.* Instead, relax and take a cab or walk. Remember, the fun is everywhere, so you don't really have to go anywhere. Parking along any parade route is not allowed 2 hours before and 2 hours after the parade. In addition, although you'll see people leaving their cars on the "neutral ground" (the median strip), it's illegal to park there, and chances are good that you'll be towed. Traffic in New Orleans is never worse than *in the hour after a parade.*

> ⸿ *Tips* **For More Information . . .**
>
> You'll enjoy Mardi Gras more if you've done a little home-work before your trip. You'll want to get your hands on the latest edition of *Arthur Hardy's Mardi Gras Guide.* Your best bet is to contact the magazine directly (℡ **504/838-6111;** www.mardigrasneworleans.com/arthur). This invaluable guide is sold all over town and is full of history, tips, and maps of the parade routes.
>
> Also contact the **New Orleans Metropolitan Convention and Visitors Bureau,** 2020 St. Charles Ave., New Orleans, LA 70130 (℡ **800/672-6124** or 504/566-5011), and ask for current Mardi Gras information.

SAFETY   Many, many cops are out, making the walk from uptown to downtown safer than at other times of year, but, not sur-prisingly, the streets of New Orleans are a haven for pickpockets during Mardi Gras. Take precautions.

CAJUN MARDI GRAS

Mardi Gras in New Orleans sounds like too much for you, no mat-ter how low-key you keep it? Consider driving out to Cajun coun-try, where Mardi Gras traditions are just as strong but considerably more, errr, wholesome. **Lafayette,** the capital of French Acadiana, celebrates Carnival in a different manner, one that reflects the Cajun heritage and spirit. Three full days of activities lead up to Cajun Mardi Gras, making it second in size only to New Orleans's cele-bration. There's one *big* difference, though: The Cajuns open their final pageant and ball to the general public. Don your formal wear and join right in!

MASKED MEN AND A BIG GUMBO   In the Cajun country-side that surrounds Lafayette, there's yet another form of Mardi Gras celebration, one tied to the rural lifestyle. Cajuns firmly believe in sharing, so you're welcome to come along. The celebration goes like this: Bands of masked men dressed in raggedy patchwork cos-tumes (unlike the New Orleans costumes, which are heavy on glit-ter and shine) and peaked hats known as *capichons* set off on Mardi Gras morning on horseback, led by their *capitaine.* They ride from farm to farm, asking at each, *"Voulez-vous reçevoir le Mardi Gras?"* ("Will you receive the Mardi Gras?") and dismounting as the invari-able *"Oui"* comes in reply. Each farmyard then becomes a miniature festival as the revelers *faire le macaque* ("make monkeyshines") with song and dance, much drinking of beer, and other antics loosely labeled "entertainment." As payment for their show, they demand, and get, "a fat little chicken to make a big gumbo" (or sometimes a bag of rice or other ingredients).

When each band has visited its allotted farmyards, they all head back to town where there is dancing in the streets, rowdy card games, storytelling, and the like until the wee hours, and you can be sure that all those fat little chickens go into the *"gumbo gros"* pot to make a very big gumbo indeed.

You can write or call ahead for particulars on both the urban and rural Mardi Gras celebrations. For the latter, the towns of **Eunice** and **Mamou** stage some of the most enjoyable celebrations. Contact the **Lafayette Convention & Visitors Commission,** P.O. Box 52066, Lafayette, LA 70505 (© **800/346-1958** in the U.S., 800/ 543-5340 in Canada, or 337/232-3737; www.lafayettetravel.com), for more information.

THE NEW ORLEANS JAZZ & HERITAGE FESTIVAL

People call it "Jazz Fest," but the full name is the New Orleans Jazz & Heritage Festival, and the heritage is about as broad as it can get. Stand in the right place and, depending on which way the wind's blowing, you can catch as many as 10 musical styles from several continents, smell the tantalizing aromas of different food offerings, and meet a United Nations–like spectrum of fellow fest goers all at once.

In the days immediately following Katrina, one of the things lovers of the city wondered about was the fate of Fest. It seems like a trivial thing to focus on, but it wasn't. The music festival is one of the city's two largest tourist draws (Mardi Gras being the other), and much of the local economy (particularly hotels and restaurants) relies on it. But it goes deeper than that; over more than 35 years, Jazz Fest has come to encompass everything the city has to offer, in terms of music, food, and culture. That, and it's a hell of a party. When its return was announced (thanks in part to Shell Oil, the festival's first corporate underwriters, a necessary step under the circumstances), it was seen as a sign that the city really would survive, after all.

While such headliners as Sting, Van Morrison, Dave Matthews, and Bob Dylan have drawn record crowds in recent years, serious Jazz Fest aficionados savor the lesser-known acts. They range from Mardi Gras Indians to old-time bluesmen who have never played outside the Delta, from Dixieland to African artists making rare U.S. appearances to the top names in Cajun, zydeco, and, of course, jazz. The 2006 Fest had more big names—Matthews and Dylan were back, Bruce Springsteen appeared for the first time, as well as Paul Simon, Elvis Costello, and Keith Urban, among others. But the biggest worry was that local acts, the backbone of the festival and its raison d'être, would be in short supply. Many local musicians, from Fats Domino on down, lost their homes, and far too many remain exiled from their city. Their return was essential for this to be the homecoming the city deserved. To attendees' relief, the organizers pulled together a local lineup that looked very much like those of the past.

While attendance at the 2006 festival was down from previous years (though those headliners were there to ensure just the opposite), nonetheless, gone are the days when only a few hundred people came to celebrate. Now filling the infield of the Fair Grounds horse-racing track up near City Park (where the grandstand sustained considerable hurricane damage, limiting its Fest use), the festival covers the last weekend in April and the first in May. It's set up about as well as such an event can be. When the crowds get big, though—the second Saturday traditionally is the busiest—it can be tough to move around, especially if the grounds are muddy from rain. However, the crowds are remarkably well-behaved—to make a sweeping generalization, these are not the same types who come for Mardi Gras.

EVERY DAY IS A GOOD DAY   Hotel and restaurant reservations, not to mention choice plane flights, fill up months (if not a year) in advance, but the schedule is not announced until a couple of months before the event. That may mean scheduling your visit around your own availability, not an appearance by a particular band. Just about every day at Jazz Fest is a good day, however, so this is not a hardship—at least, until you learn about an extraordinary group that is playing on a day you won't be in town. Or you could do like we do: Go for the whole 11 days so you won't miss a thing.

The second Saturday does attract some of the top acts, and each year it sets a record for single-day attendance. But we feel the fun tends to diminish with that many people. Still, the tickets are cheap enough (provided you buy them in advance; prices at the gate have become rather costly) that going early in the day and leaving before the crowds get too big is a viable option. The Thursday before the second weekend (which was dropped for 2006, because of post-Katrina scheduling and other problems) is traditionally targeted to locals, with more local bands and generally smaller crowds because fewer tourists are around than on the weekends. It's a great time to hit the best food booths and to check out the shopping in the crafts areas.

Contact the **New Orleans Jazz & Heritage Festival,** 1205 N. Rampart St., New Orleans, LA 70116 (© **504/522-4786;** www.no jazzfest.com), to get the schedule for each weekend and information about other Jazz Fest–related shows around town.

JAZZ FEST POINTERS

A typical Jazz Fest day has you arriving sometime after the gates open at 11am and staying until you are pooped or until they close at around 7pm (incredibly the whole thing runs as efficiently as a Swiss train). After you leave the Fair Grounds for the day, get some dinner and then hit the clubs. Every club in the city has Jazz Fest–related bookings (of special note is the **Ponderosa Stomp,** a 3-day event featuring "unsung heroes" of the blues, rockabilly, Swamp Pop, and New Orleans R&B that ideally, after a temporary move to Memphis, will return to New Orleans in 2007). Bouncing from one club to another can keep you out until dawn. Then you get up and start all over again. This is part of the reason we think Jazz Fest is so fun.

There are also many nonmusical aspects of Jazz Fest to distract you, particularly the crafts. Local craftspeople and imported artisans fill a sizable section of the Fair Grounds with demonstrations and displays of their products during the festival. You might get to see Louisiana Native American basket making; Cajun accordion, fiddle, and triangle making; decoy carving; boat building; and Mardi Gras Indian beading and costume making.

And then there's the food. The heck with the music—when we dream of Jazz Fest, we are often thinking more about those 50-plus food booths filled with some of the best goodies we've ever tasted. The food ranges from local standbys—red beans and rice, jambalaya, étouffée, and gumbo—to more interesting choices such as oyster sacks, the hugely popular sausage bread, *cochon de lait* (a mouthwatering roast pig sandwich), alligator sausage po' boys, and quail and pheasant gumbo. There's plenty of cold beer, too, although you'll probably have to wait in some mighty long lines to get to it.

Try to purchase tickets as early as February if possible. They're available by mail through **Ticketmaster** (© **800/488-5252** or 504/ 522-5555; www.ticketmaster.com). To order tickets, get information about transportation shuttles to and from the Fair Grounds, or to find out what you are allowed to bring in to Jazz Fest, contact **New Orleans Jazz & Heritage Festival** (✆ 504/522-4786; www.no jazzfest.com). Admission for adults is $30 in advance (depending on when you buy the tickets) and $40 at the gate; $5 for children. Evening events and concerts (order tickets in advance for these events as well) may be attended at an additional cost—usually between $20 and $30, depending on the concert.

JAZZ FEST PARKING & TRANSPORTATION   Parking at the Fair Grounds is next to impossible. The few available spaces cost $35 a day, but it's rare to get a space there. We strongly recommend that you take public transportation or one of the available shuttles.

The **Regional Transit Authority (RTA)** operates bus routes from various pickup points to the Fair Grounds. For schedules contact ✆ **504/248-3900;** (www.norta.com). Taxis, though probably scarce, will also take you to the Fair Grounds at a special event rate of $3 per person (or the meter reading if it's higher). We recommend **United Cabs** (✆ **504/524-9606**).

PACKAGE DEALS   If you want to go to Jazz Fest but would rather have someone else do all the planning, consider contacting **Festival Tours International,** 15237 Sunset Blvd., Suite 17, Pacific Palisades, CA 90272 (✆ **310/454-4080;** www.gumbopages.com/festivaltours), which caters to music lovers who don't wish to wear name tags or do other hokey tour activities. Packages include accommodations, tickets, and also a visit to Cajun country for unique personal encounters with some of the finest local musicians.

If you're flying to New Orleans specifically for the festival, visit **www.nojazzfest.com** to get a Jazz Fest promotional code from a list of airlines that offer special fares during the event.

5 Tips for Travelers with Special Needs

FOR TRAVELERS WITH DISABILITIES

Be aware that while New Orleans facilities are mostly accessible (especially in the Quarter) with proprietors being most accommodating (opening narrow doors wider to fit wheelchairs and such), you are still dealing with older structures created before thoughts of ease for those with disabilities. Before you book a hotel, **ask questions** based on your needs. If you have mobility issues, you'll probably do best to stay in one of the city's newer hotels, which tend to be more spacious and accommodating. Sidewalks are often bumpy and uneven, and getting on the St. Charles streetcar might be too great a challenge.

For information about specialized transportation systems, call **LIFT** (© **504/827-7433**).

You can join **SATH** (Society for Accessible Travel & Hospitality) (© **212/447-7284**; www.sath.org), which offers a wealth of travel resources for all types of disabilities and informed recommendations on destinations, access guides, travel agents, tour operators, vehicle rentals, and companion services.

FOR GAY & LESBIAN TRAVELERS

This is a very gay-friendly town with a high-profile homosexual population that contributes much to the color and flavor of the city. You'll find an abundance of establishments serving gay and lesbian interests, from bars to restaurants to community services.

If you need help finding your way, you can stop by or call the **Gay and Lesbian Community Center,** 2114 Decatur St. (© **504/945-1103**; www.lgccno.org); hours vary, so call before stopping in.

Ambush, 828-A Bourbon St., New Orleans, LA 70116 (© **504/522-8047**; www.ambushmag.com), is a weekly entertainment and news publication for the Gulf South's gay, lesbian, bisexual, and transgender communities. *The Whiz* is another popular area publication found in many gay establishments (www.whizmag.com).

Grace Fellowship, 3151 Dauphine St. (© **504/944-9836**), and the **Vieux Carré Metropolitan Community Church,** 1128 St. Roch Ave. (© **504/945-5390**), are religious organizations that serve primarily gay congregations. Both invite visitors to attend services.

One useful website is **www.gayneworleans.com**, which provides information on lodging, dining, arts, and nightlife as well as links to other information on New Orleans gay life.

FOR SENIORS

Don't be shy about asking for discounts, but always carry some kind of identification, such as a driver's license, that shows your date of birth, especially if you've kept your youthful glow.

Also mention the fact that you're a senior when you first make your travel reservations. Many hotels offer discounts, and seniors who show their Medicare card can ride New Orleans streetcars and buses for 40¢.

Members of **AARP,** 601 E St. NW, Washington, DC 20049 (© **888/687-2277** or 225/381-2940; www.aarp.org), get discounts on hotels, airfares, and car rentals. AARP offers members a wide range of benefits, including *AARP The Magazine* and a monthly newsletter. Anyone over 50 can join.

6 Getting There

BY PLANE

Flights have been somewhat limited since Katrina, though more are being added as time passes and demand increases again. Still, you may have to have a more flexible schedule for visiting than you might like. Among the airlines serving the city's **Louis Armstrong New Orleans International Airport** are **America West** (✆ 800/235-9292;** www.americawest.com), **American** (✆ 800/433-7300; www.aa.com), **Continental** (✆ 800/525-0280 or 504/581-2965; www.continental.com), **Delta** (✆ 800/221-1212; www.delta.com), **JetBlue** (✆ 800/538-2583; www.jetblue.com), **Northwest** (✆ 800/225-2525; www.nwa.com), **Southwest** (✆ 800/435-9792; www.southwest.com), **US Airways** (✆ 800/428-4322; www.usairways.com), and **United** (✆ 800/241-6522; www.ual.com).

The airport is 15 miles west of the city, in Kenner. You'll find information booths scattered around the airport and in the baggage claim area.

BY CAR

You can drive to New Orleans via **I-10, I-55, U.S. 90, U.S. 61,** or across the Lake Pontchartrain Causeway on **La. 25.** From any direction, you'll see the city's distinctive and swampy outlying regions; if you can, try to drive in while you can enjoy the scenery in daylight. For the best roadside views, take U.S. 61 or La. 25, but only if you have time to spare. The larger roads are considerably faster.

It's a good idea to call before you leave home to ask directions to your hotel. Most hotels have parking facilities (for a fee); if they don't they'll give you the names and addresses of nearby parking lots.

Driving in New Orleans can be a hassle, and parking is a nightmare. Cabs are plentiful and not too pricey, so you really don't need a car in New Orleans unless you're planning several day trips.

Nevertheless, most major car-rental companies are at the airport including **Alamo** (✆ 800/327-9633; www.alamo.com), **Avis** (✆ 800/331-1212; www.avis.com), **Budget Rent A Car** (✆ 800/527-0700; www.budget.com), **Dollar Rent A Car** (✆ 800/800-4000; www.dollar.com), **Hertz** (✆ 800/654-3131; www.hertz.com), and **National** (✆ 800/227-7368; www.nationalcar.com).

BY TRAIN

The passenger rail lines cut through some beautiful scenery. **Amtrak** (© **800/USA-RAIL** or 504/528-1612; www.amtrak.com) trains serve the city's **Union Passenger Terminal,** 1001 Loyola Ave. The New Orleans train station is in the Central Business District. Taxis wait outside the main entrance to the passenger terminal. Hotels in the French Quarter and the CBD are a short ride away.

2

Getting to Know New Orleans

At the time of this writing, New Orleans has in many ways shrunk to its 1878 borders. It was always a manageable size (only about 7 miles long), and if you didn't count the unusual directions and the nearly impossible-to-pronounce street names, it was a very user-friendly city, with most of what the average tourist would want to see concentrated in a few areas. As it happens, those areas were the least damaged by Katrina and the flooding aftermath. Aerial maps of the flooded sections show a thin sliver of dry running alongside the river, with other little pockets here and there, nearly all corresponding to the best-known districts. While the city debates about rebuilding plans, those neighborhoods are the heart of revitalization for the city.

The greatest damage occurred from the post-Katrina flooding; the storm itself was off-center just enough so that many parts of the city experienced less damage than might be expected. The average tourist could confine him or herself to certain areas and barely know a disaster ever occurred, much less one of this magnitude. However, we encourage you to take the time to tour some of the devastated areas; it's the only way to even begin to comprehend the extent of what happened, and what will be needed in the future. Further, while neighborhoods such as the Lower 9th Ward and the Treme were not part of the regular tourist routes, the city owes much of its heart and soul to the inhabitants and history of same, and while the survival of the French Quarter and Garden District should be celebrated, the future of these neighborhoods must not be neglected if New Orleans is to flourish fully again.

The major breaches in the levee system happened at the 17th Street Canal (at the rough border between Orleans and Jefferson parishes) and the Inner Harbor Navigation Canal, known locally as the Industrial Street Canal, the border between the 9th and the Lower 9th Wards. The waters of Lake Pontchartrain rushed in until the more-or-less bowl-shaped city became a level extension of the lake itself. Because of the varying levels of higher ground, the depth of flooding sometimes varied from block to block, with the result that one stretch might have been subjected to no more than a foot or so in the street, while just a couple blocks away, the water was as deep as 6 feet. The closer one gets to the lake, the more serious the flooding, particularly north (or lakeside) of St. Claude Avenue and Claiborne Avenue in the 9th and Lower 9th Wards—the now-iconic photo of the swamped Circle Foods store was taken at the corner of Claiborne and St. Bernard Avenue, looking under the 10 freeway. However, if buildings were perched on a patch of high ground, some may have avoided serious damage while neighborhoods such as the Broadmoor section of Mid-City, far from a lakeshore, suffered deep flooding. For a detailed map of the flood levels, see the map **"Post-Katrina Flood Levels,"** on the inside back cover of this book.

Though much may have changed by the time you read this, in terms of bulldozing and rebuilding, driving through some of the flooded areas can be deceptive; if an area took on only a few feet of water, the buildings may not show many signs of damage, just the telltale brown waterline revealing the height of the flood waters, or cryptic florescent spray-painted symbols, indicating a search was done of the premises and what was found within, the graffiti of disaster. Mid-City, with its 4 to 6 feet of water, on average, looks, in part, abandoned but salvageable, while even badly flooded residential Lakeview can appear normal—unless, that is, you were to enter one of the houses that sat for weeks under as much as 12 feet of water. Within these family homes, every exposed inch might be covered in mold. As reconstruction continues, throughout the city you are likely to see piles of trash in front of many buildings, as ruined interiors are ripped out, down to the studs, in an attempt to salvage a structure.

And all of that pales compared to the utter devastation of the Lower 9th Ward, where houses were pushed into each other, as if kicked about, or in many cases, reduced to indistinguishable piles of lumber and rubble.

This chapter contains some of the ins and outs of New Orleans navigation and gives you some local sources to contact for specialized information.

1 Orientation

ARRIVING

From the airport, you can get to your hotel on the **Airport Shuttle** (© **504/522-3500**). For $13 per person (one-way), the van will take you directly to your hotel. There are Airport Shuttle information desks (staffed 24 hr.) in the airport.

Note: If you plan to take the Airport Shuttle *to* the airport when you leave, call a day in advance and let them know what time your flight is leaving. They'll tell you what time they will pick you up.

A **taxi** from the airport to most hotels will cost about $29; if there are three or more passengers, the fare is $12 per person.

From the airport, you can reach the **Central Business District (CBD)** by bus for $1.50 (exact change required). Buses run from 6am to 6:30pm. From 6 to 9am and 3 to 6pm, they leave the airport every 12 to 15 minutes and go to the downtown side of Tulane Avenue between Elks Place and South Saratoga Street; at other times, they leave every 23 minutes. The trip should take 30 to 40 minutes, depending on traffic. For more information, call the **Regional Transit Authority (RTA)** (© **504/248-3900;** www.norta.com).

VISITOR INFORMATION

The **New Orleans Metropolitan Convention and Visitors Bureau,** 2020 St. Charles Ave., New Orleans, LA 70130 (© **800/ 672-6124** or 504/566-5011; www.neworleanscvb.com), is one of the most helpful tourist centers in any major city. Not only does it have a wide array of well-written brochures that cover everything from usual sightseeing questions to cultural history, but the incredibly friendly and helpful staff can also answer almost any random question you may have.

Once you've arrived in the city, you also might want to stop by the **Visitor Information Center,** 529 St. Ann St. (© **504/568- 5661**), in the French Quarter. The center is open daily from 9am to 5pm and has walking- and driving-tour maps, and booklets on restaurants, accommodations, sightseeing, special tours, and pretty much anything else you might want to know about. The staff is friendly and knowledgeable about both the city and the state.

CITY LAYOUT

"Where y'at?" goes the traditional local greeting. "Where" is easy enough when you are in the French Quarter, the site of the original settlement. A 13-block-long grid between Canal Street and Esplanade Avenue, running from the Mississippi River to North Rampart Street, it's the closest the city comes to a geographic center.

After that, all bets are off. Because of the bend in the river, the streets are laid out at angles and curves that render north, south, east, and west useless. It's time to readjust your thinking: In New Orleans, the compass points are *riverside, lakeside, uptown,* and *downtown.* Keep in mind that North Rampart Street is the *lakeside* boundary of the Quarter and that St. Charles Avenue extends from the French Quarter, *downtown,* to Tulane University, *uptown.*

Canal Street forms the boundary between new and old New Orleans. Street names change when they cross Canal (Bourbon St., for example, becomes Carondelet St.), and addresses begin at 100 on either side of Canal. In the Quarter, street numbers begin at 400 at the river because 4 blocks of numbered buildings were lost to the river before the levee was built.

The French Quarter   Made up of about 90 square blocks, this section is also known as the *Vieux Carré* ("Old Square") and is enclosed by Canal Street, North Rampart Street, the Mississippi River, and Esplanade Avenue. The Quarter is full of clubs, bars, stores, residences, and museums; its major public area is Jackson Square, bounded by Chartres, Decatur, St. Peter, and St. Ann streets. The most historic and best-preserved area in the city, a survivor of two major fires in the 1700s in addition to Hurricane Katrina, it's likely to be the focal point of your stay.

Faubourg Marigny   This area is east of the French Quarter (on the other side of Esplanade Ave.). Over the past decade, the Marigny has emerged as one of the city's vital centers of activity, and it was fortunate that it did not experience flooding. You can still find the outlines of a small Creole suburb, and many old-time residents remain. Younger urban dwellers have moved into the area in significant numbers recently. Today, some of the best bars and nightspots in New Orleans are along Frenchmen Street, the Marigny's main drag. Along with the adjacent sections of the French Quarter, the Marigny is also a social center for the city's gay and lesbian communities.

Bywater   This riverside neighborhood is past the Faubourg Marigny and is bounded on the east by an industrial canal. It is tempting to misspeak and call it "Backwater" because, at first glance, it seems like a wasteland of light industry and run-down homes. In fact, Bywater has plenty of nice, modest residential sections. It's home to the city's artists-in-hiding, and many local designers have shops among the urban decay. This is in keeping with the history of the area, which early on was home to artisans as well as communities of immigrants and free people of color. The lower Bywater that is adjacent to the Marigny suffered relatively little damage, and looks pretty good, until one travels past St. Claude toward the lake, where there was severe flooding thanks to the breach in the Industrial Canal.

Mid-City/Esplanade Ridge Stretching north from the French Quarter to City Park, the Ridge hugs either side of Esplanade Avenue. This area encompasses a few distinct neighborhoods, all of which have certain things in common. In the 19th century, Esplanade was the grand avenue of New Orleans Creole society—the St. Charles Avenue of downriver. There is still evidence of those times, especially in the ancient oak trees forming a canopy above the road. Because of this relatively high ground, most of Esplanade escaped damaging flooding.

The oldest section of Esplanade Ridge, **Faubourg Treme,** is located directly across Rampart Street from the French Quarter. Like the Quarter, it was a dense 19th-century Creole community. Unlike the Quarter, Treme (pronounced treh-*may*) has remained almost untouched by preservationists and so has continued to be an organic residential community. It is one of the most vibrant African-American neighborhoods in New Orleans, home to more than a few of the city's best brass bands. Despite major community efforts to reclaim the neighborhood, Treme was usually plagued by severe crime; it's not advisable to walk through it at night. Hurricane and flood damage has set back this historic neighborhood, and there is fear that reconstruction may lead to the sort of gentrification that could force out families who have lived there for generations.

Central Business District Historically, **Canal Street** has been New Orleans's main street, and in the 19th century, it divided the French and American sections of the city. (By the way, there's no canal—the one that was planned for the spot never came off.)

The **Central Business District (CBD)** is roughly bounded by Canal Street and the elevated Pontchartrain Expressway (Business Route U.S. 90) between Loyola Avenue and the Mississippi River. Some of the most elegant luxury hotels are in this area. Most of the district was known as Faubourg St. Mary when Americans began settling here after the Louisiana Purchase. Lafayette Square was the center of life here during the 19th century. Parts of the CBD were relentlessly featured on the news thanks to the looters that targeted the T-shirt and sporting goods stores that line Canal Street. The Hyatt, with its many blown-out windows, also garnered plenty of attention. This may have lead to the impression that the area was devastated by the disaster, but it actually bounced back quite quickly.

Within the CBD is the **Warehouse District.** More than 20 years ago, this area was full of abandoned warehouses and almost nothing else. With the efforts of some dedicated individuals and institutions, however, it's steadily evolving into a residential neighborhood with

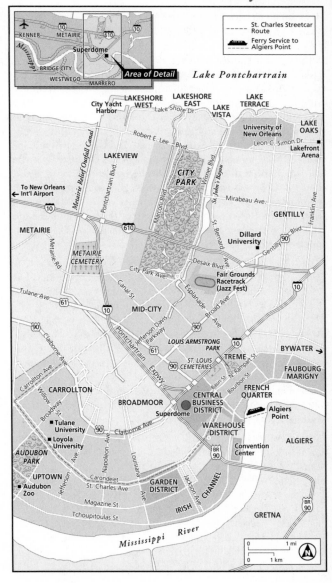

some commercial activity. Furthermore, this area also serves as the city's art gallery district, with many of the premier galleries concentrated along Julia Street.

Uptown/The Garden District Bounded by St. Charles Avenue (lakeside) and Magazine Street (riverside) between Jackson and Louisiana avenues, the Garden District remains one of the most picturesque areas in the city. Originally the site of a plantation, the area was subdivided and developed as a residential neighborhood for wealthy Americans. Throughout the middle of the 19th century, developers built the Victorian, Italianate, and Greek Revival homes that still line the streets. Most of the homes had elaborate lawns and gardens, but few of those still exist. The Garden District is located uptown (as opposed to the CBD, which is downtown); the neighborhood west of the Garden District is often called Uptown. Because it did not flood, much of Uptown looks as it always did, although some trees toppled, and many others look like they got pruned by a drunk.

The Irish Channel The area bounded by Magazine Street and the Mississippi River, Louisiana Avenue, and the Central Business District got its name during the 1800s when more than 100,000 Irish immigrated to New Orleans. As was true elsewhere in the country, the Irish of New Orleans were often considered "expendable" labor. Many were killed while employed in dangerous labor. These days, the Channel is significantly less Irish, but it retains its lively spirit and distinctive neighborhood flavor. Much of the area is run-down, but just as much is filled with quiet residential neighborhoods. To get a glimpse of the Irish Channel, go to the antiques shop district on Magazine Street and stroll between Felicity Street and Jackson Avenue.

Algiers Point Directly across the Mississippi River from the Central Business District and the French Quarter, and connected by the Canal Street Ferry, the Point is the old town center of Algiers. Because the "West Bank" of the city did not flood at all, for weeks after the storm, the city of New Orleans was almost entirely represented (and financially supported) by this overlooked original Creole suburb. Today, you can see some of the best-preserved small gingerbread and Creole cottages in New Orleans. The neighborhood has recently begun to attract attention as a historic landmark, and it makes for one of the city's most pleasant strolls.

SAFETY

As we write this, it's difficult to say anything accurate about New Orleans's crime rate. A byproduct of the evacuations has been a sharp downturn in crime statistics. The population has shrunk from 500,000 to around 75,000, though a bump should come during summer 2006, as families return in anticipation of the reopening of the public school district. There are great hopes that the deplorable social conditions that contributed to the high crime rate will be addressed over the next few years, and that New Orleans can reinvent itself accordingly.

However, the city's always-problematic police force remains troubled in the post-Katrina days, and while everyone is doing the best they can, crime probably can't stay away forever, and tourists will not be immune. While by and large the worst crime happens in areas where you are not likely to go, we want to help you avoid trouble as best you can.

The **French Quarter** is fairly safe, thanks to the number of people present at any given time, but some areas are better than others. On Bourbon Street, be careful when socializing with strangers and be alert to distractions by potential pickpocket teams. Dauphine and Burgundy are in quiet, lovely old parts of the Quarter, but as you near Esplanade, watch out for purse-snatchers. At night, stay in well-lighted areas with street and pedestrian traffic and take cabs down Esplanade and into the **Faubourg Marigny.** Conventional wisdom holds that one should not go much above Bourbon toward Rampart alone after dark, though these days it might be less of a problem than in the past. Still, it might be best to stay in a group (or near one) if you can; and if you feel uncomfortable, consider taking a cab, even if it seems silly, for the (very) short ride. In the **Garden District,** as you get past Magazine toward the river, the neighborhoods can be rough, so exercise caution.

2 Getting Around

You really don't need to rent a car during your stay. Not only is the town just made for walking (thanks to being so flat—and so darn picturesque), most places you want to go are easily accessible on foot or by some form of the largely excellent public transportation system. Indeed, we find a streetcar ride to be as much entertainment as a practical means of getting around. At night, when you need them most, cabs are easy to come by. Meanwhile, driving and parking in the French Quarter can bring grief. The streets are narrow and crowded, and many go one-way only. Street parking is minimal (and likely to attract thieves), and parking lots are fiendishly expensive. Traffic is currently a big problem, partly because so many street-lights remain out (a problem likely to be solved by the time you read this), and partly because so much action is confined to just a few small areas that all the traffic is concentrated within.

BY PUBLIC TRANSPORTATION

DISCOUNT PASSES   If you won't have a car in New Orleans, we strongly encourage you to invest in a **VisiTour** pass, which entitles you to an unlimited number of rides on all streetcar and bus lines. It costs $5 for 1 day, $12 for 3 days. Many visitors think this was the best tip they got about their New Orleans stay and the finest bargain in town. Passes are available from VisiTour vendors—to find the nearest one, ask at your hotel or guesthouse or contact the **Regional Transit Authority (RTA)** (𝒸 **504/248-3900;** www. norta.com). You can call the RTA for information about any part of the city's public transportation system.

BUSES   New Orleans has an excellent public bus system, so chances are there's a bus that runs exactly where you want to go. At press time, all rides within the city are free (thanks to FEMA, who's picking up the tab at least through June 2006). Usually, local fares are $1.25 (you must have exact change in bills or coins), transfers are an extra 25¢, and express buses are $1.25. You can get complete and updated route information by contacting the RTA (𝒸 **504/248-3900;** or **www.norta.com**) or by picking up one of the excel-lent city maps available at the Visitor Information Center, 529 St. Ann St., in the French Quarter.

STREETCARS   Besides being a national historic landmark, the **St. Charles Avenue streetcar** is also a convenient and fun way to get from downtown to Uptown and back. The line was badly damaged by the hurricane, and the famous green cars were temporarily com-mandeered to replace the damaged cars of the newly restored Canal Street streetcar line. Consequently, the St. Charles line will not be running again until late 2006, though there is a free bus running the line in the cars' absence. When in operation, the cars run 24 hours a day at frequent intervals, and the fare is $1.25 each way (you must have exact change in bills or coins). It can get crowded at rush hour and when school is out for the day. Board at Canal and Caron-delet streets (directly across Canal from Bourbon St. in the French

Quarter) or anywhere along St. Charles, sit back, and look for land-marks or just enjoy the scenery.

The streetcar line extends beyond the point where St. Charles Avenue bends into Carrollton Avenue. The end of the line is at Palmer Park and Playground at Claiborne Avenue. It will cost you another $1.25 for the ride back to Canal Street. It costs 10¢ to transfer from the streetcar to a bus.

The **riverfront streetcar** runs from the Old Mint across Canal Street to Riverview, with stops along the way. It's a great step saver as you explore the riverfront. The fare is $1.50.

The spiffy new (air-conditioned!) **Canal Street streetcar** (whose brand new cars were largely ruined by the hurricane) is again run-ning its full pre-Katrina route along Canal St. and North Carrollton to the New Orleans Museum of Art. Be prepared for jammed cars during Jazz Fest, because the line runs to within a few blocks of the Fair Grounds. Be sure you hop the right car for your destination, as some head only to the old cemeteries. One-way fares are $1.25.

BY CAR

If you must have a car, try one of the following car-rental agencies: **Avis,** 2024 Canal St. (© **800/331-1212** or 504/523-4318; www. avis.com); **Budget Rent A Car,** 1317 Canal St. (© **800/527-0700** or 504/467-2277; www.budget.com); **Dollar Rent A Car,** 1910 Airline Hwy. Kenner (© **800/800-4000** or 504/467-2285; www.dollar.com); **Hertz,** 901 Convention Center Blvd., No. 101 (© **800/654-3131** or 504/568-1645; www.hertz.com); **Swifty Car Rental,** 1717 Canal St. (© **504/524-7368**); or **Alamo,** 225 E. Air-line Hwy. Kenner (© **800/GO-ALAMO** or 504/469-0532; www. alamo.com). Many of these agencies (for a list, see p. 22) also have airport locations.

New Orleans drivers are often reckless, so drive defensively. The meter maids are an efficient bunch, so take no chances with parking meters, and carry quarters. It's probably best to use your car only for longer jaunts away from congested areas. Most hotels provide guest parking, often for a daily fee; smaller hotels or guesthouses (partic-ularly in the French Quarter) may not have parking facilities but will be able to direct you to a nearby public garage.

The narrow streets and frequent congestion make driving in the French Quarter more difficult than elsewhere in the city. The streets are one-way, and on weekdays during daylight hours, Royal and Bourbon streets between the 300 and 700 blocks are closed to auto-mobiles. Also, the blocks of Chartres Street in front of St. Louis

Cathedral are closed at all times. Driving is also trying in the Central Business District, where congestion and limited parking make life difficult for the motorist. Do yourself a favor: Park the car and use public transportation in both areas.

Once you get into more residential areas such as the Garden District and off main drags such as St. Charles Avenue, finding where you're going becomes quite the challenge. Street signs are often no bigger than a postcard and hard to read at that, while many came down in the hurricane and may not be replaced by the time you need them. At night they aren't even lit, so deciphering where you are can be next to impossible. If you must drive, we suggest counting the number of streets you have to cross to tell you when to make turns rather than relying on street signs.

BY TAXI

Taxis are plentiful in New Orleans. They can be hailed easily on the street in the French Quarter and in some parts of the Central Business District, and they are usually lined up at taxi stands at larger hotels. Otherwise, telephone and expect a cab to appear in 3 to 5 minutes. The rate is $2.50 when you enter the taxi and $1.60 per mile thereafter. During festival time, the rate is $4 per person (or the meter rate if it's greater) no matter where you go in the city. It is a $10 fee for transfers between hotels no matter how short the ride. The city's most reliable company is **United Cabs** (© **504/524-9606;** www.unitedcabs.com).

Most taxis can be hired for a special rate for up to five passengers. It's a hassle-free and economical way for a small group to tour far-flung areas of the city (the lakefront, for example). Within the city you pay an hourly rate; out-of-town trips cost double the amount on the meter.

ON FOOT

We can't stress this enough: Walking is by far the best way to see this town. There are too many unique and sometimes glorious sights to want to whiz past them. Sure, sometimes it's too darn hot or humid to make walking attractive, but there is always a cab or bus nearby. Drink lots of water if it's hot and pay close attention to your surroundings. If you enter an area that seems unsafe, retreat.

BY FERRY

The Canal Street ferry is one of the city's secrets—and it's free for pedestrians. The ride takes you across the Mississippi River from the foot of Canal to Algiers Point (25 min. round-trip), and it affords great views of downtown. Once in Algiers, you can take a walking tour of the old Algiers Point neighborhood and tour Mardi Gras World. At night, with the city's glowing skyline reflecting on the river, a ride on the ferry can be quite romantic. The ferry also does carry car traffic, in case you'd like to do some West Bank driving.

FAST FACTS: New Orleans

American Express The local office (℡ 800/508-0274) is in the Central Business District. It's open weekdays from 9am to 5pm.

Babysitters Ask at your hotel about babysitting services. If your hotel doesn't offer help finding child care, try calling **Accent on Children's Arrangements** (℡ 504/524-1227).

Convention Center The Ernest N. Morial Convention Center (℡ 504/582-3000) is at 900 Convention Center Blvd.

Emergencies For fire, ambulance, and police, dial ℡ **911.** This is a free call from pay phones. At the time of this writing, 911 response was often very slow, because of limited personnel. It is an infrastructure problem the city hopes to have adequately addressed before too long.

Hospitals Again, because so many residents, including medical personnel, have been displaced by the hurricane, and their offices or hospitals permanently closed, medical care in New Orleans is far more limited than it should be. If you have an ongoing problem or condition that may require very specific medical care, please take the time to find out what the current situation is before planning your trip. If no one is available at your hotel or guesthouse, call or go to the emergency room at **Ochsner Clinic Foundation,** 1516 Jefferson Hwy. (℡ **504/842-3460**), or the **Tulane University Medical Center,** 1415 Tulane Ave. (℡ **504/588-5800**).

Liquor Laws The legal drinking age in Louisiana is 21, but don't be surprised if people much younger take a seat next to you at the bar. Alcoholic beverages are available round-the-clock, 7 days a week. You're allowed to drink on the street but not from a glass or bottle. Bars will often provide a plastic "go" cup so that you can transfer your drink as you leave (and some have walk-up windows for quick and easy refills). *One warning:* Although the police may look the other way if they see a pedestrian who's had a few too many (as long as he or she is peaceful and is not bothering anyone), they have no tolerance at all for those who are intoxicated behind the wheel.

Newspapers & Magazines To find out what's going on around town, you might want to pick up a copy of the daily **Times-Picayune** (**www.nola.com**) or **Offbeat** (www.offbeat.com), a monthly guide (probably the most extensive one available) to the city's evening entertainment, art galleries, and special events. It can be found in most hotels, though it's often hard to locate toward the end of the month. The **Gambit Weekly** (www.bestofneworleans.com) is the city's free alternative paper and has a good mix of news and entertainment information. It comes out every Thursday. The paper conducts an annual **"Best of New Orleans"** readers' poll; check its website for the results.

Pharmacies The 24-hour pharmacy closest to the French Quarter is **Walgreens**, 1801 St. Charles Avenue, ✆ **504-561-8331**. A Walgreens with regular hours (daily 8am–10pm) is at 134 Royal (at Iberville) in the Quarter (✆ **504/525-2180**). There is also a 24-hour **Rite Aid** at 3401 St. Charles Ave. (✆ **504/896-4575**), which is more convenient if you're staying Uptown or in the Garden District.

Post Office The main post office is at 701 Loyola Ave. There's also a post office in the World Trade Center at 2 Canal St. If you're in the Quarter, you'll find a post office at 1022 Iberville St. If you have something large or fragile to send home and don't feel like hunting around for packing materials, go to **Royal Mail & Parcel**, 828 Royal St. (✆ **504/522-8523**), in the Quarter, or **Mail Box Pack & Ship**, 1201 St. Charles (✆ **504/524-5080**), uptown. The latter also has pickup service.

Radio WWOZ (90.7 FM) is *the* New Orleans radio station. They say they are the best in the world, and we won't disagree. New Orleans jazz, R&B, brass bands, Mardi Gras Indians, gospel, Cajun, zydeco—it's all here. Don't miss music historian (and former White Panther activist, memorialized in a song by John Lennon) John Sinclair's shows (at press time, Wed 11am–2pm and Sun 2–5am), which got him named Best DJ in *OffBeat*'s annual poll. The city's NPR station is **WWNO** (89.9 FM). Tulane's station, **WTUL** (91.5 FM), also plays very interesting music.

Safety Be careful while visiting any unfamiliar city. In New Orleans, in particular, don't walk alone at night and don't go into the cemeteries alone at any time during the day or night. Ask around locally before you go anywhere; people will tell you if you should take a cab instead of walking or using public transportation. Most important, if someone holds you up and demands your wallet, purse, or other personal belongings, don't resist.

Taxes The sales tax in New Orleans is 9%. An additional 4% tax is added to hotel bills for a total of 13%. There is also a nightly tax of 50¢ to $2 based on the number of rooms a hotel has.

Time Zone New Orleans observes Central Standard Time, the same as Chicago. Between the first Sunday in April and the last Saturday in October, daylight saving time is in effect. (A new law will extend daylight saving in 2007; clocks will change the second Sun in Mar and the first Sun in Nov.) During this period, clocks are set 1 hour ahead of standard time. Call ✆ 504/828-4000 for the correct local time.

Traveler's Aid Society You can reach the local branch of the society at ✆ 504/584-1111.

Weather For an update, call ✆ 504/828-4000.

3

Where to Stay

The path of Hurricane Katrina and the resulting flooding left the main areas of the city with the greatest concentration of hotels largely unscathed. Hotels that did have minor leaks and the like and could be treated or repaired easily reopened almost immediately. (The Royal Sonesta never closed, providing shelter to many during the actual hurricane!) By the end of October 2005, 75% of the hotels, representing 21,000 rooms in downtown, were operational. And by January 1, 2006, 95% were back in business.

And how do those New Orleans hotels look? Pretty much the same as always, and in some cases, even better, as some properties took advantage of the downtime to upgrade. Still, even pre-Katrina, most New Orleans hotels were in old, slightly decaying buildings, and an air of must and mold was a not infrequent component. Things rarely look fresh and new in New Orleans; wear and tear is part of the atmosphere even in ordinary times.

So where should you stay? Usually, these choices don't matter that much. If you're doing your New Orleans trip right, you shouldn't be doing much sleeping. But you do have to put your change of clothes somewhere, and so here are a few tips. Don't stay on Bourbon Street unless you absolutely have to or don't mind getting no sleep. The open-air frat party that is this thoroughfare does mean a free show below your window, but it is hardly conducive to . . . well, just about anything other than participation in the same.

A first-time visitor might also strongly consider not staying in the Quarter at all. Try the still-beautiful Garden District instead. Though the streetcar that usually connects to this area is temporarily out of service—a free bus is running its route—it's an easy commute to the Quarter, and it's closer to a number of wonderful clubs and restaurants. However, during crowded times (Mardi Gras, for example), just finding anything might have to be good enough.

After all, serious New Orleans visitors often book a year in advance for popular times.

If you are concerned about staying in damaged areas, most of the hotels listed below are in the largely undamaged French Quarter and Garden District. The exception is the Mid-City area, which is discussed below. You can decide for yourself if such proximity makes you uncomfortable.

All of the guesthouses in this chapter are first-rate. If you want more information, we highly recommend the **Bed & Breakfast, Inc., Reservation Service** ★★★ (© **800/729-4640,** 504/481-9073, or 504/342-4861; **www.historiclodging.com**), which represents about 20 establishments in every section of the city. Prices range from $75 to $252 a night. The service can also often find a room for you on relatively short notice.

As a general rule, just to be on the safe side, always book ahead in spring, fall, and winter. Right now, hotels are still filled with recovery workers, but how long that will continue is hard to predict. Hence, booking in advance is a very good idea. And if your trip will coincide with Mardi Gras or Jazz Fest, book *way* ahead—up to a year in advance if you want to ensure a room. You should also be aware that rates frequently jump more than a notch or two for Mardi Gras and other festival times, and often have a 4- or 5-night minimum requirement.

In addition to the accommodations reviewed below, we've also covered some of our favorites that remain closed at press time (p. 76). We encourage you to check in with them to see when or if they've reopened their doors; we hope and expect they will soon. Also, keep in mind that accommodations that are open are dealing with persistent staff shortages. This may mean less than swift and flawless service (often room service is limited or suspended, valet parking discontinued, and maid service scaled back to the basics), though every establishment is doing its best to fill in gaps.

The rates we've given in this chapter are for double rooms and do not include the city's 11% hotel tax. Realize that rates often shift according to demand. The high end of the range is for popular times like Mardi Gras and Jazz Fest, and the low end is for quieter periods like the month of December.

Where to Stay in New Orleans

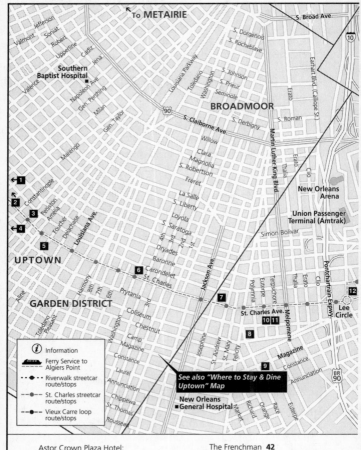

Astor Crown Plaza Hotel:
   The Alexa **37**
Ashton's Bed & Breakfast **39**
B&W Courtyards Bed & Breakfast **43**
Chimes B&B **4**
The Columns **3**
Cotton Exchange **35**
Courtyard by Marriott **16**
Dauphine Orleans Hotel **40**
The Depot at Madame Julia's **14**
Drury Inn & Suites **29**
The Fairmont New Orleans **34**

The Frenchman **42**
The Grand Victorian Bed & Breakfast **6**
Hampton Inn Garden District **5**
Hilton New Orleans
   Riverside Hotel **18**
Holiday Inn Downtown-
   Superdome **33**
Holiday Inn Express **36**
Homewood Suites **31**
Hotel InterContinental **28**
Hotel Monaco **28**
The House on Bayou Road **38**

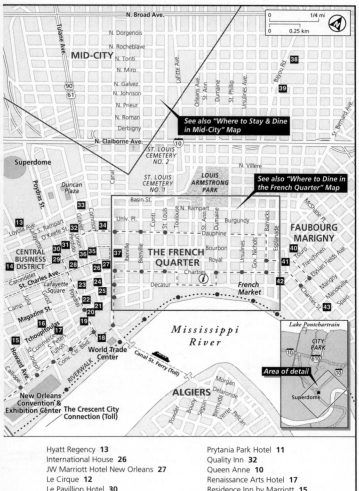

N. Broad Ave.

0   1/4 mi
0   0.25 km

N. Dorgenois
N. Rocheblave
MID-CITY N. Tonti
N. Miro
N. Galvez
N. Johnson
N. Prieur
N. Roman
Derbigny

Tulane Ave.
Lafitte Ave.
Orleans Ave.
Dumaine
St. Ann
St. Philip
Ursulines Ave.
Bayou Rd.
St. Bernard Ave.

38
39

See also "Where to Stay & Dine in Mid-City" Map

N. Claiborne Ave.

Superdome

Poydras St.

Duncan Plaza

Canal

ST. LOUIS CEMETERY NO. 2

ST. LOUIS CEMETERY NO. 1

LOUIS ARMSTRONG PARK

N. Villere

See also "Where to Dine in the French Quarter" Map

Basin St.

33

Univ. Pl.   N. Rampart   Burgundy

Conti   St. Louis   Toulouse   St. Ann   Dumaine   Barracks

13
32 **34**
30 **31** **36** **35** **37**
29   **28**   **26** **27**
14
23 **24**
22 **25**
20 **21**
19
16 **17**
15 **18**

Dauphine
Bourbon
Royal
Chartres
Decatur

THE FRENCH QUARTER

Ursulines
Gov. Nichols
Esplanade

FAUBOURG MARIGNY

McShane Pl.
Touro
Frenchmen
Elysian Fields Ave.
Marigny
Mandeville
Spain

41
42
43

Chartres St.

French Market

Loyola Ave.
S. Rampart
O'Keefe Ave.
Union
Perdido
Gravier
Common

CENTRAL BUSINESS DISTRICT

St. Charles Ave.
Carondelet
Poydras
St. Charles Ave.
Camp
Julia
Magazine St.
Tchoupitoulas
Commerce
S. Peters
Fulton
Conv. Ctr. Blvd.

Lafayette Square

Howard Ave.
St. Joseph
Calliope

RIVERWALK

World Trade Center

Canal St. Ferry (Toll)

Mississippi River

New Orleans Convention & Exhibition Center

The Crescent City Connection (Toll)

ALGIERS

Morgan
Delaronde
Brooklyn
Bouny
Seguin
Bermuda
Verret
Pelican

Lake Pontchartrain

CITY PARK

10
610

Area of detail

Superdome

Hyatt Regency **13**
International House **26**
JW Marriott Hotel New Orleans **27**
Le Cirque **12**
Le Pavillion Hotel **30**
Loews New Orleans Hotel **19**
Loft 523 **24**
Maison Perrier Bed & Breakfast **1**
The McKendrick-Breaux House **9**
Park View Guest House **2**
The Pelham **25**
Pontchartrain Hotel **7**

Prytania Park Hotel **11**
Quality Inn **32**
Queen Anne **10**
Renaissance Arts Hotel **17**
Residence Inn by Marriott **15**
Royal Street Inn & R Bar **41**
St. Charles Guesthouse **8**
St. James Hotel **22**
W New Orleans **20**
The Whitney-A Wyndham Historic Hotel **23**
Windsor Court **21**

1 The French Quarter

VERY EXPENSIVE

For hotels in this section, see the "Where to Stay in the French Quarter" map on p. 43.

Hotel Maison de Ville ✷✷   A member of *The Small Luxury Hotels of the World,* the Maison de Ville took advantage of their basic storm damage (leaks and such) to do a major renovation—new floors, new beds, new minibars, new paint—all the things that were standing between it and its former sterling reputation as the most romantic and charming property in the Quarter. At this hotel, where Tennessee Williams was a regular guest in room no. 9, most of the rooms surround an utterly charming courtyard (complete with fountain and banana trees), where it's hard to believe you're in the thick of the Quarter. Rooms (some of which have very tall ceilings and very tall—as in you need steps to reach them—beds) vary dramatically in size; however, some can be downright tiny, so ask when you reserve, as price is no indicator of size. Be careful you don't get a room overlooking the street—Bourbon is less than half a block away and makes its sorry presence known.

The far more spacious Audubon Cottages (larger than many apartments, some with their own private courtyards), located a few blocks away and including a small, inviting pool, can go for less than the cramped queen rooms in the main hotel (and are farther from the hubbub of Bourbon). All rooms are thoroughly lush, with nice touches like feather beds, and the service is helpful and courteous. A wonderful romantic getaway—we just hope the continental breakfast (in both locations) will also get an upgrade and be less disappointing!

727 Toulouse St., New Orleans, LA 70130. ✆ **800/634-1600** or 504/561-5858. Fax 504/528-9939. www.maisondeville.com. 16 units, 7 cottages. $199–$249 double and queen; $219–$259 king; $329–$399 suite; $219–$329 1-bedroom cottage; $599–$699 2-bedroom cottage; $770–$960 3-bedroom cottage. AE, DC, DISC, MC, V. Valet parking $25. **Amenities:** The Bistro restaurant (p. 86); outdoor pool; access to nearby health club; concierge; room service 7am–10pm; massage; laundry service; dry cleaning; shoeshine; computer terminal. *In room:* A/C, TV, Wi-Fi, minibar, hair dryer.

Melrose Mansion ✷   A standout even on a street full of mansions in a town full of pampering guesthouses, the Melrose Mansion has long combined luxury resort living with the best guesthouse offerings. Unfortunately, it seems lately to be resting on its laurels. Service, once impeccable, is less so, and the breakfasts, once handsome feasts, now tend toward the prepackaged and ordinary. It still

Where to Stay in the French Quarter

Bienville House 13	Hotel Maison de Ville 16	New Orleans Guest House 26
Bourbon Orleans Hotel–	Hotel Monteleone 10	Omni Royal Orleans 15
A Wyndham Historic Hotel 20	Hôtel Provincial 29	Olde Victorian Inn 25
Bourgoyne Guest House 23	Hotel Ste. Hélène 14	Place d'Armes Hotel 21
Chateau LeMoyne–	Hotel St. Marie 18	Prince Conti Hotel 7
French Quarter 4	Hotel Villa Convento 28	Ramada Plaza Hotel–
Chateau Sonesta Hotel	Lafitte Guest House 27	The Inn on Bourbon 17
New Orleans 3	Lamothe House 32	Ritz-Carlton, New Orleans 1
Cornstalk Hotel 22	Le Richelieu Hotel 31	Royal Sonesta 8
Dauphine Orleans Hotel 6	Maison Dupuy 19	Soniat House 30
The Garlands Historic	The Marriott 11	St. Louis 9
Creole Cottages 24	Maison Orleans 2	Wyndham New Orleans
Grenoble House 5	Melrose Mansion 33	at Canal Place 12

remains a charming old mansion, beautifully renovated, but it may no longer be justifying its high cost (for which, please note, it has a very strict cancellation policy). The rooms vary from classic Victorian antiques to lighter country-style decor; bathrooms can be small, but plush bathrobes and linens help.

937 Esplanade Ave., New Orleans, LA 70116. ℂ 800/650-3323 or 504/944-2255. Fax 504/945-1794. www.melrosegroup.com. 20 units. $225–$250 double; $325–$425 suite. Rates include continental breakfast and cocktail hour. AE, DC, DISC, MC, V. Parking $23. **Amenities:** Heated outdoor pool. *In room:* A/C, TV, minibar.

Ramada Plaza Hotel—The Inn on Bourbon   The justification for staying at this pricey chain hotel is the location: the former site of the 1859 French Opera House—the first opera house built in the United States (it burned down in 1919). Party animals should note that this means the hotel is right in the middle of the liveliest action on Bourbon. If you have a serious commitment to sleeping, though, choose another place to stay, or at least request an interior room. There's a modestly good-looking, vaguely Southern decor in the guest rooms, which all have king-size or double beds. The Bourbon Street Cafeteria serves breakfast.

541 Bourbon St., New Orleans, LA 70130. ⓒ 800/535-7891 or 504/524-7611. Fax 504/568-9427. www.innonbourbon.com. 186 units. $219–$299 double. AE, DC, DISC, MC, V. Valet parking $20. **Amenities:** Bar; outdoor pool; fitness room; concierge; jewelry shop; gift shop; laundry service; dry cleaning; express checkout. *In room:* A/C, TV, minibar, coffeemaker, hair dryer.

Royal Sonesta ⭐⭐ The Royal Sonesta brags that it never closed, providing refuge during and after Katrina, bless its heart. As one of the classiest hotels in the Quarter, the contrast between the boisterous hurly-burly of Bourbon Street and the Sonesta's marbled and chandeliered lobby—complete with a face-lift that has made it even more elegant—couldn't be greater. Inside, all is quiet and gracious, and if your room faces the courtyard (complete with a large pool), you are in another world altogether. Big and bustling, this is considered the only acceptable, top-flight Bourbon Street hotel, though noise is still a problem in rooms that face Bourbon. But because the Sonesta is so large, reaching nearly to Royal Street, unless you do have one of those rooms, you won't believe you are so close to such craziness. Rooms underwent a major renovation a couple of years ago, adding posher bedspreads and the like, but the designers miscalculated by including an enormous combo armoire/TV cabinet—leaving scant few inches between it and the end of the king-size beds. New bathrooms gleam with marble and tile, but don't bring a cat inside if you want to swing it. *Note:* This is the best place in the Quarter to catch a cab; they line up at the corner.

300 Bourbon St., New Orleans, LA 70130. ⓒ 800/SONESTA or 504/586-0300. Fax 504/586-0335. www.royalsonestano.com. 500 units. $249–$389 double; $479–$1,250 suite. AE, DC, DISC, MC, V. Parking $23 car, $25 oversize. **Amenities:** 2 restaurants; bar; pool; exercise room; concierge; business center; room service 7am–2am; massage. *In room:* A/C, TV, minibar, hair dryer, iron/ironing board, safe.

Soniat House ⭐⭐⭐ The recipient of endless tributes from various prestigious travel journals, the wonderful and romantic Soniat House lives up to the hype. It is classic Creole—the treasures are hidden off the street. Inside you will find a perfect little hideaway, an oasis of calm that seems impossible in the Quarter. The beyond-efficient staff will spoil you, and the sweet courtyards, candlelit at night, will soothe you. What a relief that they only had a few broken windows in terms of storm damage.

Rooms do vary, if not in quality then at least in distinction. All have antiques, but if you want, say, high ceilings and really grand furniture (room no. 23 has a 17th-c. bed), you are better off in the main house or the suite-filled annex across the street. The rooms in the old kitchen and other buildings are not quite as smashing by comparison. On the main property, bathrooms are small, but across the street they gain size, not to mention Jacuzzi bathtubs, custom decor, and antique furnishings. Our only real complaint is the extra charge ($13) for the admittedly delicious, but small, breakfast.

1133 Chartres St., New Orleans, LA 70116. ℂ **800/544-8808** or 504/522-0570. Fax 504/522-7208. www.soniathouse.com. 33 units. $265–$325 double; $395–$675 suite. AE, MC, V. Valet parking $25. Children over 12 welcome only in rooms that accommodate 3. **Amenities:** Access to nearby health club and business center (no charge); concierge; same-day laundry service and dry cleaning. *In room:* A/C, TV, Wi-Fi, fax (in suites), hair dryer, safe.

EXPENSIVE

Chateau LeMoyne—French Quarter   ✿

The Chateau LeMoyne is in a good location, just around the corner from Bourbon Street but away from the noise and not far from Canal. It's a nice surprise to find a Holiday Inn housed in century-plus-old buildings, but the ambience stops at your room's threshold. Once inside, matters look pretty much like they do in every Holiday Inn—too bad. Famed architect James Gallier designed one of these 19th-century buildings (some of which had some roof damage), and you can still see bits of old brick, old ovens, and exposed cypress beams here and there, along with a graceful curving outdoor staircase. You wish they'd made more of their space, but even the spacious courtyard feels oddly sterile.

301 Dauphine St., New Orleans, LA 70112. ℂ **888/465-4329** or 504/581-1303. Fax 504/523-5709. www.chateaulemoyneneworleans.com. 171 units. $139–$239 double; $259–$459 suite. Extra person $15. AE, DC, DISC, MC, V. Valet parking $25. **Amenities:** Restaurant (breakfast only); bar; outdoor pool; room service 7am–11pm. *In room:* A/C, TV, Wi-Fi, coffeemaker, hair dryer, iron/ironing board.

Chateau Sonesta Hotel New Orleans   ✿✿

On the site of the former D. H. Holmes Canal Street department store (1849), the Chateau Sonesta Hotel maintains the structure's 1913 facade. Thanks to Canal Street flooding, the hotel had to renovate over 50% of their guest rooms (which are now quite spiffy and fresh), plus their famous Clock Bar. Many feature balconies overlooking Bourbon or Dauphine streets, which you might want to avoid if you are a light sleeper. High ceilings and a fairly spacious layout, not to mention that proximity to Bourbon, make this a potentially well-priced (if slightly generic) choice, already popular among business groups for its meeting rooms and location. At the Canal Street entrance is a statue of Ignatius Reilly, hero of *A Confederacy of Dunces,* whom we first met when he was waiting, as all of New Orleans once did, "under the clock." The old Holmes clock, now located in a bar, was for decades the favored rendezvous point for *tout* New Orleanians. (Both clock and Ignatius rode out the storm inside.)

800 Iberville St., New Orleans, LA 70112. ℂ **800/SONESTA** or 504/586-0800. Fax 504/586-1987. www.chateausonesta.com. 251 units. $99–$350 double; $285–$798 suite. Extra person $40. Children under 17 stay free in parent's room. AE, DC, DISC, MC, V. Valet parking $25. **Amenities:** Restaurant; bar; heated outdoor pool; exercise room; concierge; tour desk; gift shop; room service 6:30am–11pm; babysitting; laundry service; dry cleaning. *In room:* A/C, TV w/pay movies, dataport, minibar, coffeemaker, hair dryer, iron/ironing board.

Dauphine Orleans Hotel 🏵🏵

Severe roof damage meant a number of this relaxed hotel's rooms were spoiled. Like other establishments with similar problems, the hotel took advantage of this otherwise unfortunate situation and embarked on a complete renovation of all rooms, a process that should be fully completed by August 2006. Once again, you will be able to stay on a relatively quiet and peaceful block of the Quarter, just a block from the action on Bourbon Street, something you wouldn't know if you were sitting in any of its three secluded courtyards. Guests tend to like the atmosphere a lot. The hotel's back buildings were once the studio of John James Audubon, and the "patio rooms" across the street from the main building were originally built in 1834 as the home of New Orleans merchant Samuel Herrmann. Wi-Fi is available in public areas of hotel.

415 Dauphine St., New Orleans, LA 70112. ℂ **800/521-7111** or 504/586-1800. Fax 504/586-1409. www.dauphineorleans.com. 111 units. $149–$269 double; $289 patio room; $179–$399 suite. Rates include continental breakfast and afternoon tea with welcome drink coupon. Extra person $20. Children under 17 stay free in parent's room. AE, DC, DISC, MC, V. Valet parking $18. **Amenities:** Bar; outdoor pool; small fitness room; Jacuzzi; concierge; complimentary French Quarter and downtown transportation; babysitting; laundry service; dry cleaning; guest library. *In room:* A/C, TV, minibar.

The Garlands Historic Creole Cottages 🏵🏵

A hidden gem across a side street from Armstrong Park, which makes it not the best location in town (at least, pre-hurricane), the inn is completely safe thanks to a good security fence, with some of the nicest accommodations in the city, set on the grounds of the former Claude Treme plantation. Creole cottages like the three-room Queen Elizabeth feature big sexy canopy beds, wide pine board floors, exposed brick walls, a fireplace, a big oval soaking tub, and good-taste furniture. Some come with kitchens and small living rooms, while other rooms are smaller (since units vary in size, ask when booking), but all are impeccably maintained, and the whole place is set in small delightful Southern gardens. The breakfast includes dishes like curried eggs with crabmeat on puff pastry, and there are often snacks, like homemade brownies, around. Parking space is plentiful, and staff includes two sweet dogs. All in all, a remarkable getaway unlike anything else in the immediate Quarter area.

1129 St. Philip St., New Orleans, LA 70116. © **800/523-1060** or 504/523-1372. Fax 504/523-1951. www.garlandsguesthouse.com. 15 units. $119–$199 double; special events higher. Rates include breakfast. AE, MC, V. Parking $10. Pet-friendly. **Amenities:** Jacuzzi, Wi-Fi. *In room:* A/C, TV.

Hotel Monteleone ☆☆

Opened in 1886, the Monteleone is the largest hotel in the French Quarter (and was home to Truman Capote's parents when he was born!), and it seems to keep getting bigger without losing a trace of its trademark charm. Because of its size, you can almost always get a reservation here, even when other places are booked. Everyone who stays here loves it, probably because its staff is among the most helpful in town. One recent guest who stayed here with a child with disabilities raved about the facilities.

The rooms were just freshly renovated—in fact, they were just finished about 2 weeks before the storm!—but there is still some difference in terms of size and style. Some of the new rooms sparkle, others are sort of bland, and the old ones have a faded gentility, in a *Barton Fink* 1940s way. Executive suites are just big rooms but have the nicest new furniture, including four-poster beds and Jacuzzis.

One of the city's best-kept secrets is the rooftop pool; on a recent visit, we were among a handful of folks lounging on the flower-filled deck high above the street noise, with unencumbered views of the city—mind you, you can see the devastation from here—and beyond.

214 Royal St., New Orleans, LA 70130. © **800/535-9595** or 504/523-3341. Fax 504/561-5803. www.hotelmonteleone.com. 570 units. $199–$275 double; $360–$2,500 suite. Extra person $25. Children under 18 stay free in parent's room. Package rates available. AE, DC, DISC, MC, V. Valet parking $27 car, $32 small SUV. **Amenities:** 3 restaurants; 2 bars (for info on the Carousel Bar, see p. 193); heated rooftop pool (open year-round); fitness center (understocked but with fabulous views of the city and river); spa; concierge; room service 6:30am–11pm; babysitting; laundry service. *In room:* A/C, TV, dataport, Wi-Fi, minibar, coffeemaker, hair dryer, iron/ironing board, safe.

Lafitte Guest House   Here you'll find the best of both worlds: antique living just blocks from Bourbon Street mayhem (though the Lafitte's cute little parlor seems almost antithetical to rowdy merriment). The three-story brick building, with wrought-iron balconies on the second and third floors, was constructed in 1849 and had a fair amount of water damage, especially to the walls, which required new drywall for about 60% of the building. The result is that the whole building got a needed face-lift with fresh paint, carpets, and the like, and the hotel reopened in March 2006. Each room has its own Victorian flair, with either antiques or top-quality reproductions, and top-quality linens on the beds, plus memorable touches such as pralines on the pillow, sleeping masks, and sound machines with soothing nature noises.

1003 Bourbon St., New Orleans, LA 70116. (*C*) **800/331-7971** or 504/581-2678. Fax 504/581-2677. www.lafitteguesthouse.com. 14 units. $159–$229 double. Extra person $25. Rates include continental breakfast. AE, DISC, MC, V. Parking $15. **Amenities:** 24-hr. concierge. *In room:* A/C, TV, Wi-Fi, hair dryer, iron/ironing board.

Maison Dupuy *✫*   Thanks to roof damage and some flooding, this hotel needed a complete renovation. It fully reopened around April 1, 2006, looking essentially the same as it did before. Which is a relief; while rooms aren't remarkable (and that hasn't changed much with the renovations), they are comfortable. We often forget to recommend this place, but that's a mistake. A little out of the main French Quarter action and a tad closer than some might like to dicey Rampart (though the hotel is entirely safe), the Maison Dupuy, with its seven town houses surrounding a good-size courtyard and a heated pool, is warm and inviting. Though floor space and balconies (with either courtyard or street views—the former is quieter) vary, the staff is friendly and helpful, the courtyard of sufficiently pleasing ambience, and the location—a quiet end of the Quarter, near a bar with pool tables (a rarity in town)—puts it right in the "oh, they've got rooms available? why not?" category. All that, plus a darn good restaurant (**Dominique's,** reviewed on p. 88) make this a recommendable place. The French Quarter Bistro offers a more casual breakfast, lunch, and dinner.

1001 Toulouse St., New Orleans, LA 70112. (*C*) **800/535-9177** or 504/586-8000. Fax 504/525-5334. www.maisondupuy.com. 200 units. $99–$269 superior double; $149–$299 deluxe double with balcony; $329–$838 suite. AE, DC, DISC, MC, V. Valet parking $24 when available. **Amenities:** Restaurant; bar; heated outdoor pool; 24-hr. exercise room; concierge; room service 6am–midnight; babysitting; same-day laundry service and dry cleaning. *In room:* A/C, TV, minibar, hair dryer, iron/ironing board, safe.

Omni Royal Orleans ★★ *Kids*   Despite being part of a chain, this is an elegant hotel that escapes feeling sterile and generic. This is only proper given that it is on the former site of the venerable 1836 St. Louis Exchange Hotel, one of the country's premier hostelries and a center of New Orleans social life until the final years of the Civil War. The original building was finally destroyed by a 1915 hurricane, but the Omni, built in 1960, is a worthy successor (not to mention one that suffered no damage from the recent hurricane), enjoying a prime location smack in the center of the Quarter. Furnishings in the guest rooms have grave good taste, full of muted tones and plush furniture, with windows that let you look dreamily out over the Quarter. Service is swift and conscientious—altogether an especially worthwhile choice.

621 St. Louis St., New Orleans, LA 70140. ℂ **888/444-OMNI** in the U.S. and Canada or 504/529-5333. Fax 504/529-7089. www.omniroyalorleans.com. 346 units. $169–$339 double; $339–$950 suite; $1,100–$1,500 penthouse. Children under 18 stay free in parent's room. AE, DC, DISC, MC, V. Valet parking $28 plus tax. **Amenities:** Restaurant; 2 bars; heated outdoor pool; health club; concierge; business center; florist; sundries shop and newsstand; salon; barbershop; 24-hr. room service; massage; babysitting; Wi-Fi; emergency mending and pressing; complimentary shoeshine. *In room:* A/C, TV, dataport, minibar, coffeemaker, hair dryer, iron/ironing board, safe.

The Saint Louis   Right in the heart of the Quarter, The Saint Louis is a small hotel that surrounds a lush courtyard with a fountain. But it's somewhat disappointingly dull for what ought to be a charming boutique hotel. Some rooms have private balconies overlooking Bienville Street, and all open onto the central courtyard. Some of the rooms are getting a redo with new carpet, drapes, and furniture, to help freshen up a slightly stodgy (and sometimes even shabby) decor. An additional wing with pricey units featuring parlors and kitchenettes is being added. The otherwise uninteresting bathrooms do have bidets. Some third-floor rooms have balconies. The courtyard is sometimes tented, blocking the view of it from the fourth and fifth floors.

730 Bienville St., New Orleans, LA 70130. ℂ **800/535-9111** or 504/581-7300. Fax 504/679-5013. www.stlouishotel.com. 98 units. $145–$335 double; $345–$375 suite. Children under 18 stay free in parent's room. AE, DC, MC, V. Valet parking $19. **Amenities:** Restaurant; access to nearby health club; concierge; room service for breakfast; laundry service. *In room:* A/C, TV.

Wyndham New Orleans at Canal Place ★   At the foot of Canal Street (though spared the flooding experienced there), the Wyndham is technically *in* the French Quarter—but not quite *of* it. It is literally *above* the Quarter: The grand-scale lobby, with its fine paintings and antiques, is on the 11th floor of the Canal Place tower. The guest rooms are on the floors above; each has a marble foyer and bathroom, and fine furnishings (including particularly good pillows). Needless to say, this hotel provides some of the city's most expansive views of the river (there is no devastation visible from here) and the French Quarter.

100 Iberville St., New Orleans, LA 70130. ℂ **800/996-3426** or 504/566-7006. Fax 504/553-5120. www.wyndham.com. 438 units. $159–$309 double. Ask about packages and specials. AE, DISC, MC, V. Valet parking, self-parking $15. **Amenities:** Restaurant; bar; heated pool; privileges at a nearby 18-hole golf course; concierge; tour desk; 24-hr. room service; laundry service; dry cleaning; direct elevator access to Canal Place shopping center, where guests can use the health center free of charge, or visit the barbershop, salon, and stores. *In room:* A/C, TV, dataport, minibar, coffeemaker, hair dryer, iron/ironing board.

MODERATE

Bienville House 🍴🍴 A nice little Quarter hotel, better than most (thanks to a combo of location, price, and room quality) though not as good as some (owing to a lack of specific personality). It's generally sedate, except perhaps during Mardi Gras, when the mad gay revelers takeover—as they do everywhere, truth be told. The truly friendly and helpful staff adds a lot of welcoming spirit. Rooms, only a few of which had any storm damage, mostly have high ceilings; kings have four-poster beds and slightly more interesting furniture than doubles. Some rooms have balconies overlooking the small courtyard that features a good pool for a dip, and all have the standard amenities of a fine hotel. Note that the Iberville Suite is so large it actually made us laugh out loud—and we mean that in a good way.

320 Decatur St., New Orleans, LA 70130. ℂ **800/535-7836** or 504/529-2345. Fax 504/525-6079. www.bienvillehouse.com. 83 units. $89–$650 double. Rates include continental breakfast. AE, DC, DISC, MC, V. Valet parking $20 cars, $25 SUVs. **Amenities:** Restaurant; outdoor pool; room service Tues–Sat 5–10pm. *In room:* A/C, TV, dataport, coffeemaker, hair dryer, iron/ironing board.

Bourbon Orleans Hotel—A Wyndham Historic Hotel 🍴 A lot of hotels claim to be centrally located in the French Quarter, but the Bourbon Orleans really is. And, while many hotels *claim* to have an interesting history, this one actually does: The oldest part of the hotel is the Orleans Ballroom, constructed in 1815 as a venue for the city's masquerade, carnival, and quadroon balls. Today the hotel occupies three buildings. Neither French Regency-style rooms nor the freshly gussied lobby were damaged by the hurricane, which is fortunate considering the pre-Katrina $15.5-million face-lift they'd just received. (Some service areas were hit.) The rooms for the mobility-impaired are well designed. Some rooms have only armoires, no closets, and some have balconies. Rooms that end in "17" (417, 517, and so forth) have views up Bourbon Street, but if you want to escape noisy street excitement, ask for an interior room. Beds are too firm while bathrooms are long and narrow and feature Golden Door Spa toiletries. Small rooms are cozy but not unbearable, though if occupied by two people they had better like each other. We are fond of the two-story town-house rooms, with exposed brickwork on the walls, and the beds upstairs in a romantic loft. It's classy and sexy, good for a multiple-day stay.

717 Orleans St., New Orleans, LA 70116. ℂ **504/523-2222.** Fax 504/525-8166. www.bourbonorleans.com. 220 units. $139–$199 petite queen or twin; $189–$329 deluxe king or double; $239–$489 junior suite; $299–$599 town house suite; $272–$482 town house suite with balcony. Extra person $30. AE, DC, DISC, MC, V. Valet parking $30. **Amenities:** Restaurant; bar; outdoor pool; concierge; room service 6:30am–10pm; same-day dry cleaning; nightly shoeshine. *In room:* A/C, TV, fax, dataport, Wi-Fi, coffeemaker, hair dryer, iron/ironing board, safe.

Bourgoyne Guest House *(Value*

This is an eccentric place, with an owner to match. If you dislike stuffy hotels and will happily take things a little worn at the edges (though in spots less so lately thanks to some post-Katrina repairs) in exchange for a relaxed, hangout atmosphere, come here. Accommodations are arranged around a nicely cluttered courtyard, the right spot to visit and regroup before diving back out onto Bourbon Street (whose main action begins just a few feet away). Studios are adequate little rooms with kitchens and bathrooms that appear grimy but are not (we saw the strong potions housekeeping uses; it's just age). The Green Suite is as big and grand as one would like, with huge tall rooms, a second smaller bedroom, a bigger bathroom, and a balcony overlooking Bourbon Street. For price and location, it's a heck of a deal, maybe the best in the Quarter.

839 Bourbon St., New Orleans, LA 70116. ℂ **504/525-3983** or 504/524-3621. 5 apts. $92 studio double; La Petite Suite $120 double; Green Suite $130 double, $160 triple, $190 quad. AE, MC, V. *In room:* A/C, unstocked fridge, coffeemaker, iron/ironing board.

The Cornstalk Hotel *(*

Thanks to the famous fence out front, this might be better known as a sightseeing stop than a place to stay, but consider staying here anyway. (They reopened in mid-Apr 2006.) A gorgeous Victorian home on the National Register of Historic Places, it's nearly as pretty inside as out. Additionally, the location couldn't be better—it's almost at the exact heart of the Quarter on a busy (but not noisy) section of Royal. The 200-year-old building withstood the storm extremely well, requiring only some new paint, and, on the inside, the need for some minor replacements of curtains, carpets, and paint.

If you are looking for period charm, look no further. The high-ceilinged rooms have fireplaces or stained-glass windows, and some have plasterwork (ceiling medallions, scrolls, and cherubs) from old plantations. The room with the largest bed is spectacular, while the rest are charming—you feel as if you have gone back 100 years. Unfortunately, that also applies to things like the plumbing (look for low-flow, spitting shower heads).

Oh, the fence? Well, it's at least 130 years old (photos indicate it might be even older), is made of cast iron, and looks like cornstalks painted in the appropriate colors. A portion of it was stolen during the Katrina days, but a security guard spotted a culprit carrying the missing section, and chased him down. With that fragment successfully retrieved, the fence was repaired and restored. When the building was a private home, Harriet Beecher Stowe stayed here—a trip that inspired her to write *Uncle Tom's Cabin*.

915 Royal St., New Orleans, LA 70116. ℂ **800/759-6112** or 504/523-1515. Fax 504/522-5558. www.travelguides.com/home/cornstalk. 14 units. $75–$185 double. Rates include continental breakfast. AE, MC, V. Limited parking $15. *In room:* A/C, TV, Wi-Fi.

Hôtel Provincial ℛ   Don't mention this to the owners, who are sensitive about it, but word from the ghost tours is that the Provincial is haunted, mostly by soldiers treated here when it was a Civil War hospital. It must not be too much of a problem, though, because guests rave about the hotel and never mention ghostly visitors. With flickering gas lamps, no elevators, no fewer than five patios, and a tranquil setting, this feels less like a hotel than a guest-house. Both the quiet and the terrific service belie its size, so it seems smaller and more intimate than it is. It's also in a good part of the Quarter on a quiet street off the beaten path. Regular rooms are dark but roomy, and most contain a mix of antique and reproduction furniture. *Note:* With such a pretty pool area, it's a shame there isn't much in the way of lounging or shade.

1024 Chartres St., New Orleans, LA 70116. ℂ **800/535-7922** or 504/581-4995. Fax 504/581-1018. www.hotelprovincial.com. 94 units. $79–$289 double. Packages available. AE, DC, DISC, MC, V. Valet parking $18. **Amenities:** Restaurant; bar; pool. *In room:* A/C, TV, dataport, hair dryer, iron/ironing board.

Hôtel St. Marie   Location, location, location. Just a little above Bourbon Street on an otherwise quiet street, this hotel should be on your list of "clean and safe backup places to stay if my top choices are full." Surrounding a sterile courtyard with a drab pool (which you will nonetheless bless the heavens for in summer), rooms are generic New Orleans in dark colors, with standard-issue, mock-European hotel furniture. Note that king rooms are more pleasant than doubles, and corner rooms are more spacious, which includes the otherwise dinky bathrooms (a few of which have odd red lights that could really cause major ocular damage). Some rooms have balconies overlooking the street and courtyard. Hallways are not numbered and can be dim, which could make a tipsy late-night return a challenge.

827 Toulouse St., New Orleans, LA 70112. ☏ 800/366-2743 or 504/561-8951. Fax 504/571-2802. www.hotelstmarie.com. 100 units. $129–$199 double. AE, DC, DISC, MC, V. Valet parking $20. **Amenities:** Restaurant; bar; limited room service (during dining-room hours); laundry service; dry cleaning. *In room:* A/C, TV, dataport, coffeemaker, hair dryer, iron/ironing board.

Hotel Villa Convento ☞
Local tour guides say this was the original House of the Rising Sun bordello, so if you have a sense of humor (or theater), be sure to pose in your bathrobe on your balcony so that you can be pointed out to passing tour groups. With its rather small public spaces and the personal attention that its owners and operators, the Campo family, give to their guests, the Villa Convento has the feel of a small European inn or guesthouse and does a lot of repeat business. The building is a Creole town house; some rooms open onto the tropical patio, others to the street, and many have balconies. Weirdly, there is better decor in those lower, lesser (by virtue of minimal windows) rooms. A few rooms got some leaks that required sheet rock replacement, a similar story told in many hotels around town.

616 Ursulines St., New Orleans, LA 70116. ☏ 800/887-2817 or 504/522-1793. Fax 504/524-1902. www.villaconvento.com. 25 units. $89–$105 double; $155 suite. Extra person $10. Rates include continental breakfast. AE, DC, DISC, MC, V. Parking $6. *In room:* A/C, TV, hair dryer, iron/ironing board.

The Lamothe House Hotel ☞
Somehow, a shiny new hotel doesn't seem quite right for New Orleans. More appropriate is slightly faded, somewhat threadbare elegance, and The Lamothe House neatly fits that bill. The Creole-style plain facade of this 1840s town house hides the atmosphere you are looking for—a mossy, brick-lined courtyard with a fish-filled fountain and banana trees and rooms filled with antiques that are worn in the right places but not shabby. It's a relief, then, that Katrina-motivated renovations will only spruce the place up, without altering the charm. All of the antique furniture remains, while new roofs, cleaned up brick

walls, some old carpet swapped out for non-moisture (and thus, musty-smelling) tiles, and fresh coats of paint everywhere will only give the old girl the right kind of primping and pampering. In the end, says the manager, "It's still going to have the same atmosphere." A continental breakfast is served in a second-floor dining room that just screams faded gentility. It's a short walk to the action in the Quarter. On a steamy night, sitting in the courtyard breathing the fragrant air, you can feel yourself slip out of time.

621 Esplanade Ave., New Orleans, LA 70116. ℂ 800/367-5858 or 504/947-1161. Fax 504/943-6536. www.lamothehouse.com. 30 units. $74–$275 double. Rates include continental breakfast and afternoon sherry. AE, DISC, MC, V. Free parking, except special events. **Amenities:** Pool, Wi-Fi in common areas. *In room:* A/C, TV, hair dryer, iron/ironing board, fridge, safe.

Le Richelieu 🦋 *Kids*   Roof damage led to the loss of about 40 rooms, and a subsequent to-the-studs renovation, though the hotel reopened in April 2006. First a row mansion, then a macaroni factory, and now a hotel, this building has seen it all. It's at the Esplanade edge of the Quarter—a perfect spot from which to explore the Faubourg Marigny. Le Richelieu is good for families (despite the surcharge for children), being out of the adult action and with a nice pool. The McCartney family thought so; Paul, the late Linda, and their kids stayed here for some months long ago while Wings was recording an album. Besides the enormous VIP suite, rooms are standard high-end motel rooms, though nearly half have been fully refreshed, of course, and many with balconies. All overlook either the French Quarter or the courtyard. Le Richelieu is the only hotel in the French Quarter with free self-parking on the premises.

1234 Chartres St., New Orleans, LA 70116. ℂ 800/535-9653 or 504/529-2492. Fax 504/524-8179. www.lerichelieuhotel.com. 86 units. $95–$180 double; $200–$550 suite. Extra person or child $15. Honeymoon and seasonal packages available. AE, DC, DISC, MC, V. Complimentary parking. **Amenities:** Restaurant; bar; outdoor pool; concierge; room service 7am–9pm. *In room:* A/C, TV, unstocked fridge, hair dryer, iron/ironing board.

Place d'Armes Hotel 🦋 *Kids*   Parts of this hotel seem a bit grim and old, though its quite large courtyard and amoeba-shaped pool are ideal for hanging out and may make up for it. Plus, it's only half a block from the **Café du Monde** (p. 120)—very convenient when you need a beignet at 3am. This also makes it a favorite for families traveling with kids. Rooms are homey and furnished in traditional style; however, 32 of them do not have windows and can be cell-like—ask for a room with a window when you reserve.

625 St. Ann St., New Orleans, LA 70116. ℂ **800/366-2743** or 504/524-4531. Fax 504/571-3803. www.placedarmes.com. 80 units. $129–$199 double; $190–$219 courtyard room. Rates include continental breakfast. AE, DC, DISC, MC, V. Parking $20. **Amenities:** Outdoor pool. *In room:* A/C, TV, coffeemaker, hair dryer, iron/ironing board.

Prince Conti Hotel ℛ   This tiny but friendly hotel with a marvelously helpful staff (some of whom are decent tour guides in their off-hours) is in a great location right off Bourbon and not generally noisy. Second-floor rooms all have fresh striped wallpaper and antiques, but quality varies from big canopy beds to painted iron bedsteads. Bathrooms can be ultra-tiny, with the toilet virtually on top of the sink. Travelers with kids should stay at the hotel's sister location, the Place d'Armes (see above), because it is farther from Bourbon and has a pool.

830 Conti St., New Orleans, LA 70112. ℂ **800/366-2743** or 504/529-4172. Fax 504/636-1046. www.princecontihotel.com. 53 units. $129–$199 double; $215–$275 suite. AE, DC, DISC, MC, V. Valet parking $20. **Amenities:** Restaurant; piano bar; breakfast cafe; room service 7–10am; laundry service. *In room:* A/C, TV, coffeemaker, iron/ironing board.

INEXPENSIVE

New Orleans Guest House ℛ   Run for many years by genial Ray Cronk and Alvin Payne, this guesthouse is a little off the beaten path (just outside the French Quarter across N. Rampart St.), but it's painted a startling hot, Pepto-Bismol pink, so it's hard to miss.

Rooms, which had to be completely renovated post-Katrina (the establishment was closed for 6 months) thanks to roof damage in both the old Creole main house (1848) and in what used to be the slave quarters, are simple—call it motel Victorian, with small bathrooms. Each has a unique color scheme (not hot pink, in case you were worried). Room no. 7, with its own private balcony, is perhaps the nicest. The courtyard is a veritable tropical garden (which came through the storm just fine) with banana trees, more green plants than you can count, some intricately carved old fountains, and a fluffy cat.

1118 Ursulines St., New Orleans, LA 70116. ℂ **800/562-1177** or 504/566-1177. Fax 504/566-1179. www.neworleans.com/nogh. 14 units. $89–$119 double; $109–$135 queen or twin; $119–$150 king or 2 full beds. Rates include continental breakfast. Extra person $35. AE, MC, V. Free parking. *In room:* A/C, TV, Wi-Fi, hair dryer, iron/ironing board.

2 The Faubourg Marigny

The Faubourg Marigny is a very distinct neighborhood from the French Quarter, though they border each other and are just an easy walk apart. Like the French Quarter, the Faubourg Marigny didn't experience flooding after the storm. This arty and bohemian neighborhood may be better for a younger crowd who wants to be near the French Quarter without actually being in it.

For hotels in this section, see the "Where to Stay in New Orleans" map on p. 40.

MODERATE

B&W Courtyards Bed & Breakfast ☆☆   The deceptively simple facade hides a sweet and very hospitable little B&B (which escaped any storm damage), complete with two small courtyards and a fountain. It's located near the bustling nighttime Frenchmen scene, a 10-minute walk or $5 cab ride (at most) to the Quarter. Owners Rob Boyd and Kevin Wu went to ingenious lengths to turn six oddly shaped spaces into comfortable rooms. No two rooms are alike—you enter one through its bathroom. All are carefully and thoughtfully decorated. Rob and Kevin are adept at giving advice—and strong opinions—not just about the city but also about their own local favorites. Breakfast is light (fruit, homemade breads) but beautifully presented. Prepare to be pampered—they take good care of you here.

2425 Chartres St., New Orleans, LA 70117. © **800/585-5731** or 504/945-9418. Fax 504/949-3483. www.bandwcourtyards.com. 8 units. $99–$250 double. Rates include continental breakfast. AE, DISC, MC, V. Free parking available on street. **Amenities:** Jacuzzi; business center. *In room:* A/C, TV, dataport, Wi-Fi, coffeemaker, hair dryer, iron/ironing board.

The Frenchmen ☆   This is seen by some as a small, sweet, and slightly funky inn, very popular with in-the-know regular visitors who think of it as quintessential New Orleans (though since it escaped any Katrina-related destruction, does that make it less so?). Some others think it's a total dump. We say that if worn carpet gives you the heebie-jeebies, assume that this place is not for you. But all new carpet, and in some cases, new tile floors, newly painted (in bright colors!) rooms, and new beds may change that impression. Nonetheless, the funk remains and for some, that's a good thing. The Frenchmen feels out of the way, but in some respects, the location can't be beat. It's just across from the Quarter and a block away from the lively nightlife of The Frenchmen section of the Faubourg Marigny.

Housed in two 19th-century buildings that were once grand New Orleans homes, rooms vary in size considerably, and some are very small indeed, and a little dingier than we would like, which is a shame, since they all have great bones. We wish someone would sweep in with better color choices and more antiques, to prime and primp this place into the charmer it deserves to be. Standard rooms have one double bed, some rooms have private balconies, and others have a loft bedroom with a sitting area. A small pool and Jacuzzi are in the inn's tropical courtyard, where you can often find guests hanging out.

417 Frenchmen St. (at Esplanade Ave.), New Orleans, LA 70116. ℂ 800/831-1781 or 504/948-2166. Fax 504/948-2258. www.frenchmenhotel.com. 27 units. $74–$299 double. Rates include breakfast. AE, DISC, MC, V. Free parking, except special events. **Amenities:** Pool; Jacuzzi. *In room:* A/C, TV, fridge, hair dryer, iron/ironing board, safe.

INEXPENSIVE

The Royal Street Inn & R Bar ⊛   This is an offbeat, happening little establishment in a residential neighborhood with plenty of street parking and regular police patrols. It's loose but not disorganized, and there couldn't be a better choice for laid-back travelers. Breakfast isn't served, but the inn still bills itself as a B&B. That's because here B&B stands for bed-and-*beverage*—the lobby is the highly enjoyable **R Bar** (p. 194). You check in with the bartender, and as a guest, you get two complimentary cocktails.

Regular rooms are small but cute, like a bedroom in a real house but with doors that open directly to the street. Suites, the best value near the Quarter, are well sized, accommodating up to four, and feature kitchenettes as well as their own names and stories. The Ghost in the Attic is a big room (complete with a mural of said ghost) with sloping ceilings, pleasing for those with starving-artist garret fantasies who don't like to give up good furniture. We love the addition of a brand-new, smashing suite, with two large bedrooms (one does double duty as half of the cavernous living room) plus two freestanding fireplaces. With a large balcony and plenty of gorgeous old new Orleans atmosphere, this is a great hang out/party space, perfect for two couples.

1431 Royal St., New Orleans, LA 70116. ℂ 800/449-5535 or 504/948-7499. Fax 504/943-9880. www.royalstreetinn.com. 5 units. $100–$250. Rates includes tax and bar beverage. AE, DISC, MC, V. Street parking available—purchase permit from the management. **Amenities:** Bar. *In room:* A/C, TV.

3 Mid-City/Esplanade

Mid-City hasn't gotten the same attention that the hardest hit neighborhoods have, but it did sustain a great deal of flood damage, with some portions taking on 6 feet or more of water. However, it's not the clear, outright devastation of the worst areas—more the quiet emptiness of abandonment and stasis, with streets full of buildings waiting for the next move by uncertain business owners and residents. However, that could easily change for the better, and the area may be bustling with reconstruction by the time you read this. Be assured that no establishment reopened unless they had little or no damage. The House on Bayou Road and Ashton's Bed & Breakfast are in the Bayou St. John neighborhood, which is bouncing back promisingly, and looks, at this writing, nearly as good as the Quarter and Garden District, though land phone lines remain largely inoperable at press time. The remaining two establishments are in areas that are recovering block by block. Both are either on or right off Canal Street, a fast car ride to the Quarter.

EXPENSIVE

The House on Bayou Road ★★★ If you want to stay in a rural and romantic setting but still be near the French Quarter, try The House on Bayou Road, quite probably the most smashing guesthouse in town. Just off Esplanade Avenue, this intimate Creole plantation home, built in the late 18th century, has been restored by owner Cynthia Reeves, who oversees an operation of virtual perfection. Like many places, the buildings and grounds were hit by the storm. The pretty little Creole cottage got smashed by a tree and is out of service for awhile, but the main building now sports a new purple tile roof. The big old barn is also gone, but the owner shrugs; this was a change in the works anyway, and now she has room for further expansion. The lovely gardens were badly battered, and are coming back slowly, but within a year or two they should be as lush and lovely as ever.

Each room is individually decorated to a fare-thee-well—slightly cluttered, not quite fussy, but still lovingly and aesthetically done. The Bayou St. John Room (the old library) holds a queen-size four-poster bed and has a working fireplace; the Bayou Delacroix has the same kind of bed and a wonderfully large bathtub. The extensive grounds are still a pleasure to stroll and there's an outdoor pool, Jacuzzi, patio, and screened-in porch. Expect a hearty plantation-style breakfast, and during the day and in the evening there's access to a minifridge filled with beverages.

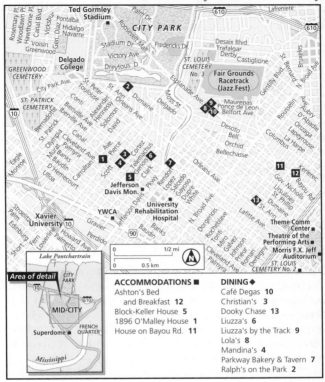

ACCOMMODATIONS ■
Ashton's Bed
    and Breakfast **12**
Block-Keller House **5**
1896 O'Malley House **1**
House on Bayou Rd. **11**

DINING ◆
Café Degas **10**
Christian's **3**
Dooky Chase **13**
Liuzza's **6**
Liuzza's by the Track **9**
Lola's **8**
Mandina's **4**
Parkway Bakery & Tavern **7**
Ralph's on the Park **2**

2275 Bayou Rd., New Orleans, LA 70119. ℂ **800/882-2968** or 504/945-0992. Fax 504/945-0993. www.houseonbayouroad.com. 8 units, 2 cottages. $155–$320 double. Rates include full breakfast. AE, MC, V. Free off-street parking. **Amenities:** Restaurant; outdoor pool; Jacuzzi. *In room:* A/C, TV, Wi-Fi, dataport, minibar, hair dryer, iron/ironing board.

MODERATE

Ashton's Bed & Breakfast ⌖ This charming guesthouse sustained one enormous dramatic hole on the side of the main house, which meant half the guest rooms needed repairs. (Look for photos of damage and repairs on their website and admire their tenacity!) In true lemonade-from-lemons style, they have used this as an opportunity to improve those same rooms, adding crown molding, ceiling medallions, and other touches they had long wanted anyway, resulting in rooms that are sweetly upgraded, while rooms in the rear service wing are as nice as ever. Those with personal space and privacy issues might want to head to room no. 3, which is most grand, with a four-poster bed and a nice bathroom with a claw-foot tub. Virtually all the rooms have wide wooden floorboards. A full breakfast is served, featuring such local dishes as *pain perdu* and eggs Sardou. That they stuck it out despite such damage is more than admirable.

2023 Esplanade Ave., New Orleans, LA 70116. ℂ **800/725-4131** or 504/942-7048. Fax 504/947-9382. www.ashtonsbb.com. 8 units. $105–$170 double. Rates include full breakfast. AE, DISC, MC, V. Free parking. *In room:* A/C, TV, dataport and Wi-Fi, minibar, hair dryer, iron/ironing board, robes.

Block-Keller House 𝒢𝒢 This inn is a splendid choice for someone who wants both the classic Victorian B&B experience but also guiltily wants a room with modern amenities (Berber carpet, Jacuzzi tubs, and the like). Six feet of water destroyed their beautifully designed basement-level rooms, which they are not rebuilding at this time. (Once the neighborhood comes back they intend to return their attention to it.) The ground-floor rooms had no damage, which was deeply fortunate, leaving intact the gorgeous Victorian details (including a newly refurnished parlor), with fireplaces and grand old beds. The gardens are being redesigned and replanted, adding flowers in the space formerly shaded by a once-grand oak tree. At this writing, they do not have daily maid service, though towels will be replaced and beds will be made each day. Fear not, the amiable hosts are very experienced in B&B running, and it shows in everything they do; we loved the continental breakfast, which included feather-light buttermilk biscuits, hard-cooked eggs, fresh cantaloupe and strawberries, and all the trappings. All in all, this place is a delight in looks, style, and service, and as the neighborhood regains its feet, it will only become more desirable. Say hello for us to resident labs Milo and Buster.

3620 Canal St., New Orleans, LA 70119. ℂ **877/588-3033** or 504/483-3033. Fax 504/483-3032. www.blockkellerhouse.com. 5 units. $90–$135. Rates include breakfast. AE, MC, V. **Amenities:** Internet access. *In room:* A/C, TV.

The 1896 O'Malley House 𝒢 This is another beautifully restored home turned B&B, in a building dating back to, you guessed it, 1896. A foot of water (look for the watermark on the marble fireplace!) prompted the need for new downstairs furniture and all new wiring, but the guest rooms were unaffected and they were able to save the original floors. Many of the original details, including marvelous tile on the various fireplaces in several of the rooms, are still intact. Second-floor rooms are larger, and most have Jacuzzi tubs. The third floor is a clever use of design and space, with formerly dull wood walls turned most striking by pickling the wood to a lighter color (ask to see the photos of the mysterious science equations found scrawled on one wall). These rooms are smaller and more garretlike, though, frankly, they pale in desirability only if you really, *really* want that classic high-ceilinged look. The breakfast is fresh and filling.

120 S. Pierce St., New Orleans, LA 70119. Ⓒ **866/226-1896** or 504/488-5896. Fax 504/483-3791. www.1896omalleyhouse.com. 8 units. $99–$145; $175 for special events. Rates include continental breakfast. AE, MC, V. Often closed for part of Aug. Pet-friendly. *In room:* A/C, TV, dataport and Wi-Fi, hair dryer, iron/ironing board on request.

4 Central Business District (CBD)

For hotels in this section, please see the "Where to Stay in New Orleans" map on p. 40.

VERY EXPENSIVE

Hilton New Orleans Riverside Hotel 🍴 (Kids)   The Hilton is blessed with a central location—right at the riverfront near the World Trade Center of New Orleans, the New Orleans Convention Center, and the Aquarium. It's a self-contained complex of nearly a dozen restaurants, bistros, and bars; two gift shops; a full and exceptional racquet and health club; and a huge exhibition space. In addition, Harrah's Casino and the Riverwalk Marketplace are accessible from the hotel's lobby, which contains a nine-story atrium (some of the windows broke and let in rainwater, requiring renovation on the second floor, although that affected only the original check-in location). This is a top choice for families. Guest rooms are spacious, and many have fabulous views of the river or the city.

2 Poydras St., New Orleans, LA 70140. Ⓒ **800/445-8667** or 504/561-0500. Fax 504/568-1721. www.neworleans.hilton.com. 1,600 units. $225–$475 double; $650–$2,000 suite. Special packages available. AE, DC, DISC, MC, V. Valet parking $27, self-parking $22. **Amenities:** 2 restaurants; 2 bars; eligible for membership ($27 for 3 days) in the hotel's Rivercenter Racquet and Health Club; concierge; airport transportation; 24-hr. room service; laundry service; dry cleaning; pressing service. *In room:* A/C, TV, dataport, minibar, coffeemaker, hair dryer, iron/ironing board.

Hotel InterContinental 🍴   The red granite Hotel InterContinental rises from the heart of the CBD within walking distance of the French Quarter and the Mississippi River attractions. Some minor flooding required repairs to some of the public areas, but it was fully functional before Mardi Gras. It's an elegant, old-fashioned—or what passes for that in this brave new Ian Schragerized world—hotel, clearly targeting a certain kind of business traveler who isn't impressed by the hip minimalists springing up everywhere. You should consider it, too. Rooms are done in dark wood furniture (mattresses are nothing special) with similarly woodsy strong greens and reds; bathrooms are small but dignified. Call it masculine in a slightly frilly way. All the rooms are decently sized. Some rooms have balconies that overlook the courtyard, although said courtyard is modern and industrial in appearance.

444 St. Charles Ave., New Orleans, LA 70130. (© 800/327-0200 or 504/525-5566. Fax 504/585-4350. http://new-orleans.interconti.com. 479 units. $305–$325 double; $500–$2,000 suite. AE, DC, DISC, MC, V. Valet parking $25. **Amenities:** The Veranda (p. 111); Pete's Pub serving lunch daily; bar; outdoor rooftop pool; health club (focusing on cardiovascular machines); concierge; business center; gift shop; barbershop and salon; 24-hr. room service; laundry service; dry cleaning. *In room:* A/C, TV, dataport, minibar, coffeemaker, hair dryer, iron/ironing board, safe.

JW Marriott Hotel New Orleans *&*

The hotel formerly known as Le Meridian and ever so briefly as the New Orleans Grand is so committed to appearing classy that it covers the electrical cords of its lamps with shirred designer fabric. You can't fault the location on Canal right across from the Quarter (excellent for viewing Mardi Gras parades), but ultimately, it's elegant but boring—yes, we're spoiled—more for business travelers who don't plan on spending much time in their rooms. Double rooms have extra-wide twin beds (a sure sign they aren't catering to families), with a chaise longue in the king room and sofas in doubles. The hotel had a pre-Katrina multi-million-dollar face-lift to bring the place up to higher standards, which means it looks just a little fresher.

614 Canal St., New Orleans, LA 70130. (© 888/364-1200 or 504/525-6500. Fax 504/525-8068. www.jwmarriottneworleans.com. 494 units. $184–$355 double; $1,000–$3,500 suite. AE, DC, DISC, MC, V. Valet parking $27. **Amenities:** Restaurant; 2 bars; heated outdoor pool; health club (offering free aerobics and spinning classes); 24-hr. concierge; business center; gift shop; jewelry store; salon; 24-hr. room service; babysitting; laundry service; dry cleaning. *In room:* A/C, TV, dataport, minibar, coffeemaker, hair dryer, iron/ironing board, safe.

Loft 523 *&*

Some flooding and other storm-related structural issues, plus staffing shortages, led to this hotel's closure until mid-April 2006, but renovations have come along nicely and it should be as good, if not better, than ever, with original style and vibe intact. Each of these spacious loft-style units, in an old carriage and dry-goods warehouse in the Central Business District, is a marvel of

Spending the Night in Chains

For those of you who prefer the predictability of a chain hotel, there's a **Marriott** *丸* at 555 Canal St. at the edge of the Quarter (*©* 800/228-9290 or 504/581-1000).

In the Central Business District (CBD), check out the **Holiday Inn Express,** 221 Carondelet St. (*©* 504/962-0800), or consider the slightly spiffier **Cotton Exchange** (both flooded and looted, but reopened in Mar 2006 with completely renovated rooms, which had only cosmetic damage) next door at 231 Carondelet St. (*©* 504/962-0700). It shares facilities with the Holiday Inn in the historic building of the same name. **Residence Inn by Marriott** *丸*, 345 St. Joseph St. (*©* 800/331-3131 or 504/522-1300), and a **Courtyard by Marriott** *丸*, 300 Julia St. (*©* 504/598-9898), are both a couple of blocks from the convention center. Both experienced some looting, but were reopened not long after Katrina. The **Homewood Suites,** at 901 Poydras St., is pretty dazzling, in a cookie-cutter way (*©* 504/581-5599), while the **Quality Inn,** at 210 O'Keefe Ave., had some flooding to the main level, but reopened almost immediately (*©* 504/525-6800).The **Holiday Inn Downtown–Superdome** *丸* is, natch, right by the Superdome at 330 Loyola Ave. (*©* 800/HOLIDAY or 504/581-1600).

modern design, sort of a Jetsons-futuristic-meets-NYC-minimalist-fantasy—those wanting plushy and overstuffed will be miserable as soon as they see the concrete floors. Beds are surprisingly comfortable platforms, with Frette linens. A Sony CD/DVD Surround Sound system adds sonic warmth, and the bathrooms are so big you could fit the entire ReBirth Brass Band inside. But here's where Loft 523 breaks from N.Y./L.A. detached cool: Throughout are reminders of the building's provenance—old wood planks form the floor downstairs, turn-of-the-20th-century tin ceiling tiles outfit the elevators, and columns from the old warehouse decorate the lounge. It is the second smoke-free hotel in the city (its sibling, the International House [p. 65], was the first).

523 Gravier St., New Orleans, LA 70130. *©* 800/633-5770 or 504/200-6523. Fax 504/200-6522. www.loft523.com. 18 units (3 of them penthouses). $259–$359 double; $859–$1,100 suite. AE, DC, DISC, MC, V. Valet parking $28. **Amenities:** Lounge; health club. *In room:* A/C, TV, Wi-Fi, remote-control stereo system, hair dryer, iron/ironing board, safe.

Windsor Court ✸✸✸   There may be a finer hotel on the conti-
nent, but it can't be found in New Orleans. The unassuming, somewhat office-building exterior (which had minimal storm damage) is
camouflage for the quiet but posh delights found within. Two corridors downstairs are mini-galleries that display original 17th-,
18th-, and 19th-century art. Everything is very, very chic and consequently just a little chilly. It's not too stiff for restless children, but
it still feels more like a grown-up hotel. The level of service is
extraordinarily high.

The accommodations are exceptionally spacious, with classy, not
flashy, decor. Almost all are suites (either really big, or downright
huge) featuring large bay windows or a private balcony overlooking
the river (ask for a river view) or the city, a private foyer, a large living room, a bedroom with French doors, a large marble bathroom
with particularly luxe amenities (plush robes, thick towels, a ham-
per, extra hair dryers), two dressing rooms, and a "petite kitchen."

300 Gravier St., New Orleans, LA 70130. ✆ **888/596-0955** or 504/523-6000. Fax
504/596-4513. www.windsorcourthotel.com. 324 units. $195–$450 deluxe guest
room; $245–$475 junior suite; $285–$525 full suite; $600–$1,500 2-bedroom
suite; $2,000–$3,500 penthouse. Children under 12 stay free in parent's room. AE,
DC, DISC, MC, V. Valet parking $28. **Amenities:** Restaurant; lounge; health club
w/resort-size pool, sauna, and steam room; concierge; 24-hr. suite service (much
more than your average room service); in-room massage; laundry service; dry cleaning. *In room:* A/C, TV, minibar, hair dryer, iron/ironing board, safe, robes.

W New Orleans ✸✸   While we have strong feelings indeed about
staying in more New Orleans–appropriate, site-specific accommodations, we cheerfully admit that this is one fun hotel, and what is
New Orleans about if not fun? There are certainly no more playful
rooms in town, done up as they are in reds, blacks, and golds—
frosty chic, to be sure, but oh, so comfortable, thanks to feather
everything (pillows, comforters, beds—and yes, allergy sufferers,
they have foam alternatives). There are nifty amenities and gewgaws
galore; suites offer little different from the rooms except more space
and, indeed, more of everything (two TVs, two DVD players, two
bathrooms, one Ouija board). Windows blew out on one side of the
building, damaging those very suites, but the W brand identity
means that once they are renovated they will look the same once
again. Not all rooms have views, but the ones that do, especially
those of the river, are outstanding. The ultra-chic bar was designed
by hip bar/club owner Rande "Mr. Cindy Crawford" Gerber. We do
wish this whole experience wasn't so, well, New York, but then
again, we find ourselves having so much fun it's kinda hard to get all
that worked up about it.

333 Poydras St., New Orleans, LA 70130. ℂ **800/522-6963** or 504/525-9444. Fax 504/581-7179. www.whotels.com. 423 units. $469–$900 double. AE, DC, DISC, MC, V. Valet parking $28. **Amenities:** Restaurant; bar; pool; fitness center; concierge; business services; 24-hr. room service; massage. *In room:* A/C, TV/VCR, minibar, coffeemaker, hair dryer, iron/ironing board, safe, CD player.

EXPENSIVE

Astor Crowne Plaza Hotel: The Alexa   This boutique hotel wannabe is connected to the larger and more traditionally elegant Astor Crowne Plaza by a series of corridors and elevators, which makes for confusion if no one at the front desk warns you about this or lets you know that all the major facilities—like the business center, health club, and pool—are over at the sister property. Then why, you may ask, should you stay here rather than there? It's cheaper. Rooms are narrow and small—as in you-can-kick-the-wall-at-the-end-of-the-bed-if-you-are-tall size, though the exposed brick wall and period-style furniture helps. Guests have access to two good restaurants, making this hotel a smart bet for the solo business traveler (rooms with two double beds are much too cramped) with no claustrophobia issues.

119 Royal St., New Orleans, LA 70130. ℂ **888/884-3366** or 504/962-0600. Fax 504/962-0601. www.astorcrowneplaza.com. 192 units. $99–$269 double; $450 suite. AE, DC, DISC, MC, V. **Amenities:** Restaurant; bar; pool; fitness room; concierge. *In room:* A/C, TV, dataport, hair dryer, iron/ironing board, safe-deposit box.

Hotel Le Cirque   A smart, sharp, and chic version of the generic business hotel—sort of like a Crowne Plaza (no coincidence; Crowne Plaza owns them), if it was done up in chartreuse and that new misty gray-blue that's all the rage. Oddly, it's not set up as a business hotel, lacking amenities such as separate dataports, but it does offer 4,000 square feet of meeting space. Rooms are average size; the ones with king-size beds are a bit cramped thanks to all the furniture crammed in along with it (chair, desk, TV). Queen rooms are even smaller. *A tip:* The hotel offers rides in a complimentary town car (first-come, first-served) anywhere within a 2-mile radius.

936 St. Charles Ave., New Orleans, LA 70130. ℂ **800/684-9525** or 504/962-0900. Fax 504/962-0901. www.neworleansfinehotels.com. 138 units. $69–$299 double. AE, DC, DISC, MC, V. **Amenities:** Concierge; limited car service; limited-hour room service; babysitting; laundry service; dry cleaning. *In room:* A/C, TV, hair dryer, iron/ironing board, safe.

International House 🐟🐟🐟   A standout from the start, the International House has set a new standard with its creative design and meticulous attention to detail. Record company and film execs should love it, but so should anyone who's had enough of Victorian sweetness and needs a palate cleanser. Here, a wonderful old Beaux Arts bank building has been transformed into a modern space that still pays tribute to its locale. Consequently, in the graceful lobby, classical pilasters stand next to modern wrought-iron chandeliers.

Interiors are the embodiment of minimalist chic. Rooms are simple with muted, monochromatic (okay, beige) tones, tall ceilings and ceiling fans, up-to-the-minute bathroom fixtures, but also black-and-white photos of local musicians and characters, books about the city, and other clever decorating touches that anchor the room in its New Orleans setting. The commitment to hip, cool, and groovy means dark corridors and hard-to-read room numbers, and although the big bathrooms boast large tubs or space-age glassed-in showers, they do come off as a bit industrial. But compensations include cushy touches such as feather pillows, large TVs, your own private phone number in your room, and CD players with CDs.

On top of all this, the hotel went smoke-free in January 2005, only the second (other than its sibling, Loft 523) in the city. Both are also instituting "green" measures to make the hotel more environmentally responsible.

221 Camp St., New Orleans, LA 70130. (*C*) **800/633-5770** or 504/553-9550. Fax 504/553-9560. www.ihhotel.com. 119 units. $149–$379 double; $369–$1,799 suite. AE, DC, DISC, MC, V. Valet parking $28. **Amenities:** Lemon Grass restaurant (p. 110); bar; health club; 24-hr. concierge; gift shop; room service 8am–10pm; dry cleaning. *In room:* A/C, TV w/pay movies, CD player, dataport, minibar, hair dryer, iron/ironing board.

Loews New Orleans Hotel *fifi*   The stylish, spanking-new Loews hotel is a sharp-dressed combo of modern and *moderne,* with judiciously applied sprinkles of New Orleans flavor. Maybe it's the newness of the place (the new luster has not really worn off even despite a few storm-blown windows) or that the front desk has a photo-tile collage featuring black-and-white shots of iconic local images. Maybe it's the fact that Loews was willing to renovate the adjoining Piazza D'Italia (a local landmark that had gone to seed; be sure to wander amid its fountain and neon-lit glory one evening). Whatever it is, we are quite smitten. The bright and spacious rooms are decorated with art by a local photographer and feature goose-down comforters and pillows. Bathrooms are small, but granite and wood vanities make up for the lack of space. Views vary from river to partial river plus piazza to New Orleans city skyline, which get better the higher up you go. Note that the hotel's lowest floor is the 11th, so this is not the choice for those with vertigo or other high-floor issues.

Possibly best of all: Loews has a "Loews Loves Pets" policy, which practically encourages Fido to come join in the fun. The terrific restaurant **Café Adelaide** is reviewed on p. 108.

300 Poydras St., New Orleans, LA 70130. © **800/23LOEWS** or 504/595-3300. www.loewshotels.com. 285 units. $149–$279 luxury units; $189–$319 grand luxury units. AE, DC, DISC, MC, V. Valet parking $28. Pet-friendly (no deposit). **Amenities:** Restaurant; bar; pool; workout room; spa; concierge; business center; 24-hr. room service; babysitting; laundry service; dry cleaning. *In room:* A/C, TV, dataport, minibar, hair dryer, iron/ironing board, safe, CD player, video games, umbrella.

The Pelham   This small hotel, in a renovated building (which had some minor structural damage that was soon fixed) that dates from the late 1800s, is one of the new wave of boutique hotels. From the outside and in its public areas, The Pelham feels like an upscale apartment building. If you're not interested in staying right in the Quarter or you're looking for something with less public atmosphere than a hotel and more anonymity than a B&B, this is a good option.

444 Common St., New Orleans, LA 70130. © **888/856-4486** or 504/522-4444. Fax 504/539-9010. www.neworleansfinehotels.com. 60 units. $79–$399 double. AE, DC, DISC, MC, V. Parking $19 cars, $22 trucks plus tax. **Amenities:** Concierge; laundry service. *In room:* A/C, TV, dataport, hair dryer, iron/ironing board, safe.

Renaissance Arts Hotel ⚑   The Renaissance brand is the Marriott's attempt at a hip, W-style hotel, a place for younger business travelers to feel a bit better about themselves. Don't expect painters in the lobby, splattering like Pollock or staging suspicious performance-art gags. What "arts" here means is that the designers made a concerted effort to incorporate art, specifically local art, into the decor. But the theme gets stronger once you enter the hallways, and comes into stronger focus in the rooms, which are hung with the works of several Louisiana artists (from Lafayette-based Francis Pavy to New Orleans's highly recommended Studio Inferno glassworks). The rooms feel less forcedly playful than those over at the Pere Marquette, and are well sized (look for a connecting room to get extra square footage) and include down pillows and covers.

700 Tchoupitoulas St., New Orleans, LA 70130. © **504/613-2330.** Fax 504/613-2331. www.marriott.com. 217 units. $189 double. AE, DC, DISC, MC, V. Valet parking $23. **Amenities:** Restaurant; bar; pool; health club; concierge; business center; gift shop; room service 6am–11pm; babysitting; laundry service; dry cleaning; newspaper delivery. *In room:* A/C, TV, CD player, high-speed Internet access, minibar, coffeemaker, hair dryer, iron/ironing board, safe.

St. James Hotel ⚑   A fine preservation job has given what could have been an eyesore derelict (if historic) building a new useful function. Actually, this is two different buildings, one of which used to be—get this!—the St. James Infirmary, sung about so memorably by many a mournful jazz musician. But because the restorers had to make do with a non-uniform space, rooms vary in size and style, and a few lack windows. All rooms have been freshly renovated (some rooms had some rain damage thanks to blown windows; like many hotels, needed repairs were used as an excuse to do some timely freshening up), have marble bathrooms, and two suites and a room share a small, private brick courtyard with a fountain—a nice setup for a small group. There is a teeny-weeny pool—you might be forgiven for considering it really just a large puddle with nice tile. Overall, this is a good and friendly find, located just a block or two within the CBD.

330 Magazine St., New Orleans, LA 70130. (C) 888/856-4485 or 504/304-4000. www.saintjameshotel.com. 86 units. $99–$299 double. AE, DC, DISC, MC, V. Valet parking $20. **Amenities:** Pool; health club; concierge; room service Mon–Sat 6:30–10am; babysitting; laundry service; dry cleaning. *In room:* Coffeemaker, hair dryer, iron/ironing board, safe.

The Whitney—A Wyndham Historic Hotel ☞ A grand old
bank building has been cleverly converted into a fine modern hotel. The unique results include gawk-worthy public spaces; be sure to look up at all the old, fanciful, wedding-cake-decoration plaster-work and help us wonder how the heck safecrackers got past those thick slab doors. Best of all is the imposing lobby, full of stately pil-lars, now part restaurant but also still part working bank—it puts other swellegant establishments in town to shame.

Rooms are a little too stately to classify as true business efficient but also a little too generic to make this a proper romantic getaway. Having said that, we found the beds most comfortable and the bath-rooms spacious. Overall, The Whitney has more character than your average upscale chain. If you are a hoity-toity businessman, you will probably like it a lot. And if you are a preservationist, you will prob-ably like it even more.

610 Poydras St., New Orleans, LA 70130 (C) 800/996-3426 or 504/581-4222. Fax 504/207-0100. www.wyndham.com. 93 units. $169–$229 double. AE, DC, DISC, MC, V. Valet parking $22. **Amenities:** Restaurant; private dining room; lobby bar; fitness center; business services; room service (temporarily discontinued due to staff shortages). *In room:* A/C, TV, CD player, dataport, coffee- and tea-making facilities, hair dryer, iron/ironing board.

MODERATE
Drury Inn & Suites *Value* This family-owned chain looks
all too generic outside, but inside is a pleasant surprise, with

grander-than-expected public spaces and rooms that are fancier than those in the average chain, not to mention clean and new. All have high ceilings (except for those on the fifth floor) and a decent amount of square footage, though bathrooms are small (with sinks in the dressing area). A nice little heated rooftop pool, a small exercise room, and a generous comp breakfast make this a good bargain for the area.

820 Poydras St., New Orleans, LA 70112. © **800/DRURYINN** or 504/529-7800. Fax 504/581-3328. www.druryhotels.com/properties/neworleans.cfm. 156 units. $149 double; $189 suite. Rates include full breakfast and weekday evening cocktails. AE, DC, DISC, MC, V. Parking $15. **Amenities:** Heated pool; exercise room; laundry service; dry cleaning. *In room:* A/C, TV, minifridge, coffeemaker, hair dryer, iron/ironing board, microwave, whirlpool tubs (in some suites).

Le Pavillon Hotel 🦋   Established in 1907 in a prime Central Business District location, Le Pavillon was the first hotel in New Orleans to have elevators. It's now a member of Historic Hotels of America. The lobby is stunning (despite some blown-out windows and resulting harm), just what you want in a big, grand hotel, with giant columns and chandeliers. The standard guest rooms are all rather pretty and have similar furnishings, but they differ in size. Bay Rooms are standard with two double beds and bay windows. Suites are actually hit-or-miss in terms of decor, with the nadir being the mind-bogglingly ugly Art Deco Suite. Much better is the Plantation Suite, decorated in—you guessed it—antiques including pieces by Mallard, C. Lee (who, as a slave, studied under Mallard), Mitchell Rammelsberg, Belter, Badouine, and Marcotte. The pool area got scruffed up a bit, but has been retiled. Late-night peanut butter and jelly sandwiches plus chocolates and milk are offered in the lobby.

833 Poydras St., New Orleans, LA 70112. © **800/535-9095** or 504/581-3111. Fax 504/522-5543. www.lepavillon.com. 226 units. $149–$179 double; $599–$1,695 suite. AE, DC, DISC, MC, V. Valet parking $28. **Amenities:** Restaurant; bar; heated outdoor pool; fitness center; whirlpool spa; concierge; 24-hr. room service; babysitting; laundry service; dry cleaning. *In room:* A/C, TV, dataport, Wi-Fi, minibar, hair dryer, iron/ironing board.

INEXPENSIVE

The Depot at Madame Julia's 🦋 *(Finds)*   The Depot is an alternative to more commercial hotels in the Central Business District. Already rather funky pre-Katrina, the outside is a bit more battered these days, though improvements are ongoing. Shingles came off the roof thanks to low-flying helicopters, but the interior problems were minimal. Low prices and a guesthouse environment mean a number of good things but also mean shared bathrooms, rooms on the small and cozy side, and a location that, although quiet on the weekends, can get noisy in the mornings as the working neighborhood gets going, especially given the amount of construction these days. It's a quick walk or a short streetcar ride from the Quarter, which makes it an affordable alternative to the Quarter's much more expensive accommodations. The budget-conscious and those who prefer their hotels with personality will consider this a find.

748 O'Keefe St., New Orleans, LA 70113. ℂ 504/529-2952. Fax 504/529-1908. 25 units, all with shared bathrooms. $65–$85 double. Rates include breakfast. Cash or personal checks (only by check if paid in advance). Off-street parking available. *In room:* A/C.

5 Uptown/The Garden District

For hotels in this section, see the "Where to Stay & Dine Uptown" map on p. 71 or the "Where to Stay in New Orleans" map on p. 40.

VERY EXPENSIVE

Pontchartrain Hotel 🐾   This fabulous grand dame really took a beating during the post-Katrina days. Most of the rooms were looted and smashed up, with about 20% also getting weather-wrecked thanks to blown-out windows. Slowly but surely the destruction is being repaired, which means that eventually, just about everything, from TVs to furniture, will be new, or at least, refreshed. This will ultimately be a good thing, since in recent years the hotel (despite a nice pre-Katrina redo) has been best known for faded grandeur and evocative atmosphere. Long a local landmark, it was the place for the likes of Rita Hayworth and Aly Kahn to tryst, courtesy of adjoining suites—we can only hope this marks a renaissance for what has always been, and will always be, despite it all, a mighty romantic spot. Note that rooms are more spacious than many typical hotel rooms (although any room ending in 01 or 09 is going to be on the smaller side).

2031 St. Charles Ave., New Orleans, LA 70140. ℂ **800/777-6193** or 504/524-0581. Fax 504/529-1165. www.pontchartrainhotel.com. 118 units. $95–$380 double. Extra person $10; during special events $25. Seasonal packages and special promotional rates available. AE, DC, DISC, MC, V. Parking $18. **Amenities:** Restaurant; bar; access to nearby spa w/health club and outdoor pool; 24-hr. room service. *In room:* A/C, TV, coffeemaker, hair dryer, iron/ironing board, safe.

EXPENSIVE

The Grand Victorian Bed & Breakfast 🐾🐾   Owner Bonnie Rabe confounded and delighted her new St. Charles neighbors

Where to Stay & Dine Uptown

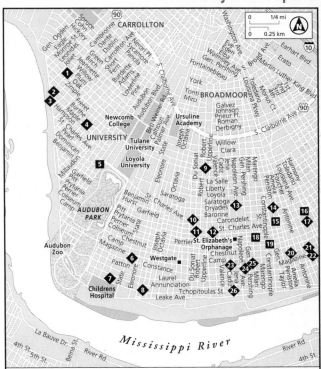

DINING ◆

Bluebird Cafe **17**
Brigtsen's **2**
Casamento's **24**
Clancy's **7**
Dante's Kitchen **3**
Dick & Jenny's **26**
Dunbar's
   Creole Cooking **9**
Franky & Johnny's **8**
Gautreau's **10**
Jacques-Imo's **1**
La Boulangerie **23**
La Crêpe Nanou **11**
La Petite Grocery **25**

Lilette **20**
Martin Wine Cellar
   and Delicatessen **14**
Martinique Bistro **6**
Mystic Café **21**
Pascal's Manale **13**
PJ's Coffee &
   Tea Company **4**
Slim Goodies Diner **22**
Upperline **12**

ACCOMMODATIONS ■

Chimes B&B **19**
The Columns **15**
Hampton Inn Garden District **16**
Maison Perrier Bed & Breakfast **18**
Park View Guest House **5**

when she took a crumbling Queen Anne–style Victorian mansion right on the corner of Washington (2 blocks from Lafayette cemetery and Commander's Palace) and resurrected it into a showcase B&B. The location makes its porches and balconies a perfect place to view Mardi Gras parades.

The stunning Victorian rooms are full of antiques (each has an impressive four-poster or wood canopy bed—though a couple are small thanks to their vintage). Linens, pillows, and towels are ultra plush, and some bathrooms have big Jacuzzi tubs. A generous continental breakfast is served, and friendly Bonnie is ready with suggestions on how to spend your time.

2727 St. Charles Ave., New Orleans, LA 70130. ℭ 800/977-0008 or 504/895-1104. Fax 504/896-8688. www.gvbb.com. 8 units. $150–$350 double. Rates include continental breakfast. AE, DISC, MC, V. *In room:* A/C, TV, dataport, hair dryer, iron/ironing board.

Maison Perrier Bed & Breakfast ☞

This B&B claims to be the equivalent of a four-star resort. Certainly, the level of service offered is very high. And rooms initially impress; each is large and has a (nonworking) fireplace ornamented with dazzling original tile. But if you look closely, you will notice the rooms lack the substantive good taste and comfort of other local B&Bs; furniture usually consists of modern copies and not great ones, linens and mattresses are not top quality, and the overall decor is not as well thought out as in peer establishments. The least impressive room is also the cheapest, a modest space just off the kitchen. Breakfast is large, prepared by a resident cook who knows the way to a guest's heart is through Southern specialties such as puff pancakes and Creole grits. There is also a fully stocked honor bar, along with a weekend wine-and-cheese party and daily snacks like fresh-baked brownies.

4117 Perrier St. (2 blocks riverside from St. Charles Ave., 3 blocks downtown from Napoleon Ave.), New Orleans, LA 70115. ℭ 888/610-1807 or 504/897-1807. Fax 504/897-1399. www.maisonperrier.com. $79–$260 double. Rates change according to season and include breakfast. AE, DISC, MC, V. Parking available on street. **Amenities:** Concierge; business center; laundry service. *In room:* A/C, TV, dataport, minibar, hair dryer, iron/ironing board, Wi-Fi.

The McKendrick-Breaux House ☞☞

This is one of the best B&Bs in town, run by a team that has been in the bed-and-breakfast game for enough years that theirs is a smooth and charming operation. The rooms are done in impeccably good taste (barely touched by the storm—they reopened 3½ weeks afterward, housing FEMA types!), with high-quality mattresses and pillows, and each has its own style; the ones in the main house have claw-foot tubs and (sadly nonworking) fireplaces. Third-floor rooms (reached by a steep, narrow staircase) evoke classic garret quarters, with exposed brick walls (we swoon over room no. 38). Rooms in the second building are somewhat larger; the first-floor units are slightly more modern in appearance (but have large bathrooms), which is probably why we like the ones on the second floor (especially the front room, and the deep-purple walls and bright-green bathroom wainscoting of room no. 33).

1474 Magazine St., New Orleans, LA 70130. © **888/570-1700** or 504/586-1700. Fax 504/522-7138. www.mckendrick-breaux.com. 9 units. $135–$235 double. Rates include tax and breakfast. AE, MC, V. Limited free off-street parking. **Amenities:** Jacuzzi in courtyard. *In room:* A/C, TV, dataport, Wi-Fi, hair dryer, iron/ironing board.

Queen Anne 🐕   A somewhat different take on lodging from the same folks who bring you the Prytania Park Hotel (see below), this was a one-family home for 130 years. The owners had to pass muster with the mayor, the governor, and the park service when they renovated it, and the result is perhaps the grandest building for a B&B in town. Inside the stately rooms, however, the furnishings are a bit sterile—hotel-room furniture masquerading as antique (though mattresses are top of the line). The Queen Anne is not our first choice for decor, but the stately rooms (each of which has some exquisite detail like beautifully tiled nonworking fireplaces or 10- to 14-ft. ceilings) pull it off. The inn is nicely located near the Mardi Gras parade route.

1625 Prytania St., New Orleans, LA 70130. Registration is at the Prytania Park Hotel on Terpsichore St. between Prytania St. and St. Charles Ave. © **888/498-7591** or 504/524-0427. Fax 504/522-2977. www.thequeenanne.com. 12 units. $99–$129 double; $159–$179 during special events. Rates include continental breakfast. AE, DC, DISC, MC, V. Free self-parking. **Amenities:** Laundry service. *In room:* A/C, TV, unstocked fridge, microwave, hair dryer, safe.

MODERATE

Chimes Bed & Breakfast 🐕🐕🐕 *(Finds)*   Barely closed even during the hurricane (they were housing the Reuters news service within a week or two of the disaster), this is a real hidden gem, one that truly allows you to experience the city away from the typical tourist experience. The Chimes is in a less fashionable but more neighborhood-like portion of the Garden District, just 2 blocks off St. Charles Avenue. Your hosts, Jill and Charles Abbyad, have run this B&B (located in the old servants' quarters behind their house, surrounding a small, sweet courtyard) for 20 years, and their experience shows.

Rooms vary in size from generous to downright cozy. All have antiques (including romantic old beds) but are so tastefully under-decorated, particularly in contrast to other B&Bs, that they feel pos-itively Zen. An ambitious continental breakfast is served in the hosts' house, and chatting with them can be so enjoyable you might get off to a late start. The Abbyads' friendliness and charm are among the reasons they have so many loyal, repeat customers. New amenities focusing on business traveler needs only give you more reasons to stay here.

1146 Constantinople St., New Orleans, LA 70115. © **800/729-4640** (for reserva-tions only); or 504/899-2621 (Chimes direct); or 504/453-2183 (owner's cell). www.chimesneworleans.com and www.historiclodging.com/chimes.html. e-mail chimes@historiclodging.com. 5 units. $130–$155 double in season; $86–$140 off season. Rates include breakfast. Look for featured specials online. AE, MC, V. Lim-ited off-street free parking. Well-behaved pets accepted. **Amenities:** Business cen-ter. *In room:* A/C, TV, dataport, Wi-Fi, coffeemaker, hair dryer, iron/ironing board.

The Columns ⊛   New Orleans made a mistake when it tore down its famous (and often grand) bordellos. The next best thing is The Columns, whose interior was used by Louis Malle for his film about Storyville, *Pretty Baby.* Please don't lounge around the lobby in your underwear, however, even if it is Victorian (the underwear, not the lobby). Built in 1883, the building is one of the city's greatest exam-ples of a late-19th-century Louisiana residence. The grand, columned porch remains a highly popular evening scene thanks to the bar inside. The immediate interior is utterly smashing; we chal-lenge any other hotel to match the grand staircase and stained-glass-window combination.

Unfortunately, the magnificence of the setting was long hurt by the rather casual attitude toward the place's potential. Meanwhile, during Katrina, the roof blew off, causing extensive water damage throughout, requiring a total top-to-bottom renovation (the long ordeal should be over by the time you read this), though that beau-tiful stained-glass window was not, thankfully, touched. Since this is a place that has long needed freshening and substantial upgrades, this is actually good news. It even has central air-conditioning and TVs in the rooms now! We will see what this means for what ought to be a deeply romantic hotel. It should give a whole new life to a deserving locale, that always has, and perhaps now more than ever, been a symbol of iconic New Orleans.

3811 St. Charles Ave., New Orleans, LA 70115. © **800/445-9308** or 504/899-9308. Fax 504/899-8170. www.thecolumns.com. 20 units. $160–$230 double. Rates include full breakfast. AE, MC, V. Parking available on street. **Amenities:** Bar. *In room:* A/C, TV, Wi-Fi.

Hampton Inn Garden District   This is a top choice for a chain hotel, if you don't mind being a bit out of the way (we don't—it's quite nice up here on St. Charles in a grand section of town that is generally not overly touristed but is right on the Mardi Gras parade route). The public areas are slightly more stylish than those found in other chains, and there are welcome touches such as free coffee in the lobby and complimentary cheese and tea served daily from 6 to 7pm. The style does not extend to the rooms, however, which are pretty mundane, though some of them got some rain damage, and subsequent renovations; consequently, they're fairly fresh. But even the older ones aren't *that* bad—and with all kinds of personality-enhancing details (decent photos for artwork, ever-so-slight arts-and-crafts detailing on furniture, and big TVs) hidden in that bland color scheme.

3626 St. Charles Ave., New Orleans, LA 70115. ⓒ **800/292-0653** or 504/899-9990. Fax 504/899-9908. www.hamptoninn.com. 100 units. $129–$159 double. Rates include continental breakfast, free local calls, and free incoming faxes. AE, DC, DISC, MC, V. Free parking. **Amenities:** Small outdoor lap pool; laundry service; dry cleaning. *In room:* A/C, TV, dataport, coffeemaker, hair dryer, iron/ironing board.

Park View Guest House ⓡ   Built in the late 1800s as a boardinghouse for the World Cotton Exchange, this is an inn crossed with a B&B, which means a front desk staffed 24/7, and proper public areas. But it's far uptown, so if you can't live without Bourbon Street and bars mere steps from your hotel entrance, then this is not the place for you. The stunning location on St. Charles (with a streetcar stop right opposite, so it's easy to get to and fro the Quarter), makes it well worth considering. Still, we wish they were more careful with their decor, a mix of antiques and sometimes truly bad modern furniture. If this sort of aesthetic mistake bothers you as much as it does us, try no. 9 (two antique wood beds, nice old fireplace, large balcony, new bathroom) or no. 17 (big bathroom, better furniture). Most of the rooms are spacious, and those downstairs, while just off the public areas, are grander still.

7004 St. Charles Ave., New Orleans, LA 70118. ⓒ **888/533-0746** or 504/861-7564. Fax 504/861-1225. www.parkviewguesthouse.com. 22 units, 17 with private bathroom. $85–$155 double. Rates include continental breakfast. Extra person $10. AE, DISC, MC, V. Parking available on street. *In room:* A/C.

Prytania Park Hotel   This 1840s building (which once housed Huey Long's girlfriend) is now equal parts motel and funky simulated Quarter digs. Rooms, some of which had minor wind and rain damage (and were quickly fixed), vary: Some have been redone to the owner's pride (adding darker wood tones and four-poster beds plus bathrooms that still have a Holiday Inn feel), but we kind of prefer the older section with its pine furniture, tall ceilings, and nonworking fireplaces.

1525 Prytania St. (enter off Terpsichore St.), New Orleans, LA 70130. ℂ 800/862-1984 or 504/524-0427. Fax 504/522-2977. www.prytaniaparkhotel.com. 62 units. $80–$90 double. Extra person $10. Rates include continental breakfast. Children under 12 stay free in parent's room. Seasonal rates and special packages available. AE, DC, DISC, MC, V. Off-street parking available. *In room:* A/C, TV, Wi-Fi, minibar, microwave.

INEXPENSIVE

St. Charles Guesthouse   Our first choice for budget travelers who have spent time in European pensions and aren't looking for the spick-and-span hotel experience. The place took a beating during Katrina, from siding that came off, ceilings that came down, and looting that left the rooms in a sad state. But the tenacious owners have been busy fixing it up—it reopened in January 2006, with plans for further renovation like new carpets, beds, and light fixtures. You can't beat the quiet, pretty location, especially for first-time New Orleans visitors, simply because it gets you out of the engulfing Quarter and into a different part of town. Rooms are plain and vary wildly in size—from reasonably spacious to "small and spartan" (the management's words)—and also range from low-end backpacker with no air-conditioning to larger chambers with air-conditioning and private bathrooms. But even the latter are funky and funny, with that slight touch of New Orleans decay—the walls are on the thin side and the plumbing is unreliable— that many of us find more bemusing than bothersome. Still, the atmosphere is the best of New Orleans: high ceilings, antiques (or just old furniture), a long staircase, and best of all, a banana-tree-lined courtyard with a pool, featuring a daily continental breakfast with a variety of carbs (muffins, biscuits, bread) and fresh juices.

1748 Prytania St., New Orleans, LA 70130. ℂ **504/523-6556.** Fax 504/522-6340. www.stcharlesguesthouse.com. 35 units, 23 with private bathroom. $45–$95 double. Rates include continental breakfast. AE, MC, V. Parking available on street. **Amenities:** Outdoor pool. *In room:* No phone.

6 Scheduled to Reopen

IN THE FRENCH QUARTER

Hotel Ste. Hélène ✦ *Value*   In the shadow of the Omni Royal Orleans, its grand across-the-street neighbor, the Hotel Ste. Hélène could easily be overlooked. But in our opinion, this is what a slightly funky Quarter hotel should be—and you can't beat its close-to-Jackson-Square location.

The scheduled reopening is **spring 2006.**

508 Chartres St., New Orleans, LA 70130. ② **800/348-3888** or 504/522-5014. Fax 504/523-7140. 26 units.

Maison Orleans 🦋🦋   This special addition to the Ritz-Carlton is for those who say "I would stay at the Ritz if only it were even nicer and had even better service." *Voilà!* This place, originally designed as a special boutique hotel, but now operating as the Ritz's Club Level, is attached to the Ritz, and has, get this, 24-hour butler service.

The Maison Orleans is scheduled to reopen alongside the Ritz in **September 2006.**

904 Iberville St., New Orleans, LA 70112. ② **504/670-2900.** Fax 504/670-2864. www.maisonorleans.com. 75 units.

Olde Victorian Inn 🦋🦋   A small but sweet little B&B with new post-Katrina owners, whose plans were uncertain at press time.

914 N. Rampart St., New Orleans, LA 70116. ② **800/725-2446** or 504/522-2446. www.oldevictorianinn.com. 4 units.

Ritz-Carlton, New Orleans 🦋🦋   Sentimentalists that we are, we were deeply sad to see the venerable Maison Blanche department store go the way of Woolworth's, D. H. Holmes, and other Canal Street shopping landmarks. But for the city's sake, we were pleased to have a Ritz-Carlton take its place, preserving the classic, glazed terra-cotta building and bringing a high-end luxury hotel to the Quarter. We would rather find our luxury in a less—how shall we say—*generic* way, but we can't deny that with name-brand recognition comes a reliable standard.

The Ritz was occupied during the hurricane and aftermath, and as such, took a beating. A major renovation and restoration should revive it beautifully; it has plans to reopen in **December 2006.**

921 Canal St., New Orleans, LA 70112. ② **800/241-3333** or 504/524-1331. Fax 504/524-7675. www.ritzcarlton.com. 452 units.

IN THE CENTRAL BUSINESS DISTRICT

The Fairmont New Orleans 🦋🦋   New Orleanians still sometimes think of this as the Roosevelt, and today's Fairmont Hotel upholds its predecessor's tradition of elegance. The marbled and columned lobby runs a full block and is famous for its over-the-top decorations at Christmas time. President Bill Clinton stayed here for many of his New Orleans overnights.

The Fairmont is scheduled to reopen in steps from **September to November 2006.**

123 Baronne St., New Orleans, LA 70112. 🄲 **800/441-1414** or 504/529-7111. Fax 504/529-4764. www.fairmont.com. 700 units.

Hotel Monaco 🄲🄲 🄚ids   There is much to like about this surprisingly whimsical boutique hotel, which recently took over (and beautifully preserved) the 1925 Masonic Temple. It's self-consciously quirky (check out the seashell fireplace in the lobby sitting area), but who cares when that translates to faux-fur throws on the beds (which also have down comforters and mosquito-net half-canopies), leopard-patterned bathrobes, and, upon request, an in-room goldfish?

Hotel Monaco plans to reopen in **summer 2006.**

333 St. Charles Ave., New Orleans, LA 70130. 🄲 **866/561-0010** or 504/310-2777. Fax 504/561-0036. www.monaco-neworleans.com. 250 units.

Hyatt Regency 🄲   Now infamous thanks to the many wire photos showing a side of the building all but stripped of its windows, the corporate-style Hyatt was always best simply as a base for the Superdome (near which it is conveniently located) or for conventions. Renovations, naturally, will take longer because of that extensive damage.

The projected reopening is **spring 2007.**

500 Poydras Plaza, New Orleans, LA 70113. 🄲 **800/233-1234** or 504/561-1234. Fax 504/587-4141. www.neworleans.hyatt.com. 1,184 units.

4

Where to Dine

New Orleans restaurant matriarch Miss Ella Brennan says that whereas in other places, one eats to live, "In New Orleans, we live to eat." Never was that more apparent than when the first high-pro-file restaurant—as it happens, a Brennan family restaurant, Bacco—reopened in the French Quarter post-Katrina. You can only imagine what that meant for the spirits and souls of the intrepid locals. Each returning restaurant is greeted with cries of pleasure and relief; it's a sign that normalcy, and good times, are returning to the city. But it's more than that; it's the return of family. Returning restaurants are packed and generally remain that way.

Still, as we write this, there are some concerns. Nearly all the reopened establishments are in the Quarter and Uptown (and in unflooded Jefferson Parish); while hundreds have reopened (includ-ing those in Jefferson), they represent only a fraction of the thou-sands that operated pre-hurricane. (Some remain closed because they are in deep-water areas, and proprietors are waiting to find out the future of those neighborhoods before making a firm commit-ment to returning; while others had either extensive flood or storm damage that needed renovation; and still more simply had a great deal of seafood in fridges that had no power for weeks or months on end, requiring entirely new equipment, and often long waits for insurance to pay for same. For a list of these restaurants, see the sec-tions "Planning to Reopen," p. 122, and "Will They Reopen?" p. 127.) And while it's wonderful when the high-profile folks return, New Orleans cuisine is not just about old-line fancy-pants places. It's also about the corner po' boy shops, and Miss Willie Mae's Scotch House, home to fried chicken so heavenly she was celebrated by a major culinary organization not long before the floodwaters destroyed her restaurant. In one of the shows of grace that emerged from adversity, local restaurateurs and others have banded together to help her rebuild. Further problems exist because of damage caused to local suppliers of significant New Orleans ingredients, many of whom lost buildings to flood and other hurricane damage.

Where to Dine in New Orleans

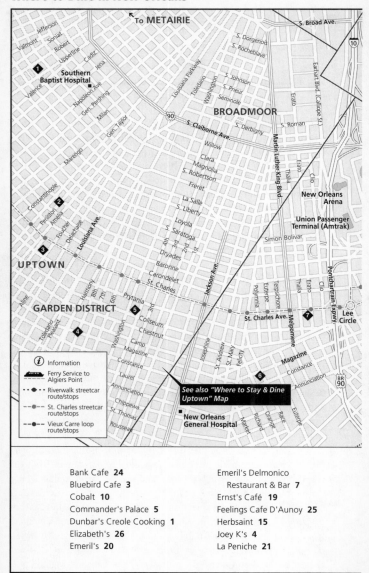

Bank Cafe **24**
Bluebird Cafe **3**
Cobalt **10**
Commander's Palace **5**
Dunbar's Creole Cooking **1**
Elizabeth's **26**
Emeril's **20**

Emeril's Delmonico
    Restaurant & Bar **7**
Ernst's Café **19**
Feelings Cafe D'Aunoy **25**
Herbsaint **15**
Joey K's **4**
La Peniche **21**

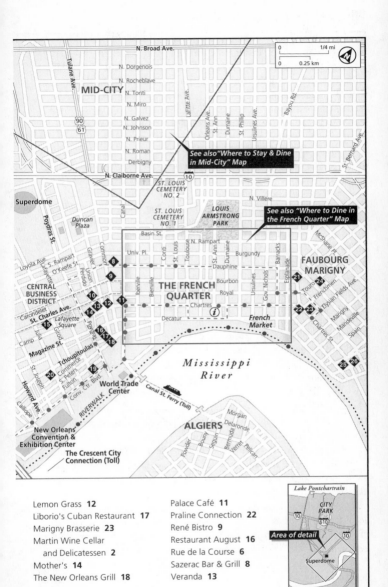

MID-CITY

N. Broad Ave.
N. Dorgenois
N. Rocheblave
N. Tonti
N. Miro
N. Galvez
N. Johnson
N. Prieur
N. Roman
Derbigny

N. Claiborne Ave.

Tulane Ave.

90
61

Lafitte Ave.
Orleans Ave.
St. Ann
Dumaine
St. Phillip
Ursulines Ave.

Bayou Rd.

St. Bernard Ave.

See also "Where to Stay & Dine in Mid-City" Map

Superdome

Duncan Plaza

Poydras St.

Canal

ST. LOUIS CEMETERY NO. 2

ST. LOUIS CEMETERY NO. 1

LOUIS ARMSTRONG PARK

N. Villere

See also "Where to Dine in the French Quarter" Map

FAUBOURG MARIGNY

Loyola Ave.
S. Rampart
O'Keefe St.
Gravier
Common
Union
Perdido

CENTRAL BUSINESS DISTRICT

Carondelet
St. Charles Ave.
Gravier
Magazine St.
Camp
Julia
Lafayette Square

Tchoupitoulas
Commerce
S. Peters
Fulton
Conv. Ctr. Blvd.
RIVERWALK

8
9
10
11
12
13
14 17 12
15
16 17 18
20
19

Basin St.
Univ. Pl.
Conti
St. Louis
Toulouse
N. Rampart
St. Ann
Dumaine
Burgundy
Iberville
Bienville
Dauphine
Bourbon
Royal
Chartres
Decatur

THE FRENCH QUARTER

Ursulines
Gov. Nichols
Barracks
Esplanade

(i)

French Market

McShane Pl.
Touro
Frenchmen
Elysian Fields Ave.
Marigny
Mandeville
Spain
Chartres St.

21 24
22 23

25 26

Mississippi River

Howard Ave.
St. Joseph
Calliope

World Trade Center

Canal St. Ferry (Toll)

New Orleans Convention & Exhibition Center

The Crescent City Connection (Toll)

ALGIERS

Morgan
Delaronde
Pelican
Bermuda
Seguin
Bouny
Powdir
Verret

0   1/4 mi
0   0.25 km

Lake Pontchartrain

CITY PARK

10
610

Area of detail

10

Superdome

As we write this, Crystal hot sauce was in such scant supply, with a somewhat uncertain future (it's not going to return to its New Orleans factory), that avid fans were stockpiling it like gold. Still, other essentials—CDM coffee, Zatarain's spices, Angelo Brocoto's Italian cookies, Hubig's Pies, and Leidenhelmer French bread (the best for po' boys)—are either all back in production in some form, or should be soon. Meanwhile, the quality of the food has hit a particular high, as diminished help means chefs are more in charge of their kitchens than ever. Further, extensive state and federal government testing of both the fish and the water have alleviated concerns about the safety of the seafood. As one local restaurateur said "It's not the fish—it's the people who are a mess." To the fish of the Gulf, Katrina was just another big storm. The oyster beds were hard hit, with somewhere between 30% and 40% destroyed, and harvesting happening faster than reproduction for a while, so expect shellfish to be in short supply until fall 2006. But you can make up for it with shrimp, which bury themselves at the bottom of the ocean to escape a storm's fury, and are currently a boom crop. The biggest problem for fish is supply, because a large number of Gulf fishermen and shrimpers lost their boats.

You should also further keep in mind that all times and prices in the following listings are subject to change as restaurants regain their feet, and are able to hire enough staff (as people return to town) to cover normal hours. That's the optimistic view; the pessimistic, but equally realistic, is that some struggling places may find these reconstruction days too difficult, and close permanently, or sell. You should call in advance to ensure the accuracy of anything significant to you. If a phone number is out of service, try calling information for a new listing; if that doesn't work try the website (or e-mail); if that doesn't work, try driving by when you're in town.

While it is true that the New Orleans food scene will not be the same until Commander's Palace is back, it is equally true it won't be the same until one can once again readily get a classic shrimp or hot sausage po' boy, dressed, of course, and a nectar snowball from a local family that has been making those things for generations. We sincerely hope that within a short time, such elements will be restored to their rightful places. But the essential point is this: As long as there are people in New Orleans, there will be food made, food worth talking about, and so regardless, we believe that even now, and ever more so in the future, once again, during your trip to

New Orleans, you will find yourself talking less about the sights and more about food—if not constantly about food. What you ate already, what you are going to be eating later, what you wish you had time to eat. And what you intend to eat on your return to this city where food is life.

1 The French Quarter

EXPENSIVE

Antoine's ☞ CREOLE   Owned and operated by the same family for an astonishing 160 years, Antoine's sustained some of the most dramatic Katrina damage in the otherwise relatively untouched Quarter; an exterior wall crumbled, poignantly exposing the inside of the restaurant. After some initial concern, the restaurant is fine, though not all of its 15 dining rooms have reopened. With its massive menu (more than 150 items), it was once the ultimate in fine dining in New Orleans and has over the years played host to local bigwigs and international figures from the Duke and Duchess of Windsor to Pope John Paul II. But subtle murmurs about a decline in quality have become outright complaints. Still, it's hard to ignore a legend, especially one we came so close to losing, and so you may wish to investigate for yourself. Locals—loyal customers all, mind you—will advise you to focus on starters and dessert and skip the entrees. You might order a side of creamed spinach, classic comfort food. Oysters Rockefeller (served hot in the shell, and covered with a mysterious green sauce—Antoine's invented it and still won't give out the recipe) will live up to its rep.

713 St. Louis St. ✆ **504/581-4422.** www.antoines.com. Reservations recommended. Jacket required and tie recommended at dinner. Main courses $22–$38. AE, DC, MC, V. Mon and Thurs–Sat 5:30–9:30pm; Sun 11am–2pm.

Arnaud's ☞☞ CREOLE   Arnaud's seems to have the lowest profile of all the classic old New Orleans restaurants, but undeservedly so, since it tops them in quality. You need to try at least one venerable, properly New Orleans atmospheric establishment, and that one should be Arnaud's. In addition to the formal (and seriously New Orleans) dining room, it now has a more casual jazz bistro featuring lovely lunches (currently suspended but likely to resume by the time you read this) that put the other grande-dame establishments to shame. Apart from the signature appetizer, shrimp Arnaud (boiled shrimp topped with a spicy rémoulade sauce), we love the crabmeat Ravigotte (generous amounts of sweet lump crabmeat tossed with a Creole mustard–based sauce, hearts of palm, and other veggies). It's hard to find a better turtle soup. Delicious fish dishes include snapper or trout Pontchartrain (topped with crabmeat), the spicy pompano Duarte, and pompano David and tuna Napoleon, good choices for those watching waistlines. Any filet mignon entree is superb (the meat is often better than what's served in most steak-houses in town). Desserts aren't quite as magnificent, but the Chocolate Devastation is worth trying, and one crème brûlée fan said Arnaud's was the best she'd ever had.

Arnaud's also operates a less formal, less expensive brasserie, **Rémoulade** (p. 95), right next door.

813 Bienville St. © 866/230-8895 or 504/523-5433. www.arnauds.com. Reservations requested. Jackets requested in main dining room at dinner. Main courses $19–$36. AE, DC, DISC, MC, V. Daily 6–10pm; Sun jazz brunch 10am–2:30pm.

Bacco 𝒢𝒢 ITALIAN/CREOLE   Any affection we already had for Bacco increased exponentially the day, about a month after Katrina, it became the first major Quarter restaurant to reopen. Did it matter the menu was limited to five items, all grilled and served on plastic dinnerware? Heck, no. It was New Orleans food, again, and even taking obvious joyful bias into account, it was delicious. (President Bush dined there just a few days later, during his first post-hurricane trip to the city.) Now back to its regular menu, Bacco is romantic and candlelit at night, more affordable and casual at lunchtime. Don't expect spaghetti and marinara sauce here. Instead, think rich, arresting creations such as *ravioli ripieni di formaggio,* featuring four creamy cheeses all melting into a sauce of olive oil, tomatoes, and browned garlic. Or try the *cannelloni con fungi,* stuffed with wild mushrooms and fresh herbs, and covered in a goat cheese and chive sauce. Truffle pasta made us so happy we asked for the recipe. Because this is a Brennan (the most prominent name in New Orleans dining) restaurant, desserts are generally above average— including possibly the best version of tiramisu we've ever had.

310 Chartres St. © 504/522-2426. www.bacco.com. Reservations recommended. Main courses $15–$31. AE, DC, MC, V. Daily 11:30am–2pm and 6–10pm.

Bayona 𝒢𝒢 INTERNATIONAL   Bayona's reputation as one of the top restaurants is so earned that patrons have been known to burst into applause driving by. Chef-owner Susan Spicer is a local treasure—it was a *frisson* of pleasure to learn she had returned to the kitchen post-Katrina. Unlike Bayona's wine cellar, which was lost to the hurricane, the lovely courtyard survived and only adds to the pleasures of the experience.

Where to Dine in the French Quarter

Acme Oyster House **2**

Angeli on Decatur **47**

Antoine's **20**

Arnaud's **9**

Bacco **14**

Bayona **24**

Bella Luna **42**

Bourbon House Seafood **3**

Brennan's **21**

Broussard's **23**

Café au Lait **13**

Café Beignet **11**

Café du Monde **37**

Café Giovanni **4**

Café Maspero **36**

Café Sbisa **45**

Central Grocery **43**

Clover Grill **41**

Court of Two Sisters **30**

Dickie Brennan's
    Steakhouse **3**

Dominique's **26**

Felix's Restaurant
    & Oyster Bar **7**

Galatoire's **6**

Irene's Cuisine **44**

Johnny's Po Boys **17**

K-Paul's **16**

La Madeleine **38**

La Marquise **34**

Le Bistro **29**

Louisiana Pizza Kitchen **48**

Maximo's **46**

Meauxbar **28**

Mr B's Bistro **8**

Muriel's **33**

Napoleon House **18**

Nola **15**

Olde N'Awlins Cookery **22**

The Pelican Club **12**

Peristyle **27**

Petunia's **25**

Ralph & Kacoo's **35**

Red Fish Grill **1**

Remoulade **10**

Rib Room **19**

Royal Blend Coffee
    and Tea House **31**

Sekisui Samurai Sushi **5**

Stanley **39**

Stella! **32**

Tujague's **40**

85

Be sure to begin with the outstanding cream of garlic soup, a perennial favorite. Appetizers include grilled shrimp with cilantro sauce and black-bean cakes, and delicate, flavorful veal sweetbreads sautéed with scallions and diced potatoes in sherry vinaigrette. Knockout entrees have included medallions of lamb loin with a lavender honey aioli (a mayonnaise-based sauce) and a zinfandel demiglace; a perfectly grilled pork chop with a stuffing of fontina cheese, fresh sage, and prosciutto; and yet another lamb dish, this one topped with goat cheese, that may have been the best lamb we've ever tasted. Heaven.

430 Dauphine St. ℂ **504/525-4455**. www.bayona.com. Reservations required at dinner, recommended at lunch. Main courses at lunch $10–$14, at dinner $24–$28. AE, DC, DISC, MC, V. Mon–Thurs 11:30am–2pm and 6–9:30pm; Fri 11:30am–2pm and 6–10pm; Sat 6–10:30pm.

The Bistro 🦊🦊🦊 INTERNATIONAL   This tiny jewel of a bistro, part of the superb Hotel Maison de Ville, had some water damage calling for the usual renovations, but they reopened by Mardi Gras with their usual menu and sterling service. Be sure to find it; it is easy to overlook among the higher-profile choices in the French Quarter. But it's a favorite among in-the-know locals, who think of it as a training ground for new chefs who then go on to make a splash at their own restaurants (as Susan Spicer has at Bayona). Patrons also bask in the warm Gallic glow of hospitality emitted by longtime maitre d' Patrick, who will remember your name and your favorite dish. The menu seems fairly stable, but even if it changes you can expect uniformly delicious dishes, such as recent entrees like roasted pavé of salmon stuffed with crab, shrimp, and scallops, or game dishes like pistachio-crusted pannéed rabbit "Benson" with yam brabants and a brandy, dijon, and rabbit jus with capers. Sides such as lavender-mashed potatoes or yam Lyonaisse soufflé show wit. It's also an excellent choice for lunch, with selections like the rich country pâté, lovely salads, and especially the signature dish of mussels with thick french fries and homemade mayonnaise.

In the Hotel Maison de Ville, 727 Toulouse St. ℂ **504/528-9206**. www.maisonde ville.com. Main courses $29–$39. AE, DISC, MC, V. Mon–Sat 11am–2pm; Thurs–Sat 6–10pm.

Bourbon House Seafood 🦊 SEAFOOD   The most recent entry from Dickie Brennan, this modern take on the classic New Orleans fish house, both aesthetically and gastronomically, was able to reopen a mere five weeks post-storm, and since then has hosted names as big as First Lady Laura Bush. It's a big, cheerful room with balcony seating perfect for spying or canoodling. The menu features all kinds of fish, from fresh boiled or raw seafood to entrees like baked fish Grieg (soft, tender fish in a meunière sauce that is neither overpowering nor overly buttery) and grilled Gulf fish on a ragout of local legumes. There's fried stuff as well, like crab claws with a mustardy rémoulade sauce.

144 Bourbon St. (C) **504/522-0111.** www.bourbonhouse.com. Reservations recommended. Main courses at lunch $8.50–$20, at dinner $19–$27. AE, DISC, MC, V. Sun–Thurs 11:30am–9pm; Fri–Sat 11:30am–10pm.

Brennan's ⊛ FRENCH/CREOLE   For more than 40 years, breakfast at Brennan's has been a New Orleans tradition, a feast that has surely kept many a heart surgeon busy. Their lengthy closure was tough on New Orleans traditionalists, but what can you do when the third-floor freezer defrosts and all kinds of putrid water ruins the floors and walls of the back house? Renovate slowly, that's what; you can't rush repairing 200-year-old cypress. But you can't keep a grande dame down; after all, 30 years ago, the roof burned off. Reopened in late-April 2006, in time to celebrate their 60th anniversary, Brennan's is a lesson in New Orleans survival, and of course, diet. Don't expect any California health-conscious fruit-and-granola options here; this multicourse extravaganza is unabashedly sauce- and egg-intensive. It's also costly—it's not hard to drop $50 on breakfast—so you might be better off sticking with the fixed-price meal (though it often limits your choices).

417 Royal St. (C) **504/525-9711.** www.brennansneworleans.com. Reservations recommended. Main courses $20–$39; fixed-price lunch $35; fixed-price 4-course dinner $39. AE, DC, DISC, MC, V. Daily 8am–2:30pm and 6–10pm. Closed Christmas.

Broussard's ⊛ CREOLE   Unfairly dismissed as a tourist trap (which, in truth, it was for some years), Broussard's is a perfectly fine alternative if your top choices are booked up. Chef Gunther Preuss and his wife, Evelyn, own the place, which includes an elegant, formal dining room and a lovely courtyard, and were dedicated even from the early days post-Katrina to reopening their restaurant, even if they had to use frozen, not fresh, fish for awhile. Such a little thing, but recall, "Gunther has a way with crab," claims his press material, and once we stopped giggling over that turn of phrase, we have had to admit it is true. Chef takes his seafood seriously. Try the appetizer of crabmeat Florentine, which includes spinach and is covered in a brie sauce. Be sure to order the baked filet of redfish Herbsaint (a local anise-flavored liqueur), clever and delicious in its components, which include impossibly sweet crabmeat and lemon risotto.

819 Conti St. ℂ **504/581-3866**. www.broussards.com. Reservations recommended. No jeans, shorts, sneakers, or T-shirts. Main courses $22–$36. AE, MC, V. Tues–Sat 5:30–10pm.

Café Giovanni ℱ ITALIAN

Though Chef Duke LoCicero has won culinary awards, Café Giovanni is kind of a mixed bag, thanks to a combo of fine food, lackadaisical service, and—of course—the dreaded (or highly enjoyable, depending on your conversational needs during dinner and your love of schmaltz) opera-singing waiters (to be found Wed, Fri, and Sat nights). Still, any place that serves the gastronomic wonder that is fresh, buttery crescenza cheese on panettone *pain perdu* (Italian Christmas cake merged with local French toast . . . kinda), smeared over foie gras and topped off with a reduction sauce that ought to be illegal, well, we can overlook a little operatic noise. And we are glad that their storm-related problems were minimal enough that they were able to reopen at the end of October 2005, when operating restaurants were so sacred.

117 Decatur St. ℂ **504/529-2154**. www.cafegiovanni.com. Main courses $16–$26. AE, DISC, MC, V. Daily 5:30–10pm.

Court of Two Sisters *Overrated* CREOLE

This is probably the prettiest restaurant in town (thanks to a huge, foliage-filled courtyard located in a 2-c.-old building; luckily, roof damage was not significant, though they lost a tree, and some of their wisteria, but it bloomed again in the spring, and everything's looking pretty lush again), but even major ambience can't obscure the problems with the food. You'll find the only daily jazz brunch in town here, but it suffers from the typical buffet problem—too many dishes, none of which succeed except maybe the made-to-order items like eggs Benedict. Avoid the vinegary seviche, but try the seafood slaw (we give it a thumbs up). Dinner may be even worse; apart from a Caesar salad (made in the traditional style, at tableside), there is little, if anything, to recommend. It's a pity, because you can't ask for a better setting.

613 Royal St. ℂ **504/522-7261**. www.courtoftwosisters.com. Reservations recommended for dinner and brunch. Main courses $18–$30; fixed-price menu $39; brunch $23. AE, DC, DISC, MC, V. Daily 9am–3pm and 5:30–10pm.

Dickie Brennan's Steakhouse ℱℱ STEAK

One of a handful of Quarter locales that had water damage (due to the restaurant's below-street-level placement, the place flooded), this carnivore's delight reopened at the end of April, with lunch not planned to

return until fall 2006, though that's always subject to more optimistic possibilities. Carnivores should be pleased with this particular Brennan family establishment, which has the feel of a
contemporary clubhouse. All the meat is USDA Prime, and great
care is taken to cook it just as the customer dictates. The house filet
comes surrounded by quite good creamed spinach and Pontalba
potatoes (diced roasted potatoes sautéed with garlic, onions, wild
mushrooms, ham, and scallions). We rather prefer the tender, flavorful rib-eye, but do get creamed spinach on the side. Don't miss
the bananas Foster bread pudding, which proves that there can still
be new twists on this old faithful dish.

716 Iberville St. ℂ 504/522-2467. www.dickiebrennanssteakhouse.com.

Dominique's ℱ. INTERNATIONAL   Though it's been around
for a few years, Dominique's seems to have struggled to achieve a
significant profile among New Orleans restaurants. Perhaps that's
the reasoning behind some reconceptualizing of the cuisine. Pre-
Katrina, it was French-Caribbean, and although it may have had the
prettiest presentations in town, the dishes were too busy, with hit-
or-miss results. "L.A. visuals with New Orleans–size portions," said
one guest, and that about sums it up. Hits included blue crab and
coconut soup served in the actual shell (why doesn't everyone do
that?), cured wild salmon with blue-crab claw meat on a brioche,
and best of all, citrus-spiced crusted pheasant breast stuffed with
veal cheeks (you can see what we mean about the needless com-
plexity of certain dishes) with sweet-potato gnocchi.

In the Maison Dupuy Hotel, 1001 Toulouse St. ℂ 504/522-8800. www.dominiques
restaurant.com. Reservations recommended. Main courses $22–$30. AE, DC, DISC,
MC, V. Tues–Sun 6–10pm.

Galatoire's ℱ FRENCH   The venerable Galatoire's causes heated
discussions among local foodies: Is it still the best restaurant in New
Orleans or is it past its prime? This conversation was rendered
almost irrelevant when it reopened after Katrina. Walking into its
classic green-wallpaper interior, exactly as it used to be, complete
with favorite waiter John, at his post for 35 years and counting,
despite the loss of his home to flooding, was such a relief, such a
return to normalcy, that any gastronomic inadequacies are easy to
overlook. Or even welcomed; really, you don't come to Galatoire's
for cutting-edge cuisine. You come to it to eat a nice piece of fish,
perfectly sautéed or broiled, topped with fresh crabmeat. Or you
have a seafood dish with a gloopy white sauce, because that's what

you've been eating at your regular Sunday-evening dinners, where all the old waiters know your name, for years. Galatoire's, where in *A Streetcar Named Desire* Stella took Blanche to escape Stanley's poker game, is New Orleans tradition, and a symbol of everything else we could have lost, and that alone makes it worth the trip. You may not have the same experience as a knowledgeable local unless you get a waiter who can really guide you (ask for John. Everyone else does). We love the lump crabmeat appetizer (think coleslaw, only with crab instead of cabbage), the shrimp rémoulade, and the oysters Rockefeller. For an entree, get the red snapper or redfish topped with sautéed crabmeat meunière (a delightful butter sauce)—it will probably be one of the finest fish dishes you'll have during your stay. Don't miss out on the terrific creamed spinach and the puffy potatoes with béarnaise sauce, which will make you swear off regular french fries forever.

209 Bourbon St. ℂ 504/525-2021. Reservations accepted for upstairs. Jackets required after 5pm and all day Sun. Main courses $14–$27. AE, DC, DISC, MC, V. Sun noon–10pm; Tues–Sat 11:30am–10pm. Closed Mardi Gras (and prior weekend), Memorial Day, July 4th, Thanksgiving, and Christmas.

K-Paul's Louisiana Kitchen ℛ CAJUN/CREOLE

Paul Prudhomme was at the center of the Cajun revolution of the early '80s, when Cajun food became known throughout the world. His reputation and his line of spices continue today, which is probably why there is constantly a line outside his restaurant. Now, normally, we would say that although the American regional food is still good, it's not spectacular and certainly is not worth the wait (upwards of 1½ hr.). The portions are Paul-size (that is, large) and as spicy as you might imagine, but nothing that particularly special. But then again, Chef's dedication to the city, post-Katrina, is as big as all that, as he immediately got out there and started to feed everyone. Under his new charitable organization, "Chefs Cook for Katrina," K-Paul's continues to cook meals for relief and other workers who are clearing out devastated portions of the city, serving tens of thousands of meals in the process. Consequently, we are inclined toward nothing but loyalty, and point out that while we may have our own views about the food, few who come here complain.

Different menu items are offered daily, but you can't go wrong with jambalaya (spicy!) or bronzed or blackened anything (really spicy!). One vegetarian friend claims the fried eggplant dish he had there was one of his lifetime outstanding meals (you have to ask for it; it's not regularly featured on the menu).

416 Chartres St. ⓒ **504/524-7394**. www.kpauls.com. Reservations recommended. Main courses $30–$40. AE, DC, DISC, MC, V. Thurs–Sat 11:30am–2:30pm; Mon–Sat 5:30–10pm.

Muriel's ⓖⓖ CREOLE/ECLECTIC Conventional wisdom would have it that any restaurant this close to tourist-hub Jackson Square—as in, across the street from it—would have to serve over-priced, mediocre food. But then conventional wisdom notes the Gothic-parlor look to the dining rooms in the newish Muriel's (reopened by mid-October 2005) and decides to sit down just to be polite. Then conventional wisdom eats excellent seared scallops with balsamic vinegar, smoked oysters with bacon, and house salad with vanilla-bean vinaigrette, poached pears, and Stilton, following it up with perfectly grilled BBQ shrimp, equally good lamb, and Dijon-mustard-crusted salmon. Sated and fully satisfied, conventional wisdom then floats upstairs, past the table set for the in-house ghosts, and into the Séance Room, which looks like a Gypsy den crossed with a bordello, and has a drink. Conventional wisdom is reminded that rules are made to be broken and vows to tell everyone to come here.

801 Chartres St. (at St. Ann). ⓒ **504/568-1885**. www.muriels.com. Reservations suggested. Main courses at lunch $9.50–$13, at dinner $16–$26. AE, DISC, MC, V. Daily 5:30–10pm; Fri–Sun 11am–2pm.

Nola ⓖⓖ CREOLE/NEW AMERICAN This modern two-story building with a glass-enclosed elevator is the most casual and the least expensive of chef Emeril Lagasse's three restaurants—not to mention the first to reopen post-Katrina—and the most conveniently located for the average tourist. We've had frequent problems with attitude here (at least when making reservations and when showing up for them; the service thereafter is fine, if slow at times), but when the food is on, it's spectacular. Try smoked duck pizza with Brie and white truffle aioli as a starter, or any filet (we especially liked the one with red potatoes, walnuts, and bacon in a port-wine reduction, with bleu cheese and shallot crisps).

534 St. Louis St. ⓒ **504/522-6652**. www.emerils.com. Reservations recommended. Main courses $20–$32. AE, DC, DISC, MC, V. Sat 11am–2:30pm; Tues–Sun 6–10pm.

The Pelican Club ⓖ NEW AMERICAN Just a short stroll from the House of Blues, The Pelican Club is worth investigating, particularly for its reasonably priced three-course fixed-price meal. They had a lot of the usual restaurant damage (defrosting second floor refrigeration spread disgusting water throughout, causing damage and the need for extensive repair and renovation), plus the loss of their wine collection. Expect a smaller menu for the time being, as they remedy the usual staffing shortages. Once it's back to normal, you can expect the appetizers to be a bit more inventive than the entrees (you could easily make a meal of them), but everything is quite tasty. Escargots come in a tequila garlic-butter sauce (which you will probably find yourself sopping up with bread), topped with tiny puff pastries. Special salads are served each evening; a recent visit found arugula, Gorgonzola, and apple in balsamic dressing. Tender lamb comes coated in rosemary-flavored bread crumbs with a spicy pepper jelly. Interesting sides like wild-mushroom bread pudding accompany the entrees, and desserts are standouts.

312 Exchange Place. ℂ **504/523-1504.** www.pelicanclub.com. Reservations recommended. Main courses $18–$42; fixed-price early dinner $25. AE, DC, DISC, MC, V. Tues–Sat 5:30–10pm.

Peristyle ECLECTIC   When Anne Kearney gave up her seminal restaurant, local foodies went into mourning. Peristyle was regarded by many as the best in New Orleans, so this was a blow. Still, locals took heart, because new chef-owner Thomas Wolfe was behind the well-regarded Wolfe's in Metairie (currently closed post-Katrina). Different Peristyle would be, but still worthy. Unfortunately, those optimistic expectations haven't yet been borne out. A recent visit featured largely mediocre food. Perhaps it was our fault for not realizing that champagne-vanilla-bean poached oysters wouldn't work. Lump crabmeat and roasted beets was a better combination. As for entrees, roast chicken topped with apricots was juicy (not always the case in restaurants) but dumped on tasteless, dry, and pointless oven-baked crispy spatzle. Pan-seared tuna suffered from similar careless presentation. A repeat trip for the prix-fixe lunch produced a split decision; one set of appetizer and entree tasted strangely fishy (the fish in question may have been frozen) while the other combination was fine. This probably remains a work in progress, which may change a great deal in the post-Katrina days; we'll keep you informed.

1041 Dumaine St. ℂ **504/593-9535.** Reservations recommended. Main courses $24–$28. DC, DISC, MC, V. Fri 11:30am–1:30pm; Tues–Sat 6–9:30pm.

Rib Room ℛ SEAFOOD/STEAK   This is where New Orleanians come to eat beef. And who can fault their choice of surroundings? The solid and cozy Old English feel of this room (same as it always was even before Katrina) is complete with natural-brick and open ovens at the back. But while the meat is good, it is not outstanding, and the acclaimed prime rib is just a bit tough and more than lacking in flavor. There are also filets, sirloins, brochettes, tournedos, and steak *au poivre,* plus some seafood dishes. Carnivores, landlubbers, and ichthyophobes will be happier here than at one of the city's Creole restaurants, but it is not the must-do that its reputation would have you believe.

In the Omni Royal Orleans hotel, 621 St. Louis St. (C) **504/529-7045.** www.omni royalorleans.com. Reservations recommended. Main courses $24–$34. AE, DC, DISC, MC, V. Daily 6:30–10:30am, 11:30am–2:30pm (serving lunch Mon–Sat, brunch Sun), and 6–10pm.

Stella! *(fish)(fish)*   Reopened in March 2006, following a serious post-hurricane renovation, it's taken us a bit to come around to Stella!—or maybe, it took a bit for Stella! to come around to us—but we are now very fond of this charming Quarter restaurant. Maybe it's because the chef/owner, after getting all nouveau with an oyster topped with ginger and wasabi granita (an icy/spicy combo that got diners fighting over the extra portion), then dares to put potato salad on an appetizer of cornmeal-crusted oysters. Or that the tandoori-spiced salmon was juicy and came with coconut shrimp Basmati rice and mango cashew butter all of which mixed together in a jumble of pleasing Asian spices. Or it could be the playful and frivolous desserts like the powerful, but light and with the texture of ice cream, Grand Marnier and ginger crème brûlée, or that there is a Shake Du Jour (chocolate pistachio the night we were there), fabulously thick and sweet because it's made with heavy cream, or that there is Bananas Foster French toast. All this in two elegant, but not intimidating, small dining rooms. Meanwhile, the owners have opened a new cafe, Stanley, which is reviewed later in this chapter.

1032 Chartres St. (in the Hotel Provincial). (C) **504/587-0091.** www.restaurant stella.com. Reservations recommended. No shorts or tank tops. Main courses $23–$36. AE, DC, DISC, MC, V. Thurs–Mon 5:30–10pm.

MODERATE

Irene's Cuisine *(fish)(fish)* FRENCH/ITALIAN Irene's is somewhat off the regular tourist dining path, and locals would probably prefer to keep it that way, even though they often have to wait upwards of 90 minutes for a table. (A friend of ours was their third customer post-Katrina, and the sight of the place nearly empty was shocking to him!) To many, the French Provincial/Italian food is worth the wait, and you may agree.

Once you enter, you will find a dark, noisy, cluttered tavern, with friendly waiters who seem delighted you came. We were thrilled by soft-shell-crab pasta, an entirely successful Italian/New Orleans hybrid consisting of a whole fried crustacean atop a bed of pasta with a cream sauce of garlic, crawfish, tomatoes, and wads of basil leaves. The panned oysters and grilled shrimp appetizer can be magnificent, and don't forget *pollo rosemarino*—five pieces of chicken marinated, partly cooked, marinated again, and then cooked a final time.

539 St. Phillip St. ℂ **504/529-8811.** Reservations accepted only for Christmas Eve, New Year's Eve, and Valentine's Day. Main courses $14–$18. AE, MC, V. Sun–Thurs 5:30–10:30pm; Fri–Sat 5:30–11pm. Closed New Year's Day, July 4th, Labor Day, and Thanksgiving.

Meauxbar Bistro 𝒢 ASIAN/BISTRO   Rampart Street needs more places like this: a sweet neighborhood cafe that aspires to serve more than just the usual New Orleans inexpensive fare. Frozen food is rarely used, and all the dressings are made fresh, a touch you appreciate when you try the tart Roquefort onion dressing. The signature starter is ginger crawfish dumplings in a sesame dipping sauce. Entrees include lamb shanks braised 3 hours, until the meat is falling off the bone; the result is a nongreasy wonder. Coconut shrimp in a red curry sauce is very spicy with just a touch of sweet. Looking for something a little more familiar? The hamburger, topped with goat cheese or Roquefort and bacon can be cooked perfectly rare. Paired with crispy fries, it's a filling meal for $10. The apple tartin is like no other apple dish in New Orleans and worth coming for just on its own.

942 N. Rampart St. ℂ **504/569-9979.** Main courses $15–$28. AE, MC, V. Tues–Thurs 6–10pm; Fri–Sat 6–11pm.

Port of Call 𝒢𝒢 HAMBURGERS   Sometimes you just need a burger—particularly when you've been eating many things with sauces. Locals feel strongly that the half-pound monsters served at the cozy (and we mean it) Port of Call are the best in town—so you can imagine how happy locals were that they were able to reopen by October 3, 2005. The Port of Call is just a half step above a dive, but it's a convivial place. The hamburgers come with a baked potato, and there also are pizzas, excellent filet mignon, rib-eye steaks, and New York strip steaks. It's often jammed at regular eating hours.

838 Esplanade Ave. ℂ **504/523-0120.** www.portofcallneworleans.com. Main courses $6–$21. AE, MC, V. Daily 7am–1am.

Ralph & Kacoo's CREOLE/SEAFOOD   Though they suffered plenty of damage in the storm (repairs are ongoing), this is still a satisfying, reliable place for seafood, nothing we would consider writing home about, but decent. The Creole dishes are quite good, portions are more than ample, prices are reasonable, and the high volume of business means everything is fresh. Start with fried crawfish tails or the killer onion rings, and if you're adventurous, give the blackened alligator with hollandaise a try. Be sure to try the satin pie for dessert—it's a creamy, mousselike concoction of peanut butter and a thin layer of chocolate that will please even non–peanut butter fans.

519 Toulouse St. ℭ **504/522-5226**. www.ralphandkacoos.com. Reservations suggested. Main courses $14–$40. AE, DC, DISC, MC, V. Mon–Thurs 4–10pm; Fri 4–11pm; Sat noon–11pm; Sun noon–9pm.

Red Fish Grill ☙ SEAFOOD Red Fish is far better than anything else in its price range on Bourbon Street—and was the first restaurant in the city to get a health permit post-Katrina, making them the first official place to reopen (Bacco reopened the next day). Ralph Brennan's place serves many New Orleans specialties with an emphasis on—no surprise—fish. Skip the dull salads in favor of appetizers like shrimp rémoulade napoleon (layered between fried green tomatoes) or grilled shrimp and shiitake mushroom quesadillas. For your entree, go right to the fish they do so well. The signature dish is a pan-seared catfish topped with sweet potato crust and an andouille cream drizzle. It's outstanding.

115 Bourbon St. ℭ **504/598-1200**. www.redfishgrill.com. Reservations recommended. Main courses at lunch $8.75–$16, at dinner $16–$32. AE, DC, MC, V. Daily 11am–3pm and 5–11pm.

Rémoulade CREOLE/CAJUN/AMERICAN Rémoulade is certainly better than the otherwise exceedingly tourist-trap restaurants on Bourbon Street (Red Fish Grill being the exception), offering adequate local food at reasonable prices. Ignore the undistinguished jambalayas, gumbos, and so forth in favor of the fine turtle soup and shrimp rémoulade. Burgers and pizza fill out the menu. *Note:* This is one of the few places in town that serves Brocatto's Italian ice cream, which should be back in production by the time you read this. A visit for a serving of this fabulous local product (it's impossibly thick and creamy) is a mandatory pit stop for us on a hot day.

309 Bourbon St. ℭ **504/523-0377**. www.remoulade.com. Main courses $5–$17. AE, DISC, MC, V. Daily 5pm–midnight.

Sekisui Samurai ☙ JAPANESE Lord knows we love a cream sauce as much as the next person, to say nothing of our deep commitment to deep-fried anything, but sometimes something's gotta give (like our waistbands), and that's why, if we can't get our hands on a plain green salad, we end up eating sushi. If you find yourself needing a similar break, try this French Quarter sushi place (which was able to reopen in October 2005). While the crawfish tail sushi is hit-or-miss, the Crunchy Roll (a California roll topped with tempura—see, we always come back to deep-fried) and the spicy tuna roll are worth checking out, as is the enjoyably named Flying Fish Roll. They also have teriyaki.

239 Decatur St. 𝒞 504/525-9595. www.sekisuisamurai.com. Sushi $3.50–$7.50 for pieces/rolls; lunch specials $6.25–$11; dinner $15–$26. AE, DC, DISC, MC, V. Sun–Thurs 11:30am–10pm; Fri–Sat 11:30am–10:30pm.

Tujague's 🇫 CREOLE Dating back to 1856, Tujague's (pronounced *two*-jacks) is every bit as venerable as the big-name New Orleans restaurants (heck, in the bar they've got a mirror that has been in place for 150 years!), and yet no one ever mentions it— which is a shame. It may not be a knockout, but it's authentic and solid, and pretty much the same as ever (leakage from roof damage was minimal) since their reopening in November 2005. Tujague's does not have a menu; instead, each night, it offers a set six-course (it seems one course is coffee) meal. Don't expect fancy or nouvelle: This is real local food. Meals start with a sinus-clearing shrimp rémoulade, heads to a fine gumbo, then to a sample of a so-tender-you-cut-it-with-a-fork brisket, and then on to whatever is happening for an entree. There's likely to be filet mignon, but skip it (it's ordinary) in favor of items like stuffed shrimp or Bonne Femme chicken, a baked garlic number from the original owner's recipe. Finish with a classic, the right-on-the-money bread pudding.

823 Decatur St. 𝒞 504/525-8676. www.tujaguesrestaurant.com. Reservations recommended. 3-course lunch $15–$17; 6-course dinner $30–$36. AE, DC, DISC, MC, V. Daily 11am–3pm and 5–10pm.

INEXPENSIVE

Acme Oyster House 🇫🇫 SEAFOOD/SANDWICHES The Quarter's oldest oyster bar needed a $2-million renovation to recover from Katrina-related issues, but it looks pretty much as it always did, just spiffier (new floor, new tiling, new bathrooms, and best of all, newly expanded kitchen). This joint is always loud, often crowded, and the kind of place where you're likely to run into obnoxious fellow travelers. But if you need an oyster fix or you've never tried oyster shooting (taking a raw oyster, possibly doused in sauce, and letting it slide right down your throat), come here.

There's nothing quite like standing at the oyster bar, eating a dozen or so freshly shucked oysters on the half shell. (Somehow they taste better at the bar.) If you can't quite stomach them raw, try the oyster po' boy, with beer, of course, or the increasingly popular char-grilled oysters.

724 Iberville St. ⒸÞ **504/525-1157.** www.acmeoyster.com. Dozen oysters $8; po' boys $5.50–$7.50; entrees $7–$17. AE, DC, DISC, MC, V. Daily 11am–8pm.

Angeli on Decatur ⭑⭑ ITALIAN/MEDITERRANEAN   This highly welcome addition to the Quarter—it reopened almost immediately after Rita passed through—features terrific (if not particularly New Orleans–specific) food with further praise for its nearly round-the-clock hours and local delivery service. Angeli is perfect for a light, actually rather healthy meal, a much-needed alternative to some of the extravaganzas offered by more formal restaurants in town. Portions are substantial—splitting a Greek salad produced two full plates of fresh, lovely veggies and a couple of pieces of garlic bread. Add to that a small pizza (they do them all well, but the Mystical—roasted garlic, goat cheese, onions, sun-dried tomatoes— is a top choice), and you've got a tasty, affordable meal for two.

1141 Decatur St. (at Gov. Nicholls St.). ⒸÞ **504/566-0077.** Main courses $6.95–$18. No credit cards. Mon–Thurs 11am–4am; Fri–Sat 24 hr.

Café Beignet ⭑ CAFE   This is a full-service, bistro-style cafe now set in its new location in Legends Park as well as in its original on Royal Street. At breakfast you can get Belgian waffles, an omelet soufflé, bagels and lox, or brioche French toast. Items on the lunch menu include gumbo, crawfish pie, vegetable sandwiches, and salads. And, of course, beignets.

311 Bourbon St. ⒸÞ **504/525-2611.** www.cafebeignet.com. All items under $7. No credit cards. Daily 7am–5pm. Additional location 334b Royal St. ⒸÞ **504/524-5530.**

Café Maspero ⭑ SEAFOOD/SANDWICHES   Upon hearing complaints about the increasing presence in the Quarter of "foreign" restaurants, such as Subway and the Hard Rock Cafe, one local commented, "Good. That must mean the line will be shorter at Café Maspero." Locals do indeed line up for burgers, deli sandwiches (including a veggie muffuletta!), seafood, grilled marinated chicken, and so on, in some of the largest portions you'll ever run into. And there's an impressive list of wines, beers, and cocktails. Everything is delicious and is sold at low, low prices.

601 Decatur St. ⒸÞ **504/523-6250.** Main courses $4.25–$9. No credit cards. Sun–Thurs 11am–11pm; Fri–Sat 11am–midnight.

Clover Grill 👌 COFFEEHOUSE   Though we are glad in some ways that the Clover Grill has continued on as it ever was post-Katrina, we are still cross with it. Once a place where the irreverent menu ("We're here to serve people and make them feel prettier than they are.") competed with the even more outrageous staff for smart-aleck behavior, it has lost its luster. The once charmingly sassy staff is straying lately toward surly. But the burgers are still juicy and perfect, and if you get them with cheese, still cooked under a hubcap (they say it seals in the juices). We'll go out on a limb and declare them right up there with the usual favorites at the Port of Call as the best burgers in the Quarter. Breakfast is still served round-the-clock. But too many times lately we've come in at night requesting a shake, only to be told "no shakes." Unacceptable for a 24-hour diner.

900 Bourbon St. 📞 **504/598-1010.** www.clovergrill.com. All items under $8. AE, MC, V. Daily 24 hr.

Johnny's Po' Boys 👌👌 SANDWICHES   For location (right near a busy part of the Quarter) and menu simplicity (po' boys and more po' boys)—they are back to a full menu after a post-Katrina period of a shortened one—you can't ask for much more than Johnny's. They put anything you could possibly imagine (and some things you couldn't) on huge hunks of French bread, including the archetypal fried seafood (add some Tabasco, we strongly advise), deli meats, cheese omelets, ham and eggs, and the starch-o-rama that is a French Fry Po' Boy. You need to try it. *Really.* Johnny boasts that "even my failures are edible," and that says it all. The whole family is pitching in to make up for staff shortages, and that kind of dedication deserves your patronage. And they deliver!

511 St. Louis St. 📞 **504/524-8129.** All items under $11. No credit cards. Mon–Fri 8am–4:30pm; Sat–Sun 9am–4pm.

Louisiana Pizza Kitchen PIZZA   The Louisiana Pizza Kitchen, which promptly reopened post-storm in October 2005, is a local favorite for its creative pies and atmosphere. Pastas have a significant place on the menu, but diners come for the pizzas and Caesar salad. Individual-size pizzas, baked in a wood-fired oven, feature a wide variety of toppings (shrimp and roasted garlic are two of the most popular) that don't get lost in an overabundance of cheese and tomato sauce.

95 French Market Place. 📞 **504/522-9500.** www.louisianapizzakitchen.com. Pizzas $8–$12; pastas $10–$16. AE, DC, DISC, MC, V. Sun–Thurs 11am–10pm; Fri–Sat 11am–11pm. Additional location at 615 S. Carrollton Ave. 📞 **504/866-5900.** Daily noon–8pm.

Napoleon House ✦ CREOLE/ITALIAN   Folklore has it that the name of this place derives from a bit of wishful thinking: Around the time of Napoleon's death, a plot was hatched here to snatch the Little Corporal from his island exile and bring him to live in New Orleans. The third floor was added expressly for the purpose of providing him with a home. Alas, it probably isn't true: The building dates from a couple of years after Napoleon's death. But let's not let the truth get in the way of a good story, or a good hangout, which this is at any time of day, but particularly late at night (though not at this time; see below), when it's dark enough to hatch your own secret plans. Somewhere between tourist-geared and local-friendly, it serves large portions of adequate versions of traditional New Orleans food (po' boys, jambalaya), plus the only heated muffuletta in town. Luckily, this historic place sustained no storm damage, but for the foreseeable future, they have severely shortened hours.

500 Chartres St. ⓒ 504/524-9752. www.napoleonhouse.com. Main courses $3.25–$25. AE, DISC, MC, V. Fri–Wed 11:30am–6pm.

Petunia's ✦ CAJUN/CREOLE   Petunia's, located in an 1830s town house, dishes up enormous portions of New Orleans specialties like shrimp Creole, Cajun pasta with shrimp and andouille, and a variety of fresh seafood. Breakfast and Sunday brunch are popular, with a broad selection of crepes that, at 14 inches, are billed as the world's largest. Options include the St. Marie, a blend of spinach, cheddar, chicken, and hollandaise, and the St. Francis, filled with shrimp, crab ratatouille, and Swiss cheese. If you have room for dessert, try the dessert crepes or the peanut butter pie.

817 St. Louis St. (between Bourbon and Dauphine sts.). ⓒ 504/522-6440. www. petuniasrestaurant.com. Reservations recommended at dinner. Main courses at breakfast and lunch $6.95–$15, at dinner $14–$27. AE, DC, DISC, MC, V. Thurs–Tues 8am–3pm.

Stanley ✦✦ AMERICAN   Proving the truth of the adage "necessity is the mother of invention," in the days following Katrina, when the Quarter was an isolated island of intrepid survivors determined to carry on regardless, and few, if any, places to eat were open (in New Orleans, that's how you know a disaster has hit), the chef-owner of Stella! began serving sandwiches and grilling burgers on the sidewalk. This was so successful he turned this ad hoc measure into a full proper cafe. The choice of name was obvious. Certainly, Stella's crude and awkward, yet magnetic and charismatic husband would feel more comfortable in this casual and airy locale, where the burgers have already earned raves, than over in its more exotic big sister. Look for hearty, filling, sandwich-intensive breakfast and lunch fare, like eggs Benedict po' boy, corned beef hash, cornmeal crusted oyster po' boy, and even a touch of the unexpected, a Korean BBQ beef po' boy with kimchee. Here's hoping it someday turns into a late nightspot as well as a first-choice breakfast stop.

1031 Decatur St. ℭ **504/593-0006.** Everything under $12. AE, DISC, MC, V. Daily 8am–3pm.

2 The Faubourg Marigny

For the restaurants in this section, see the "Where to Dine in New Orleans" map on p. 80.

EXPENSIVE

The Bank Café ℛ ECLECTIC   So-called because it's set in a converted bank building, it's a big gorgeous spare modern room in the arty but still not overly developed Marigny. The plucky owners stuck it out through the storm (they served the night before!) and for some days after, fending off looters and trying to deal with brick damage caused by the collapse of the building next door. They reopened in December 2005. Reward their tenacity and see how they are progressing. The menu is hit-and-miss; the Bar-B-Qued shrimp features five large specimens, a generous serving for an appetizer, but it can be overcooked enough to make the shells mushy and very difficult to peel. House-made ravioli is feathery and stuffed with mushrooms and ricotta cheese. Beef carpaccio comes lightly drizzled with a creamy garlic dressing, an excellent combo. Duck and andouille gumbo is smoky, with big chunks of duck, an excellent upscale version of the dish. Desserts are microscopic, though you might want to try the chocolate cake for its accompanying chocolate-pimento ice cream for the spice kick that it leaves in the back of your throat. A grown-up space that is still maturing; we will watch it with interest.

2001 Burgundy St. ℭ **504/371-5260.** www.thebankcafe.com. Reservations suggested. Main courses $14–$26. AE, MC, V. Tues–Sun6pm–whenever.

MODERATE

Feelings Cafe ℛ AMERICAN/CREOLE   Friendly and funky, and with only minor bruising after the storm (though their piano bar has been silent since, lacking a regular player), this modest neighborhood joint serves tasty, solid (if not spectacular) food. It feels like a true local find and can be a welcome break from the scene in the Quarter or from more intense dining. Try to get a table in the pretty courtyard or on the balcony overlooking it (particularly delightful on a balmy night). Expect selections like oysters en bro-chette, pâté de maison, seafood-stuffed eggplant (shrimp, crabmeat, and crawfish tails in a casserole with spicy sausage and crisp fried eggplant), and a chocolate mousse/peanut butter pie for dessert.

2600 Chartres St. ② 504/945-2222. www.feelingscafe.com. Main courses $12–$24. AE, DC, DISC, MC, V. Thurs–Sun 6–9:30pm.

Marigny Brasserie ⋆⋆ ECLECTIC   Originally a neighborhood cafe, this is perhaps our first choice for a nice meal in the French-men/Marigny section of town—not because the food is so out-standingly innovative, but it's interesting enough, and everything we tried was pleasing to various degrees. Strongly recommended is the Serrano fig salad—aged goat cheese wrapped in Serrano ham and tossed with mixed greens in a fig vinaigrette—and the seasonal tomato and Spanish tarragon salad, one of those lovely green cre-ations that have finally started showing up on New Orleans menus. The mushroom-crusted salmon, on a bed of fragrant sesame sticky rice and topped with lump crabmeat, was juicy, and the rack of lamb comes with a sweet cherry demiglace topping.

640 Frenchmen St. ② 504/945-4472. www.marignybrasserie.com. Reservations suggested. Main courses $17–$24. AE, MC, V. Mon–Fri 11:30am–2:30pm; Sat–Sun 11am–3pm; daily 5:30–10pm.

INEXPENSIVE

Elizabeth's ⋆⋆ CREOLE   A much-beloved local breakfast shop, most noted for its praline bacon (topped with sugar and pecans—"pork candy!"—gleefully exclaimed the chef), there was consterna-tion when it changed hands since it was such a perfect little spot. Worry not; they have retained the same menu and the same ambi-ence, though not, in these post-Katrina days, real breakfast hours. That's okay; the praline bacon (and the boudin balls in a mustard sauce) remain, as do the hefty portions, and a smattering of Viet-namese-inspired dishes such as shrimp spring rolls on vermicelli. Daily specials bring items like BBQ and meatloaf. And true to their motto, it's all "real food done real good." It's a bit out of the way, in that part of the Bywater that fortunately remained dry.

601 Gallier St. ② 504/944-9272. www.elizabeths-restaurant.com. Lunch all items under $10; dinner main courses $10–$25. MC, V. Tues–Fri 10:30am–2:30pm; Sat–Sun 9am–2:30pm; Tues–Sat 5–10pm.

La Peniche Restaurant ⋆ CREOLE   A short walk into the Marigny brings you to this homey dive, thankfully, not a Katrina casualty; take the walk, because rents in the Quarter are too high for any place that looks like this to be a true bargain. It's open 24 hours, except for Wednesday, which means you are just moments away from fried fish, po' boys, burgers, and even quiche. Good brunch options exist as well, which is why it's packed during that time. Come for specials like bronzed (with Cajun spices) pork, and be sure to have some chocolate layer cake (like homemade!) and peanut-butter chocolate-chip pie.

1940 Dauphine St. ℂ 504/943-1460. All items under $15. No credit cards. Thurs 9am–Tues 2am; closed Wed.

Mona's Café & Deli ☺☺ MIDDLE EASTERN This local favorite finally expanded from its original Mid-City location into other parts of the city, with varying results. Unfortunately, the original location, which was by far the most reliable, was virtually destroyed in an arson fire, and then came the floods. For the time being, we recommend coming to this location (and ordering the marinated chicken and the basmati rice with saffron). The food is not bad, but the strictly ordinary Middle Eastern fare (hummus, kabobs, and so forth) won't make a believer out of anyone with no prior exposure to this kind of cuisine. We hope some of their other branches (including a closed Uptown location) reopen soon.

504 Frenchmen St. ℂ 504/949-4115. Sandwiches $3–$4.95; main courses $6–$14. AE, DISC, MC, V. Mon–Fri 11am–10pm; Sat 11am–11pm; Sun noon–9pm. Additional location at 4126 Magazine St. ℂ 504/894-9800.

Praline Connection CREOLE/SOUL FOOD To some NOLA residents and devotees, this might be heresy, but we think the Praline Connection is somewhat overrated. It's probably riding on sentiment and tradition; this used to be the place to come for solid, reliable, and even—once upon a time—marvelous Creole and soul food. The crowds still come, not noting that what they are getting is often dry and dull. On the other hand, they are back in business post-Katrina, which is valiant of them, especially considering how many places that serve food like it aren't coming back. It would be a terrible thing if establishments like this become rare; all the more reason to eat here, and besides—the food may well have an upswing right about now.

542 Frenchmen St. ℂ 504/943-3934. www.pralineconnection.com. Main courses $6.95–$19. AE, DC, DISC, MC, V. Daily 11am–8pm.

3 Mid-City/Esplanade

For a map of the restaurants in this section, see the "Where to Stay & Dine in Mid-City" map on p. 59.

EXPENSIVE

Ralph's on the Park *(*® BISTRO   Taking over the tired Tavern on the Park's space, this latest establishment by a scion of the Brennan family continues to uphold their reputation as first-rate restaurateurs. That's even before you get to the food, thanks to an iconic view of the Spanish moss–draped giant oaks (a bit raggedy, but still there) across the street in City Park. It's a delightful spot for lunch after a visit to the park and museum, or for an early summer evening dinner (when the light is still good). At dinner, appetizers are hit-or-miss, so you might want to focus on the entrees. The pan-seared scallops, bread-crumb-crusted drum, and glazed duckling are all sterling—and would be our top choices if we hadn't tried the lamb chops, which were the most tender we have ever eaten. Lunches, once they return, are the way to go here (though the evening menu is affordably priced), given the range of liberally portioned entrees, sandwiches, and salads. Most notable is that Ralph's has a vegetarian-specific menu (ask for it) with some well-considered options (pan-sautéed vegetable cake, crepe gateau of spinach and chard), instead of the usual veggie-friendly suspects.

900 City Park Ave. ℂ 504/488-1000. www.ralphsonthepark.com. Reservations recommended. Main courses at lunch $8–$14, at dinner $16–$29. AE, MC, V. Tues–Sat 5:30–9:30pm.

MODERATE

Café Degas *(*®® BISTRO/FRENCH   You have to love this adorable, friendly, charming French bistro—the big tree that dominated their patio (part of their structure was built around it) came down during the storm. And yet—they reopened, and pretty darn quickly, too. The loss is mourned, but the cafe is as nice as ever, just a delightful neighborhood restaurant, and one that doesn't emphasize fried food (trust us, that's a combo that's hard to find in this town!). Think quiches and real, live salads (always a happy find in this town), and simple but fun fish and meat dishes, all featuring big but straightforward flavors, presented in generous portions. You can go light (a salad, a plate of pâtés and cheeses) or heavy (filet of beef tenderloin with a green peppercorn brandy sauce)—either way, you'll feel like you ate something worthwhile. Though it's French, this is not France, and this bistro is informal enough that you can go wearing blue jeans.

3127 Esplanade Ave. ℂ 504/945-5635. www.cafedegas.com. Reservations recommended. Main courses $9.50–$20. AE, DC, DISC, MC, V. Wed–Sun 11am–3pm; Wed–Thurs 6–10pm; Fri–Sat 6–10:30pm.

Whole Lotta Muffuletta Goin' On

Muffulettas are sandwiches of (pardon the expression) heroic proportions, enormous concoctions of round Italian bread, Italian cold cuts and cheeses, and olive salad. One person cannot eat a whole one—at least not in one sitting. (And if you can, don't complain to us about your stomachache.) Instead, share; a half makes a good meal, and a quarter is a filling snack. They may not sound like much on paper, but once you try one, you'll be hooked. Believe this: Nothing tasted sweeter or more like hope than the freezer-burned one (stashed away for who could recall how many months) from Central Grocery we ate in the dark days following Katrina.

Several places in town claim to have invented the muffuletta and also claim to make the best one. (Some fancy restaurants have their own upscale version—they are often delicious but bear no resemblance to the real McCoy.) Popular opinion, shared by the author, awards the crown to Central Grocery. But why take our word for it? Muffuletta comparison-shopping can be a very rewarding pastime.

Judging from the line that forms at lunchtime, many others agree with us that **Central Grocery** ∗∗∗ , 923 Decatur St. (℃ **504/523-1620**), makes the best muffuletta—and we

Lola's ∗∗∗ SPANISH/INTERNATIONAL   "Please, oh please, don't mention Lola's in the book!" beg our local foodie friends. Why? Because this small, special place doesn't take reservations, and the nightly wait is already long as it is (it's somewhat shorter since Katrina, but surely that won't last). But we are going to spill the beans anyway while assuring you that this is worth waiting for, thanks to incredible Spanish dishes, from various paellas to starters such as garlic shrimp tapas and a heck of a garlic soup. Try to arrive 15 to 30 minutes before opening time. If you come later and there's a mob, don't be discouraged: Food comes quickly, so your wait shouldn't be too long. Don't forget to bring cash.

3312 Esplanade Ave. ℃ **504/488-6946**. Main courses $8.75–$14. No credit cards or out-of-town checks. Sun–Thurs 6–10pm; Fri–Sat 6–10:30pm.

are so glad that freezer-burned one wasn't our last! There are a few seats at the back of this crowded, heavenly smelling Italian grocery, or you can order to go. Best of all, they ship, so once you're hooked—and you will be—you need not wait until your next trip for a muffuletta fix. Take your sandwich across the street and eat it on the banks of the Mississippi for an inexpensive romantic meal (about $10 for a whole sandwich). Central Grocery makes up its sandwiches early in the day, so they are ready to go as the rush hits. This means you can sometimes get a sandwich that is just a bit less fresh. Go early, to get them shortly after they are constructed, or later, if there has been a big rush, forcing production of more later in the day.

Then there are those who swear by the heated muffulettas served at the **Napoleon House** ✿, 500 Chartres St. (✆ **504/524-9752**). Others find them blasphemous. We recommend that you start with cold and work up to heated—it's a different taste sensation. Feeling experimental? Go to **Nor-Joe's Importing Co.,** 505 Friscoe, in Metairie (✆ **504/833-9240**), where what many consider outstanding muffulettas are constructed with iconoclastic ingredients like prosciutto and mortadella.

INEXPENSIVE

Liuzza's By the Track ✿✿ CREOLE/SANDWICHES   Not to be confused with Liuzza's (p, 128), and not to be overlooked either. This Liuzza's is a near-flawless example of a corner neighborhood hole in the wall, and boy are we glad they made it through the storm. In one visit, you will either get the point or not; by the second visit, the staff will know your name. By the third visit, you might wonder why you would eat anywhere else. It's not just the fact that they serve what may be the best gumbo and red beans 'n' rice in the city, it's the monster perfect po' boys, including a drippy garlic-stuffed roast beef (with a pinch of horseradish in the mayo) and a rare BBQ-shrimp po' boy (about three dozen shrimp in a hollowed-out po' boy loaf, soaked in spicy butter). It's also the surprise of serious daily specials like "grilled crab cheese" and shish kabobs.

It's the salads as well, huge and full of leafy greens (the healthy aspects of which we like to ruin by having ours topped with fried crawfish and green-onion dressing); vegetarians will be thrilled with the portobello mushroom version. Space is at a premium (they don't have a lot of tables), and it is not out of the question that you could show up and simply never, ever get seated. (Or you could just as easily be the only diner. It's unpredictable.) Call ahead or plan for, say, lunch (the most popular time) at 11:45am instead of noon.

1518 N. Lopez. © 504/943-8667. Everything under $10. MC, V. Mon–Thurs 11am–8:30pm; Fri–Sat 11am–9pm.

Parkway Bakery and Tavern 🐟🐟 A block or so off Bayou St. John, some enterprising folks with a good sense of history resurrected a long-boarded-up, and once much-beloved po' boy shop and bakery, founded in 1922. It elicits flashbacks from old customers (though the lovingly renovated and spick-and-span interior bears no relation to the grungy last days of its old incarnation) and deep pleasure in just about everyone. Never was that more evident than the evening the intrepid owner (living at this writing in a FEMA trailer in front of his restaurant) reopened, one of the first businesses in his area to do so. About 1,000 locals came out to sample the (then) limited menu of just one po' boy (roast beef), listen to some music, and rejoice. You won't find any innovations here, just classic po' boys (the falling-apart roast beef, and the sine qua non fried oyster have their dedicated fans, while we are believers in the hot sausage and cheese topped with roast beef debris), and many a local beloved brand name like Barq's and Zapp's. The bar is good hang as well, while the bayou remains a pretty walk even if it now borders some very sad areas. But it's brave acts like this early reopening that will help revitalize a once-up-and-coming area, so go ahead—have a sandwich and a beer and toast them and their city.

538 Hagan St. © 504/482-3047. Everything under $10. AE, DISC, MC, V. Daily 11am–7pm.

4 Central Business District (CBD)

For restaurants in this section, see the "Where to Dine in New Orleans" map on p. 80.

VERY EXPENSIVE

Emeril's 🐟🐟 CREOLE/NEW AMERICAN The ubiquitous Emeril came in for some noisy flak in the days following the disaster, by some who felt he was not visible enough in supporting the city. More controversy followed, but here's the only thing worth really noting: At press time, Emeril had reopened all three of his restaurants. Keeping a business presence, and employing many is an excellent way to support the city, and that's where the matter should be left. Meanwhile, we can vouch for his first namesake restaurant. Although it may no longer be trend setting, it certainly isn't resting on its laurels in terms of quality, a remarkable feat given how long the place has been around. And while Emeril may not always be in the kitchen (what with the other restaurants and the Food Network shows), he certainly has left his original baby in some capable hands. On a recent, well-stuffed visit, there wasn't a single misstep. For starters, try the panned oysters (with tomato jam and bacon!) or Emeril's signature lobster cheesecake (a savory treat that has to be experienced at least once). Entree standouts include a precisely done BBQ salmon with onion marmalade, a brick-size pork chop paired with homemade boudin (make sure this thick, hearty piece of meat is not overcooked), and pecan-crusted redfish. BBQ shrimp comes with a heavier sauce than the classic versions of this local dish, and is paired with charming little rosemary biscuits. Emeril's influence is such that you can find variations of these dishes on menus throughout the city, but nowhere else are they as reliable, with such flawless presentation and professional preparation. Try to save part of your generously portioned meal for leftovers, so that you have room for the notable banana cream pie, a behemoth whose fat content doesn't bear thinking about, or the mini-Creole cream cheesecake, or even some delicate homemade sorbets.

800 Tchoupitoulas St. ⒞ **504/528-9393.** www.emerils.com. Reservations required at dinner. Main courses $26–$39; menu degustation (tasting menu) $65. AE, DC, DISC, MC, V. Mon–Fri 11:30am–2pm; Daily 6–10pm.

The New Orleans Grill ⒢ NEW AMERICAN   The return of this ultra-special-event place in February 2006 surely comes as a relief for locals who love their dress-up dining. Don't be deceived by the rather dull name or sometimes misleading menu descriptions. It appears to be gourmet Boy Food (all rib of this and loin of that), but that's because the descriptions don't do the final product justice. This is easily the most artful food in the city, more inventive and sophisticated than that found in any other locale. The loin of venison is thin, butter-soft slices, gorgeously arranged with caramelized cauliflower. The menu is also ambitious: The "civet of sautéed frog legs, Jerusalem artichoke velouté with pan-fried foie gras gnocchi, and shaved black truffles" probably won't encourage the timid. Having said that, the Grill has not yet found a steady course. When black drum was substituted for salmon in a dish with sautéed gnocchi and artichokes *barigoule* (braised with vegetables and wine), the results were bland, unlike the original version. Lunch has also produced some failures. But clever artistry returns at dessert, when you can thrill to chocolate fondant with slow-roasted figs and port wine and fig ice cream; a chicory coffee soufflé with a side of crema gelato and beignets; and an autumn apple tasting (apple pave, tart tartin, granita, cider caramel, apple foam, Calvados ice cream) prettily displayed in geometric shapes. If you want to dress up like serious grown-ups and take a chance on eating serious food, head here.

In the Windsor Court Hotel, 300 Gravier St. (C) **504/523-6000.** www.windsorcourt hotel.com. Reservations recommended. Main courses $16–$25 at lunch, $28–$39 at dinner. AE, DC, DISC, MC, V. Mon–Sat 7–10:30am and 11am–2pm; Sun 7–9am; Sun brunch 10:30am–2pm; Sun–Thurs 6–10pm; Fri–Sat 6–10:30pm.

EXPENSIVE

Café Adelaide 🦞🦞🦞 CONTEMPORARY CREOLE   Lots of reshuffling has happened since Katrina in the New Orleans restaurant world (to put it mildly) and this has resulted in many losses. But sometimes, the outcome is a happy one, and that's the case here, as former Commander's Palace chef Danny Trace took over after the restaurant reopened, transforming the place from a very good dining option to an excellent one, one that can stand along the best in town at any time. He's playing around with classic local dishes, made with local ingredients, but with the sort of fresh and clever twists needed to keep it all out of the Creole business-as-usual rut. Try the Louisiana boucherie (pork tenderloin with blackberry honey, tasso and andouille pie or tasso braised cabbage, and boudin crepinette) or the Tabasco soy glazed tuna (with celery root purée), or the seared duck breast (with duck cracklins cornbread and roasted tomato jam, topped with a sunny-side-up quail egg). For a change, we are going to steer you toward a savory dessert, the drunken fig bleu cheese tart. ***Note:*** at breakfast they offer the classic *pain perdu,* New Orleans's version of French toast. The drinks, especially the sweet and powerful house Swizzle Stick, make this a bar worth investigating as well.

300 Poydras St. (in the Loews Hotel). (C) **504/595-3305.** www.cafeadelaide.com. Reservations suggested. Main courses at lunch $11–$15, at dinner $16–$28. AE, DC, DISC, MC, V. Mon–Fri 7–10:30am, 11:30am–2:30pm, and 6–10pm; Sat–Sun 7–10:30am, 11am–2pm, and 6–10pm. Bar food served daily 11am–11pm.

Cuvee 🦞🦞 CONTEMPORARY CREOLE   An early return to the post-storm restaurant scene, Cuvee has since ramped it up and is producing some of the most raved-about food in town. Should you indeed end up in this cozy, brick-lined room (suggesting a wine cellar, natch), try to order the lovely spicy mirliton (a fruit that's kind of like a cross between a pear and a yucca plant) napoleon (with shrimp rémoulade) appetizer, though the pan-seared scallops with citrus beurre blanc isn't a bad second choice. We loved the pan-seared duck breast with duck confit and foie gras, combined with a Roquefort risotto—a medley that ranks among the city's best duck dishes. Don't miss the crunchy wonder that is the chocolate macadamia nut torte—it's like the ultimate candy bar.

322 Magazine St. ℭ 504/587-9001. www.restaurantcuvee.com. Reservations highly recommended. Main courses at lunch $7–$15, at dinner $18–$28. AE, DC, MC, V. Mon–Sat 6–10pm.

Restaurant August ✱ FRENCH   Harkening back to elegant New Orleans dining (Frette linens and chandeliers; classy, but the effect is more dated than nostalgic formal), but with a nouvelle twist on classic New Orleans cuisine, August has received a great deal of attention, but for our tastes, chef John Besh's contemporary French food is a bit too dainty, fussy, and expensive. Having said that, he just got nominated for a James Beard award. Pheasant comes both roasted and crispy, and desserts are unusual (especially the lavender almond milk soup with lavender mousse and lavender white chocolate parfait). Vegetarians should be warned that ham is used liberally and not wisely—it pops up even in fine dishes—but the waitstaff seems willing to make adjustments if need be. And having said all of that, Besh has become a local hero for his efforts feeding relief workers and others during those harrowing days immediately following the disaster.

301 Tchoupitoulas St. ℭ 504/299-9777. www.rest-august.com. Reservations recommended. Main courses $20–$29. AE, DC, MC, V. Fri 11am–2pm; Tues–Sat 5:30–10pm.

MODERATE

Herbsaint ✱✱ BISTRO   Herbsaint—that would be the locally made pastis found in, among other places, the popular local cocktail, the Sazerac—was one of the first (if not the first) restaurants to reopen in the CBD. As a restaurant, it's an alternative to similarly inventive, but much higher priced peers in the Quarter (here the entrees are mostly comfortably under $20), and its chef was just nominated for a James Beard award. Be sure to try the Herbsaint, tomato, and shrimp bisque—it sent us into rhapsodies, and we aren't even soup fans—and the "small plate" of shrimp with green-chile grits ("Not as good as Uglisech's," says one NOLA foodie, invoking the name of a legendary local seafood joint, "but a close second."). Salads can come delectably decorated with figs, bleu cheese, and a sherry vinaigrette. For once, vegetarians will not feel left out; the herbed gnocchi with eggplant tomato sauce is a marvelous dish, while the carnivores will be equally as pleased with the cane-braised short ribs. Or try the frogs' legs and the rabbit fricassee, because you can. The desserts are standouts; we could eat the coconut–macadamia nut pie, but that would take up space that could be occupied by the chocolate beignets with their molten boozy interior, something we could eat every day of our lives.

701 St. Charles Ave. ℂ **504/524-4114.** www.herbsaint.com. Reservations suggested for lunch and for 2 or more for dinner. Main courses $14–$24. AE, DC, DISC, MC, V. Mon–Fri 11:30am–1:30pm; Mon–Sat 5:30–9:30pm.

Lemon Grass ☙☙ VIETNAMESE   After reconciling with the ubiquitous spoilage of refrigerated items, Lemon Grass reopened its doors in December 2005. Don't feel you are missing out on local cuisine by trying the modern Vietnamese creations found in this hip Asian cafe—for one thing, New Orleans has some of the best Vietnamese restaurants in the world, outside of Vietnam. Chef Minh is as influenced by his adopted town as his homeland. Crawfish can pop up in dishes, and Minh's take on shrimp mirliton (a fruit that's kind of like a cross between a pear and a yucca plant) is well worth trying. Appetizers are terrific, one and all, but a highlight is the flash-fried oysters crusted with nuts and served with wasabi leek confit. We adore the spicy chicken roti, among the entrees, as well as the felicitously named Happy Pancake.

Next to the International House Hotel, 217 Camp St. ℂ **504/523-1200.** www.lemongrassrest.com. Reservations recommended. Main courses $13–$27. AE, MC, V. Mon–Fri 7–10am, 11am–2:30pm, and 6–10pm; Sat–Sun 8am–noon; Sat 6–11pm; Sun 6–10pm.

Liborio's Cuban Restaurant ☙ CUBAN   This Cuban cafe, after cleaning out the fridges, was able to reopen in late October 2005. It attracts many local business folk at lunchtime, but despite the crowds, that might be the best time to go, when prices are very affordable (they do seem to be needlessly high at dinnertime). Plus, it's a fun space—the chartreuse sponged walls and pillowy parachute-fabric upholstering the ceiling make for a festive and more aesthetically pleasing look than you might think from reading the description. Lazy ceiling fans and photos from the homeland put you in mind of Hemingway's Havana. Order the day's special or be like us, partial to Cuban specialties like tender, garlicky roast pork, the flatbread Cuban sandwich, and sweet fried plantains.

321 Magazine St. $\mathcal{C}$ **504/581-9680.** Reservations suggested. http://yp.bellsouth. com/sites/liboriocuban. Main courses at lunch $6.50–$14, at dinner $11–$20. AE, DC, DISC, MC, V. Mon–Sat 11am–3pm; Tues–Sat 5:30–9:30pm.

Palace Café $\mathcal{R}\mathcal{R}$ CONTEMPORARY CREOLE Housed attractively in the historic former Werlein's for Music building, there was a little bit of anxiety about this popular Brennan family restaurant, considering what a strip of desolation Canal Street was for a time there. But then it soon reopened, heralding, we hope, a new beginning for what was once New Orleans's most fashionable street, before it became a home for generic T-shirt shops and sporting goods stores. This is where to go for low-key and nonintimidating romantic dining. Be sure to order the crabmeat cheesecake appetizer, a table-pounding dish if ever there was one. For main courses, they do fish especially well (andouille-crusted fish with a cayenne beurre blanc and chive aioli, and Gulf shrimp Tchefuncte—that's toasted garlic and green onions in a Creole meunière sauce). They invented the by-now ubiquitous white chocolate bread pudding, and theirs remains the best.

605 Canal St. $\mathcal{C}$ **504/523-1661.** www.palacecafe.com. Reservations recommended. Main courses $19–$31. AE, DC, DISC, MC, V. Mon–Fri 11:30am–2:30pm; Sat–Sun brunch 10:30am–2:30pm; daily 5:30–10pm.

Tommy's $\mathcal{R}\mathcal{R}$ FRENCH/ITALIAN Those of you frustrated by the perennially long lines at Irene's in the Quarter will be delighted to know that Tommy's—the creation of Irene's eponymous cofounder—is more or less exactly the same; it has the same welcome waft of garlic that greets you from a block away and virtually the same menu. But Tommy's (which was able to reopen in November 2005) has one important difference: It takes reservations. Don't get us wrong; we love Irene's. But this space is less cramped in feel, if quite dark and chatty (forget deep conversations—the noise level is palpable). And did we mention they take reservations? So you can actually come here and not wait 2 hours before you get to dig into fantastic chicken Rosemarino, chicken marinated in an olive oil, garlic, and rosemary sauce (not dissimilar to the local BBQ-shrimp sauce you will read us rhapsodizing about in other entries), and duck Tchoupitoulas, which some consider the best duck dish in New Orleans. The nightly specials are the only real difference we can spot, and even those will seem familiar to those on the New Orleans restaurant scene, because Tommy's chef spent a number of years at Galatoire's and brought along some of their heavy-on-the-béchamel-sauce seafood dishes. Stick to the regular menu (we also recommend the deep-fried soft-shell crab on pasta, and an authoritative crawfish bisque), and revel in your ability to do so without having to stand in line. They are currently in the works to open Tommy's Wine Bar next door, yet another venue to try.

746 Tchoupitoulas St. ⓒ **504/581-1103.** Reservations preferred. www.tommys cuisine.com. Entrees $17–$23. AE, DISC, MC, V. Mon–Thurs 5:30–10:30pm; Fri–Sat 5:30–11pm.

The Veranda Restaurant ⑀ CONTINENTAL/CREOLE   This is one of the more unusual dining spaces in town, thanks to a glass-enclosed courtyard (one heck of a show during a thunderstorm—and yes, it all broke during the hurricane. But it was all repaired). Buffet buffs will think themselves in heaven with a buffet lunch option; you will find no gloppy macaroni and cheese here but rather all sorts of culinary wonders. Regular dining is less impressive but still tasty; consider Louisiana crab cakes in a light Creole mustard sauce for a starter. The Creole herb–encrusted chicken breast, and the duo of black bean and spinach ravioli in a chipotle pepper cream are other stars.

In the Hotel InterContinental, 444 St. Charles Ave. ⓒ **504/585-4383.** www.new-orleans.intercontinental.com. Reservations recommended. Main courses $16–$26. AE, DC, DISC, MC, V. Daily 10:30am–2pm and 5–10pm.

INEXPENSIVE

Ernst Café AMERICAN   The same family has run the restaurant and bar in this old brick building since 1902. Located right next to Harrah's casino and featuring live blues music on Friday and Saturday nights, it's a big local scene. Sandwiches, hamburgers, fried shrimp, salads, red beans and rice, and po' boys are offered here.

600 S. Peters St. ⓒ **504/525-8544.** www.ernstcafe.net. Main courses $7–$10. AE, DC, MC, V. Daily 11am–2am or possibly later.

Mother's ⑀⑀ SANDWICHES/CREOLE   Perhaps the proudest of all restaurants when New Orleans was named Fattest City in the U.S. was Mother's, whose overstuffed, mountain-size po' boys absolutely helped contribute to the results. They pushed past some looting and the universal food spoilage to reopen in the middle of October 2005. It has long lines and zero atmosphere, but who cares when faced with a Famous Ferdi Special—a giant roll filled with baked ham (the homemade house specialty), roast beef, gravy, and debris (the bits of beef that fall off when the roast is carved)? We can never decide between the Ferdi, the fried shrimp, or the soft shell crab, when in season, and end up getting all three.

401 Poydras St. ⓒ **504/523-9656.** www.mothersrestaurant.net. Menu items $1.75–$20. AE, DISC, MC, V. Mon–Sat 7:30am–8pm.

5 Uptown/The Garden District

For a map of restaurants in this section, see either the "Where to Dine in New Orleans" map on p. 80 or the "Where to Stay & Dine Uptown" map on p. 71.

EXPENSIVE

Brigtsen's 𝒜𝒜 CAJUN/CREOLE   There was some anxiety that Brigtsen's might not reopen post-storm, but it did, once again offering one of the loveliest evenings you'll spend in a Crescent City restaurant. In a 19th-century house that is both elegant and homey, chef Frank Brigtsen serves some of the city's best contemporary Creole cuisine. Brigtsen has a special touch with rabbit; one of his most mouthwatering dishes is an appetizer of rabbit tenderloin on a tasso-Parmesan grits cake with sautéed spinach and a Creole mustard sauce. The rabbit and andouille gumbo is delicious, intensely flavored, and well balanced. One of the most popular dishes is roast duck with cornbread dressing and pecan gravy, with the duck skin roasted to a delightful crackle. We enjoyed the pan-roasted drum fish topped with lots of lump crabmeat and chanterelle mushrooms, surrounded by a wonderful crab broth. Save room for dessert, perhaps the signature banana bread pudding with banana rum sauce.

723 Dante St. ⓒ **504/861-7610.** www.brigtsens.com. Reservations required. Main courses $19–$28; 3-course "Early Evening" dinner (Tues–Thurs 5:30–6:30pm) $17. AE, DC, MC, V. Tues–Sat 5:30–10pm.

Clancy's 𝒜𝒜 CREOLE   The food and neighborhood vibe alone should be worth the trip; it's a relief to get off the tourist path. The locals, terribly grateful their beloved favorite was largely untouched by Katrina, who cram into the smallish, oh-so-New Orleans room nightly will advise you to order the night's specials rather than sticking to the menu (though the duck dish on the menu is as good as duck gets). Do try the renowned fried oysters with brie appetizer. Recently, we tried smoked fried soft-shell crab topped with crabmeat (crab perfectly fried without a drop of grease to taint the dish), and veal topped with crabmeat and béarnaise sauce.

6100 Annunciation St. ⓒ **504/895-1111.** Reservations recommended. Main courses $17–$27. AE, DC, DISC, MC, V. Mon–Sat 5:30–10:30pm; call for updated lunch hours.

Martinique Bistro ✹ FRENCH   Because it has only 44 seats when the jasmine-scented courtyard is not open (100 with), and because Uptown restaurants are uniformly doing great business, you might have trouble getting a table. Nonetheless, this sweet little bistro, a local favorite, is no longer quite worth the long cab ride and potential wait. All that remains from the previous menu is the shrimp with sun-dried mango and curry which is still dazzling, while the flat iron steak is an unusual thick cut that, if prepared raw, can have the tender flavor of something approaching venison. Pork tenderloin and Atlantic salmon are cooked perfectly, but too heavily salted, with other promised components considerably less prominent or missing outright. Lavender-honey crème brûlée is a standout dessert. It is very likely that this limited menu will improve as time goes on and the usual issues affecting most local restaurants are resolved.

5908 Magazine St. ✆ **504/891-8495**. Reservations recommended. Main courses $15–$23. MC, V. Thurs–Sun 11am–2pm; Tues–Sun 5:30–9pm.

Upperline ✹✹✹ ECLECTIC/CREOLE   In a small, charming house in a largely residential area, the Upperline is more low-key than such high-profile places as Emeril's. In its own way, though, it's every bit as inventive. Owner JoAnn Clevenger—one of the most determined to reopen immediately following Katrina, come high water or worthless fridges—and her staff are quite friendly, and their attitude is reflected in the part of the menu where they actually— gasp!—recommend dishes at *other* restaurants. Perhaps you can afford to be so generous when your own offerings are so strong. Standout appetizers include fried green tomatoes with shrimp rémoulade sauce, spicy shrimp on jalapeño cornbread, duck confit, and fried sweetbreads. For entrees, there's moist, herb-crusted pork loin, roast duck with a tingly sauce (either plum or port wine), and a fall-off-the-bone lamb shank.

1413 Upperline St. ✆ **504/891-9822**. www.upperline.com. Reservations suggested. Main courses $20–$27. AE, DC, MC, V. Wed–Sun 5:30–9:30pm.

MODERATE

Dante's Kitchen ✹ CONTEMPORARY LOUISIANA   Dante's Kitchen has held its own against its justly fabled neighbor, Brigtsen's, offering its own takes on local cuisine for more moderate prices. Minor exterior damage and the typical rotting food issues kept them closed only a couple of months. Our last meal found us swooning over plump grilled shrimp in creamy grits, and the eminently successful combo salad of warm, pecan-crusted goat cheese, pulled pork, arugula, and pears in a mimosa-balsamic vinaigrette.

Really. Roast duck was perfect, though the cornbread dressing was dry, and an herb-crusted salmon on a pasta putanesca is deceptively healthy, so go for it.

736 Dante St. ✆ 504/861-3121. www.danteskitchen.com. Reservations for parties of 6 or more only. Lunch entrees $12, dinner $20–$24. AE, DISC, MC, V. Wed–Sun 11:30am–2:30pm and 6–10pm.

Dick & Jenny's ✹✹ ECLECTIC/CREOLE Don't let out-of-the-way-on-a-depressing-industrial-street keep you away from this marvelous restaurant. A change of ownership (to former staff members!) is the only difference post-Katrina. The room is small, and the wait may be long, so you might want to time your visit for an off-hour or day. When you do get there, you might eat as we recently did: steamed artichoke with warm brie crab dip, smoked salmon and dill cream cheese terrine with blue crab beignet and lemon aioli, a hearty white-bean-and-roast-lamb soup—and that's just the appetizers! Duck Quattro is, naturally, duck four ways (confit, foie gras, duck liver cognac flan, and seared breast with white beans).

4501 Tchoupitoulas St. ✆ 504/894-9880. Main courses $14–$23. AE, DISC, MC, V. Tues–Thurs 5:30–10pm; Fri–Sat 5:30–10:30pm.

Jacques-Imo's ✹ ECLECTIC/CREOLE/SOUL FOOD Well returned to its pre-Katrina ways, Jacques-Imo's is the type of funky, colorful neighborhood joint that the natives love. But all that good-time vibe would be for naught if the food was less than stellar—which, to be honest, some people feel it is. We've had some fine meals here, and some pretty underwhelming, certainly not worth the usual tremendous wait in line. Still, you may enjoy the serendipitous amalgam of traditional Creole, Southern soul, and New Wave innovative. The fried chicken is already a classic, and the shrimp Creole was a fine one—big fat shrimp swimming in a perfectly balanced Creole tomato sauce.

8324 Oak St. ✆ 504/861-0886. www.jacquesimoscafe.com. Main courses $17–$25. AE, DC, DISC, MC, V. Mon–Thurs 5–10pm; Fri–Sat 5–10:30pm.

La Crêpe Nanou ✹ FRENCH Voted the top French bistro in New Orleans in the Zagat survey, La Crêpe Nanou is another not-so-secret local secret. It's a romantic spot (windows angled into the ceiling let you gaze at the stars) that is simultaneously 19th century and quite modern. You can order crepes wrapped around a variety of stuffings, including crawfish. But you might want to save your crepe consumption for dessert (big and messy, full of chocolate and whipped cream) and concentrate instead on the big healthy salads and moist, flaky fish.

1410 Robert St. ① **504/899-2670.** www.lacrepenanou.com. Main courses $8.95–$17. MC, V. Tues–Sat 6–10pm.

La Petite Grocery BISTRO   Reopened soon after Katrina, this newer Uptown restaurant, a pretty, if underlit room with a relatively low noise level, generated big buzz when it opened, thanks to its pedigree (the owners are alums of the Anne Kearney Peristyle years), and thanks to some excellent reviews quickly became one of the hottest culinary spots in town. But a sampling of visits came up with one quite good, one abysmal, and the rest firmly with a vote for "fine, but forgettable." The disappointment would probably be less if the hype weren't so great. The menu features nothing you won't find in similar bistro-style restaurants in town: unmemorable braised lamb shank, pedestrian filet mignon over pommes lyonnaise, an adequate pumpkin ravioli or gnocchi topped with confit of duck—the latter an awful dish. A foie gras pâté is good enough to finish, except for the bits of connective tissue disturbingly found within on two separate visits. Bouillabaisse is flavorful, with so much seafood there was little broth. A side of celery root purée was that proper gourmet baby food texture we love. Desserts (especially the miserly-portioned cheese plate) can be skipped, with the most successful the sweet and crunchy napoleon cheesecake and the excellent house-made ice cream.

4238 Magazine St. ① **504/891-3377.** Reservations highly recommended on weekends. Main courses $18–$24. AE, DC, MC, V. Tues–Sat 6pm–whenever.

Lilette ✦ BISTRO   With just the typical spoiled food issues to clean up, this critically and commercially popular Uptown restaurant reopened quickly after Katrina. Lilette's chef John Harris trained locally under Bayona's Susan Spicer, who sent him to work in France with Michelin-starred chefs. The result is a menu of more arty playfulness than those at many other local establishments, served in a space that uses the high ceiling and tile floor to good effect, though the result is a fashionable bistro space that would not look out of place in Tribeca. You probably are better off coming here at lunch for the cheaper menu that sufficiently reflects what Harris is up to. The pulled pork sandwich is generously portioned, but can come out drier than we like. Sizzling shrimp bubbles as it arrives, just like the authentic Spanish tapas versions. Braised pork belly topped with a poached egg can be heavy rather than satisfyingly rich, but potato gnocchi in a sage brown butter sauce is light and fresh. While sandwiches are served only at lunch, any time of day you will get fancy (sometimes oddly hearty) and nicely composed dishes such as *boudin noir* (dark sausage) with homemade mustard, arugula with white balsamic vinaigrette, and grilled beets with goat cheese. Don't miss the curious signature dessert, little rounds of goat cheese crème fraîche, delicately paired with pears poached in liquid flavored with vanilla beans and raisins, topped with lavender honey, a marriage made on Mount Olympus.

3637 Magazine St. ⓒ **504/895-1636.** www.liletterestaurant.com. Reservations suggested. Main courses at lunch $8–$17, at dinner $18–$29. AE, DISC, MC, V. Tues–Sat 11:30am–2pm; Tues–Thurs 6–10pm; Fri–Sat 6–11pm.

Pascal's Manale ⚘ ITALIAN/STEAK/SEAFOOD BBQ shrimp. This 93-year-old restaurant has built its reputation on that one dish, and you should come here, if only for that. Don't expect fancy decor—the emphasis is on food and conviviality. Here you get hearty, traditional N'Awlins fare in a hearty, traditional N'Awlins setting—all the more traditional for having, like so many other buildings around town, post-Katrina mold issues (they were in some seriously deep water for over a week), that took some considerable dealing with (ask them about the thrilling tenting stories!), and caused the restaurant to be closed for some months. It's still a top-notch place for raw oysters. The BBQ shrimp sauce may no longer be the best in the city (we are more partial to the buttery wonder served over at Mr. B's), but the shrimp within it—plump, sweet, kitten-size—are. Try not to think about your arteries too much; lick your fingers, enjoy, and vow to walk your socks off tomorrow.

1838 Napoleon Ave. ⓒ **504/895-4877.** Reservations recommended. Main courses $11–$24. AE, DC, DISC, MC, V. Mon and Wed–Sat 5–9pm or 10pm ("depends on business right now!").

INEXPENSIVE

Bluebird Cafe ⚘⚘ AMERICAN Employees here tell the story of a man who awoke from an extended coma with these two words: *huevos rancheros.* As soon as possible, he returned to the Bluebird for his favorite dish. A similar scene repeats each weekend morning when locals wake up with Bluebird on the brain. Why? Because this place (which sustained no Katrina damage and reopened in October 2005) consistently offers breakfast and lunch food that can restore and sustain your vital functions. Try the buckwheat pecan waffle, cheese grits, or homemade sausage and corned beef hash. You can also build your own omelet or see why the huevos rancheros enjoys its reputation.

3625 Prytania St. ⓒ **504/895-7166.** All items under $7.95. No credit cards. Wed–Fri 7am–3pm; Sat–Sun 8am–3pm.

Casamento's *๙๙* SEAFOOD   When the fatalities attributed to Katrina are tallied, the number will not be accurate, and not just because of post-storm confusion, but because there are many deaths that can, in their way, be blamed on the stress of the storm. Surely the death of Joe Casamento, whose father founded this oyster bar and who was, for fifty years, the best oyster opener in the city, can and should be counted. Joe spent his whole life above the shop, and never took a vacation—the only restaurant he ate at other than his own in 36 years was an IHOP when he evacuated for Hurricane Ivan. Joe suffered from emphysema, and died, aged 80, the night he evacuated for Katrina, possibly in a panic over the fate of his city and the store that was his world. So eat here for him.

Not that you shouldn't do so on its own merits. The family restaurant takes oysters so seriously that it simply closes down when they're not in season. The oysters are cleanly scrubbed and well selected. You might also take the plunge and order an oyster loaf: a big, fat loaf of bread fried in butter, filled with oysters (or shrimp), and fried again to seal it. Casamento's also has terrific gumbo—perhaps the best in town.

4330 Magazine St. *๏* **504/895-9761**. www.casamentosrestaurant.com. Main courses $4.95–$11. No credit cards. Tues–Sun 11am–2pm; Thurs–Sat 5:30–9pm. Closed June to mid-Sept.

Franky & Johnny's *๙* SEAFOOD   This is a favorite local hole-in-the-wall neighborhood joint with either zero atmosphere or enough for three restaurants, depending on how you view these things. And by "things" we mean plastic checked tablecloths, a ratty but friendly bar, and locals eating enormous soft-shell-crab po' boys with the crab legs hanging out of the bread. You got your po' boys, your boiled or fried seafood platters with two kinds of salad, and goodness knows, you got your beer. They plan to be back to a full daily schedule by summer 2006.

321 Arabella St. (and Tchoupitoulas St.). *๏* **504/899-9146**. www.frankyand johnys.com. Main courses $6.95–$16. AE, DISC, MC, V. Mon–Thurs and Sat 11am–7pm; Fri 11am–9pm.

Joey K's *๙* CREOLE/SEAFOOD   This is just a little local corner hangout, though one that savvy tourists have long been hip to. Indeed, it was a tourist who told us to order the Trout Tchoupitoulas, and boy, were we happy—lovely pan-fried trout topped with grilled veggies and shrimp. Of course, at this writing, they aren't doing said trout, but right now, they've got all the fried catfish you can eat. (The trout should be back by the time you read this. They should also have longer hours, too.) Daily blackboard specials like brisket, white beans with pork chops, or Creole jambalaya won't fail to please. Order it all to go, and you'll be dining like a real Uptown local.

3001 Magazine St. ℂ 504/891-0997. www.joeyksrestaurant.com. Main courses $5.95–$13. MC, V. Mon–Fri 11am–2pm and 5–8pm; Sat 8am–8pm.

Martin Wine Cellar ✦✦✦ SANDWICHES Martin's saved us during one busy pre-Mardi Gras weekend when parades and crowds prevented us from hitting a sit-down restaurant for lunch. A gourmet liquor and food store, Martin's also has a full-service deli counter. In addition to the usual deli suspects, they offer about two dozen specialty sandwiches, elaborate concoctions like the Dave's Special: rare roast beef, coleslaw, pâté de Campagne, and special mustard on rye. We ordered it on onion bread instead, and it made our list of the Ten Best Sandwiches of All Time. (They've taken the Dave off the regular menu—it pops up occasionally as the daily special—but will make it on request. We make that request a lot.) Weekdays feature daily specials (lamb shanks, BBQ shrimp, garlic soup), gorgeous entire meals. And then there is the cheese counter, the packaged salads, and the fresh breads to explore. It's just 2 blocks lakeside of St. Charles, making this is the perfect Garden District spot for takeout or picnic fixings, though while that location undergoes post-Katrina repairs (due to reopen by summer 2006), they have opened a smaller temporary-that-may-turn-into-a-permanent-additional-location on Magazine St. with no deli counter, though it will have gourmet takeout. *Note:* It has a location in Metairie, perfect for a stop as you head to the airport.

3827 Baronne St. ℂ 504/896-7380. www.martinwine.com. Everything under $10. AE, DC, DISC, MC, V. 3500 Magazine St. (temporary location) ℂ 504/894-7420. Tues–Sat 10am–7pm. Additional location in Metairie at 714 Elmeer, in the 1200 block of Veterans Memorial Blvd. ℂ 504/896-7300.

Slim Goodies Diner ✦✦ DINER We'd already be partial to this place but when they busted out some heroic culinary moves, as the first restaurant in their neighborhood (if not in the city—seriously, Katrina had barely passed) to reopen, dodging anxious health inspectors by serving only fried eggs and other easy cleanup items on plastic dinnerware (which doesn't requiring washing, since water was not yet potable), and thus not only becoming a meeting place for stressed-out hunkered-down locals, but also demonstrating for other intrepid restaurant owners how they could do likewise, they won our hearts and loyalty forever. Come for classic diner food with modern diner clever names (not that we mind) like "Low Carbonator" and burgers named after famous folks, though we aren't sure why the Robert Johnson has bacon and blue cheese, unless it's something to do with the lengths one might go to (such as make a deal with the devil at the crossroads) in order to have such a burger. There are large salads, omelets, and even sweet potato pancakes and a biscuit topped with étouffée. A fine fun stop while you are shopping, for an Uptown breakfast or for a late night snack before seeing an even later night show. Or just come by to tell them you think they are kind of awesome.

3322 Magazine Street. ② **504/891-3447.** Daily 6am–2pm. Everything under $10. No credit cards.

6 Coffee, Tea & Sweets

Café Fleur de Lis ⭑ COFFEE/BAKERY/SANDWICHES This is a good little coffeehouse space (that also serves, as of right now, an impressive menu of mostly sandwiches and salads; this is the major post-storm difference) in an area of the Quarter sadly lacking much of this type of food. We like their freeze drinks (icy blends of coffee and chocolate) on any hot day.

307 Chartres St. ② **504/529-9641** Coffee $1.70–$3.50; main courses $3.95–$12. AE, MC, V. Mon–Sat 7am–3pm; Sun 8am–3pm.

Café du Monde ⭑⭑⭑ COFFEE Since 1862, Café du Monde has been selling café au lait and beignets (and nothing but) on the edge of Jackson Square. And boy, was its reopening one of those moments when the city knew it would be coming back. It's a must-stop on any trip to New Orleans. What's a beignet anyway? (Say ben-*yay.*) It's a square French doughnut–type object, hot and covered in powdered sugar. You might be tempted to shake off some of the sugar. Don't. Pour more on, even. At three for about $1, they're a hell of a deal. Wash them down with chicory coffee, and listen to the nearby buskers.

In the French Market, 800 Decatur St. ② **504/581-2914.** www.cafedumonde.com. Beignets (3 for $1.35). No credit cards. Daily 24 hr. Closed Christmas. Additional locations at Riverwalk Marketplace ② **504/587-0841** and 4700 Veterans Blvd. ② **504/888-9770.**

EnVie COFFEE/BAKERY/SANDWICHES A very handsome, Euro-style coffeehouse with a nice selection of drinks and pastries, some bagels and cream cheese, an actual cheese board plate, and even free Wi-Fi access. The staff is occasionally surly, but the

location is excellent if you are waiting for the clubs on Fr
to get cranking.

1241 Decatur St. ⓒ **504/524-3689.** Everything under $10. MC, V. Daily 7pm–midnight or later.

La Boulangerie ⭐⭐⭐ BAKERY

This bakery would be a jewel even if it were in a major bread city. With perhaps the only authentic baguettes in the city (the owners are from France, so they are particular about their bread, as you might guess), the loaves are crusty on the outside, soft and flavorful on the inside. But we forget about the baguettes, perfect though they may be, because of the olive bread, an oval loaf studded with olives, and just slightly greasy (in a good way) with olive oil, and the fluffy savory bleu cheese bread. Heaven.

4526 Magazine St. (Uptown). ⓒ **504/269-3777.** Loaf of bread $2–$6. No credit cards. Mon–Sat 6am–5pm. Additional location at 625 St. Charles Ave. ⓒ **504/569-1925.**

La Madeleine ⭐ BAKERY/COFFEE

La Madeleine is one of the French Quarter's most charming casual eateries, though its location means it's nearly always crowded with tourists. However, it remains closed due to staffing shortages until September 2006 or so. In the meantime, you can go to the uptown location just off St. Charles. One of a chain of French bakeries, it has a wood-burning brick oven that turns out a wide variety of breads, croissants, and brioches. Don't order their main dishes—stick with the wonderful baked goods.

547 St. Ann St. (at Chartres St.). ⓒ **504/568-0073.** www.lamadeleine.com. Pastries $1.35–$2.60; main courses $3.90–$9.25. AE, DISC, MC, V. Daily 7am–9pm. Additional location at 601 S. Carrollton Ave. (just of St. Charles) ⓒ **504/861-8662.**

P.J.'s Coffee & Tea Company ⭐ COFFEE

P.J.'s is a local institution, with 17 locations around town at last count. It offers a great variety of teas and coffees, and it roasts its own coffee beans. The iced coffee is made by a cold-water process that requires 12 hours of brewing. P.J.'s also serves mochas, cappuccinos, and lattes.

5432 Magazine St. ⓒ **504/895-2190.** www.pjscoffee.com. Coffee/tea 95¢–$4. AE, MC, V. Mon–Fri 6:30am–11pm; Sat–Sun 7am–11pm. Additional locations at Tulane University ⓒ **504/865-5705** and 644 Camp St. ⓒ **504/529-3658.**

Royal Blend Coffee & Tea House ⭐ COFFEE/SANDWICHES

To reach this place you walk through a courtyard. Order a sandwich, quiche, or salad at the counter and take it out into the courtyard. On Saturday afternoons, weather permitting, a guitarist serenades diners. If you're just in the mood for coffee and pastry, they have plenty of that, too.

621 Royal St. ℃ **504/523-2716**. www.royalblendcoffee.com. Pastries 85¢–$2.95; lunch items $3.25–$6.45. AE, MC, V. Daily 8am–4pm. Additional locations at 222 Carondelet St. ℃ **504/529-2005** and 204 Metairie Rd. in Metairie ℃ **504/835-7779**.

Rue de la Course ⚐ COFFEE   This is your basic comfy boho coffeehouse: cavernous, thanks to a very tall ceiling; manned by cool, friendly college kids; and full of locals seeking a quick pick-me-up or lingering over the paper. In addition to prepared coffee and tea, Rue de la Course sells loose tea and coffee by the pound.

3121 Magazine St. ℃ **504/899-0242**. No Credit cards. Hours vary. Additional locations at 219 N. Peters St. ℃ **504/523-0206**, 401 Carondelet St. ℃ **504/586-0401**, and 1140 S. Carrollton Ave. ℃ **504/522-8497**.

7 Planning to Reopen

Remember that many restaurants do not have working telephone numbers or updated websites, especially those which haven't yet reopened. If a particular place is important to you and you have trouble finding out about its status via phone or web, your best bet might be to drive by when you're in town.

THE FRENCH QUARTER

Bella Luna ⚐ ECLECTIC/CONTINENTAL   With its sweeping view of the Mississippi, Bella Luna is considered the most romantic restaurant in town. At this writing, after suffering serious water damage twice, the restaurant was still closed with no firm reopening date, though the owners are firm that they *will* return, and in much the same form.

When they do, definitely try the fettuccine appetizer, prepared tableside. It's a wonderfully fresh pasta, happily light for a dish that can sometimes be gluey and heavy. Skip the meat entrees in favor of fish dishes such as sautéed redfish in a sweet basil pesto crust. Even ordinary dishes like mashed potatoes are done well. Ask for a table with a good view (the closer to the windows, the better).

914 N. Peters St. ℃ **504/529-1583**. www.bellalunarestaurant.com.

Cafe Sbisa CREOLE   Right across from the French Market, Cafe Sbisa opened in 1899 and in the 1970s was one of the first restaurants to experiment with Creole cooking. This local favorite is currently closed while it undergoes post-Katrina renovations, with hopes to reopen by June 2006. We hope that they also renovate the food, which we have found in the past decidedly mediocre. BBQ shrimp came in a sauce something like heavy Worcestershire. A special of wild boar was tough and chewy and its preparation bland. A salad special, with bibb lettuce, unusual zebra tomatoes, and lemon vinaigrette, was memorable, however. You can't fault the atmosphere, which is classy and unpretentious, with live piano music some nights. The waitstaff is almost smothering in their friendly, effusive care.

1011 Decatur St. ✆ **504/522-5565.** www.cafesbisa.com.

Felix's Restaurant & Oyster Bar ★★ SEAFOOD/CREOLE Like its neighbor the Acme Oyster House, Felix's is a crowded and noisy place, full of locals and tourists taking advantage of the late hours. Each has its die-hard fans, convinced their particular choice is the superior one. Have your oysters raw, in a stew, in a soup, Rockefeller or Bienville style, in spaghetti, or even in an omelet. If oysters aren't your bag, the fried or grilled fish, chicken, steaks, spaghetti, omelets, and Creole cooking are mighty good, too.

At this writing, Felix's is still undergoing repairs, but once it reopens, its essence is likely to be the same as ever.

739 Iberville St./210 Bourbon St. (2 entrances). ✆ **504/522-4440.** www.felixs.com.

Mr. B's Bistro ★★ CONTEMPORARY CREOLE Another place that got considerable flood damage and consequently is undergoing a massive renovation, Mr. B's won't reopen until summer 2006, though once it does, we expect it will once again draw its steady group of regulars for lunch, hugely relieved to be back again at their regular tables. The food, mostly modern interpretations of Creole classics, is simple but peppered with spices that elevate the flavors into something your mouth really thanks you for. The crab cakes are as good as this dish gets. Gumbo Ya Ya is a hearty, country-style rendition with chicken and sausage, perfect for a rainy day. The Cajun BBQ shrimp are huge and plump, with a rich, thick, buttery sauce. It's so tasty it makes you greedy for every drop of sauce, completely oblivious to the silly bib they make you wear.

201 Royal St. ✆ **504/523-2078.** www.mrbsbistro.com.

MID-CITY/ESPLANADE

Angelo Brocato's Ice Cream & Confectionary ★★★ ICE CREAM/SWEETS A genuine ice-cream parlor, small but sweet, and that's even before you get to the goods. Run by the same family since 1905, in a replica of the establishments found in the founder's hometown of Palermo, they make rich Italian ice cream (made fresh daily on the premises, and tasting not quite like gelato, which they also make, but similar), cookies, and candy in the kind of atmosphere that is slowly being lost in this age of strip malls and superstores. Their area of Mid-City was severely flooded, damaging both the store and the factory out back. Fortunately for all of us, the family is committed to returning to New Orleans, and has begun serious renovations, with an eye toward reopening at some point in 2006 and finishing up that aborted centennial celebration. Thank goodness: The chocolate ice cream is one of our all-time favorites, but the fresh lemon ice and pana cotta custard have brought us to our knees. The fresh cannolis are also inspired. Right on the Canal streetcar line, it's not just nostalgia—it's still vibrant, a local tradition worthy of continuing another 100 years. And on hot days, it's vital! Come back soon!

914 N. Carrollton Ave. ✆ **504/486-1465.** www.angelobrocatoicecream.com.

CENTRAL BUSINESS DISTRICT

Cobalt ✿✿ REGIONAL AMERICAN   The precise culinary future of this restaurant was unclear at press time, but it appears something called Cobalt will reopen in this space when the Hotel Monaco gets back in business around summer 2006. We hope it's the Cobalt we knew, because it was a such a fun space, with such a fun, fun menu of kicky comfort foods, with excellent, and affordable, lunch specials.

333 St. Charles Ave. ✆ **504/565-5595.** www.cobaltrestaurant.com.

Dooky Chase's ✿ SOUL FOOD/CREOLE   This famous soul food restaurant was undergoing extensive renovations at press time, and though they had no date for reopening, they were very firm; they are committed to the city, and they *will* return. We certainly hope so. Here, classic soul food interacts gloriously with the city's French, Sicilian, and Italian traditions. Chef Leah Chase, a local legend who has been living out of a FEMA trailer across the street from her restaurant, dishes up one of the city's best bowls of gumbo—no small achievement—along with more esoteric dishes.

2301 Orleans Ave. ✆ **504/821-0535.** www.dookychaserestaurant.com.

Emeril's Delmonico Restaurant and Bar ✿✿ CREOLE   We had one of our most delightful New Orleans meals here just 3 weeks before Katrina turned that part of the world upside down. Intended as a way for Emeril to delve into variations on classic Creole dishes (and housed in a revered old restaurant space), Delmonico's was never quite as dazzling as the beautifully renovated space seemed to deserve, until it was taken over by Chef de Cuisine Shane Pritchett. We can't wait to return for appetizers like tomatoes three ways (raw with crème fraîche, dried with balsamic syrup, and fried and topped with creamy burrata); a Louisiana oyster wrapped in shredded phyllo, sitting in a creamy leak broth topped with "pearls" of caviar; salads such as spinach and arugula topped with grilled peach and a huckleberry vinaigrette; not to mention entrees such as a spectacular double-cut pork chop or the whole roasted Branzino (a Mediterranean fish that has been hard to find on this side of the Atlantic), prepared with a simple topping of pea shoots, olives, green tomato chutney, and olive oil. Get a side of the thick buttermilk battered onion rings, but save room for desserts like warm cookies still gooey from the oven, accompanied by (what else?) milk.

1300 St. Charles Ave. ℂ 504/525-4937. www.emerils.com.

Mandina's ⍟⍟ CREOLE/ITALIAN   In a city renowned for its small, funky, local joints as well as its fine-dining establishments, dis is da ultimate neighbahood N'Awlins restaurant. Tommy Mandina's family has owned and operated this restaurant and bar since the late 1800s, and the menu hasn't changed much in the last 50 years or so. Mandina's flooded deeply along with much of Mid-City, but the family is currently renovating the place, making some changes to the kitchen they had long wanted to do anyway (though there are rumors they are going to tear down and start over from scratch). A big sign boasts "We WILL return!" This is a very good thing.

And presumably, when they do, that menu won't change a bit. Standouts among the appetizers are the greasy but yummy fried onion rings, the excellent tangy shrimp rémoulade, and the crawfish cakes. Soups are always fine as well, especially seafood gumbo and turtle soup au sherry. Then go for the wonderful red beans and rice with Italian sausage, the trout meunière, the grilled trout, or our favorite comfort food, the sweet Italian sausage and spaghetti combo. Finish up with rum-soaked Creole bread pudding, and you'll have such a taste of New Orleans you'll feel like a native from da old neighbahood—back in a place that has survived against all odds.

3800 Canal St. ℂ 504/482-9179. www.mandinas.com.

René Bistrot ⍟ FRENCH   Currently undergoing the usual renovations, this chic, sophisticated, slightly snooty modern hotel bistro should be reopened by Jazz Fest. The menu isn't overwhelmingly interesting (mushroom and arugula salad with sweet beets is a nice starter), but on the other hand, they serve a perfect steak frites: The steak is pounded thin and peppered, topped with a dollop of herb butter, and the pommes frites on the side are brilliant. It's an archetype of that dish and reason enough to come here. Oh, and it's gotten lots of national accolades, including being named one of *Esquire* magazine's Best New Restaurants of 2002 and one of America's 50 Best Hotel Restaurants in *Food & Wine* magazine in May 2003. So it has its fans, who will be glad to see it return.

817 Common St. (in the Renaissance Pere Marquette Hotel). © 504/412-2580. www.renebistrot.com.

Sazerac Bar & Grill ⊛ CONTINENTAL/CREOLE   We're not sure how the Sazerac is going to look once it reopens (supposedly doing so between September and December 2006)—as it is, a pre-Katrina top-to-bottom renovation so completely redesigned the venerable watering spot (yep, the cocktail was invented in the adjoining bar, which remains unchanged from its Art Deco days) that it was unrecognizable to bewildered locals. Once they got over the confusion, they were pleased to note that a once rather claustrophobic experience has been turned into an airy one, with the room now open to the Fairmont's famous block-long lobby. Let's see what happens next.

In the Fairmont Hotel, 123 Baronne St. © 504/529-7111.

UPTOWN/THE GARDEN DISTRICT

Commander's Palace ⊛⊛⊛ CREOLE   The much-beloved Commander's is perhaps *the* symbol of the New Orleans dining scene, and for good reason. The building has been a restaurant for a century, it's at the top (more or less) of the multibranched Brennan family restaurant tree, and its chefs have gone on to their own fame and household name status (Prudhomme and Emeril ring any bells?), plus they train and produce their own outstanding locals, so the tradition keeps spreading. The building itself seemed to escape the hurricane's force, but roof leaks caused enough damage that the entire interior needed to be replaced, a long process of renovation that will keep it closed until late summer 2006. If you have as many fond memories of the place as anyone else who has dined here, don't fret; the Brennans have been quietly redoing rooms all along, and much of it was scheduled for a face-lift around now anyway.

Although our meals here have ranged from the superlative to the merely good, it's usually the whole package that brings us back time and again. The waitstaff is sharply attentive; several people pamper you throughout your meal. Executive chef Tory McPhail has worked on making the menu his own, as his predecessors did before him. Although he has retained some of the late Jamie Shannon's better-known dishes (including the tasso shrimp in pepper jelly appetizer), he's worked up some sure-to-be-signatures of his own, such as the *petite couchon baton* ("little pig on a stick"), which consists of a pork belly cooked in brown sugar and a fritter of pork *rillettes* impaled on a sugar-cane baton. He makes a daily gumbo (smoked duck on a recent visit) of relatively exotic ingredients that might convince even a committed Cajun cook to reconsider his own traditions. For dinner, try the Creole-mustard-crusted lamb, the muscadine-and-chicory-coffee-lacquered quail, or any of the Gulf fish preparations. The dessert menu continues to grow as new creations are added, and regulars refuse to let any old favorites vanish. We remain torn between the bread pudding soufflé your waiter will (justly) press upon you, the chocolate Sheba (old-fashioned, but such a dense, creamy wonder that we can't help ourselves), the chocolate molten (a generally reliable version of the cake with the oozing center), and the Creole cream cheesecake, a version of a classic so superb it got a die-hard cream-cheese hater to eat it with gusto.

1403 Washington Ave. ✆ 504/899-8221. www.commanderspalace.com.

Gautreau's ✿ CREOLE   Extensive roof damage means the usual rip-to-the-studs renovations, but Gautreau's, a classy "old-timey" restaurant, plans to reopen in summer 2006 with a new look inside, but much the same Creole menu and staff. Last time we ate there, we had the sweet mixed greens with pears, goat cheese, and a port vinaigrette—a marvelous salad in a town not known for salads. Pork chops are novel-thick, set on sweet-potato hash with braised red cabbage and apple-sage butter. Sautéed drum fish comes on caramelized-onion and spinach risotto with roasted red-pepper aioli. Flourless chocolate cake is ubiquitous in this town, but here is the place to have it, where it's soft and fudgey.

1728 Soniat St. ✆ 504/899-7397. http://ebiz.hibernia.com/gautreaus.

8 Will They Reopen?

THE FRENCH QUARTER

La Marquise ✿ PASTRIES/COFFEE/TEA/SWEETS   Tiny La Marquise serves French pastries in the crowded front room and outside on a small but delightful patio. Maurice Delechelle is the master baker here, and you'd be hard-pressed to find more delectable goodies.

There is no word on when they will reopen.

625 Chartres St. ✆ 504/524-0420.

Olde N'Awlins Cookery ⊀ CREOLE/CAJUN/SEAFOOD
The owner of this family-operated restaurant died during Katrina, and at press time, his partner was uncertain about whether she would reopen or if she would sell it. If the latter, we can only hope it will retain the charm, and the BBQ shrimp recipe, that made it so popular. If so, look for reliable Cajun and Creole favorites such as jambalaya, blackened redfish, and shrimp Creole. If the BBQ shrimp stays, don't forget to ask for plenty of extra bread to sop up the rich, buttery, spicy sauce. Housed in an 1849 building that's been a private house, a brothel, a bistro bar, and a disco, it makes use of the original old brick and a charming courtyard to create a very pleasant and decidedly New Orleans atmosphere.

729 Conti St. ⓒ **504/529-3663.**

MID-CITY/ESPLANADE

Christian's ⊀⊀ CREOLE   Ever had a three-course meal in a church? We hope you get the chance again. Christian's, doubly well named, as it's owned by Christian Ansel (whose culinary pedigree is strong; he's the grandson of a nephew of Jean Galatoire) and occupies a former church, probably won't reopen until at least late 2006.

3835 Iberville St. ⓒ **504/482-4924.** www.christiansrestaurantneworleans.com.

Ruth's Chris Steak House ⊀ STEAK   Even though branches of Ruth's Chris have popped up all over the country in the past few years, you won't get an argument locally if you pronounce this the best steak in town. This Mid-City location is the original Ruth's Chris, and if you're looking for prime beef—corn fed, custom aged, cut by hand, and beautifully prepared—this is your place. Ruth is buried in Metairie cemetery, so it's highly likely her original house o' beef will reopen, though it may do so in another location.

711 N. Broad St. ⓒ **504/486-0810.** www.ruthschris.com.

CENTRAL BUSINESS DISTRICT

Liuzza's ⊀⊀ CREOLE/ITALIAN   We are including this humble, small, and utterly wonderful neighborhood institution (since 1947) because at press time, the owners were still vacillating between returning and not (though they were leaning toward reopening), and we want to err on the side of optimism. One can't blame their hesitation; the building took on 6 feet of water (the deepest in their neighborhood), and renovations will be extensive. Still, some light will go out of the lives of regulars and anyone who loves classic New Orleans restaurants if they don't start again. If they come back, you will find us first in line for the heavenly fried onion rings or the deep-fried dill pickle slices. Still more recommended menu items are the Galboroni Pasta (spaghettini with spicy marinara sauce, pepperoni strips, and stuffed artichoke hearts) and the excellent fried seafood po' boys. It is great inexpensive food in an establishment dripping with New Orleans atmosphere—come back, come back, come back.

3636 Bienville Ave. (C) **504/482-9120.** www.liuzzas.com.

UPTOWN/THE GARDEN DISTRICT

Camelia Grill 🦀🦀 HAMBURGERS/SANDWICHES For 60 years Camelia Grill has been everyone's favorite waffle and hamburger joint. Their future was already somewhat uncertain pre-Katrina due to financial problems. At this writing, Camelia Grill remains shuttered with unconfirmed rumors spreading of a sale and new owners. Fans remain anxious and await news.

626 S. Carrollton Ave. Phone disconnected.

Dunbar's Creole Cooking 🦀🦀 SOUL FOOD For a genuine soul-food experience, come to this small, super-friendly establishment run by the very charming Tina Dunbar. A no-decor, big-kitchen place, Dunbar's caters to blue-collar locals in search of breakfast (which can run as little as $1) or lunch. You'll feast on huge, soul-warming, and generally amazing Southern dishes, including gumbo, cornbread, and bread pudding.

Dunbar's was in a deep flood zone. At press time, its future plans are uncertain.

4927 Freret St. (C) **504/899-0734.** www.dunbarscreolecooking.com.

5

Sights to See & Places to Be

A common sentiment voiced in the days immediately following Katrina was "I wish I had gotten to New Orleans again/for the first time, before this happened." The implication is that New Orleans is no longer that place the speaker wished to visit. And that's true—and yet not. By some act of grace, the most notable, from a visitor's perspective, and historic portions of New Orleans, the French Quarter, and the Garden District (along with much of the rest of Uptown) were not flooded, and escaped serious storm damage. Within those districts, many significant sights have reopened, including several fine museums and the city's sweet zoo, though ongoing budget problems have prevented others from reopening as we go to press. Those attractions not yet reopened as of this writing are listed in the section "Planning to Reopen," on p. 158. Before your visit, please call or check their websites for updated reopening information. While it is true that a geographical majority of New Orleans remains either in uneasy flux, in ruins, or in stasis, much of what the average visitor would want to see survived the disaster, and is all the more precious for it.

Still, our favorite New Orleans activities always did involve simply walking, eating, listening to music, and dancing. If that's all you do while you're visiting, we won't complain. At least you are here, and it is still here, and that may be enough, for now.

Frankly, New Orleans itself is one big sight, even now. Its distinct architecture has made it one of the most recognizable cities in America, and being nice and flat, it's just made for exploring on foot. Don't confine yourself to the French Quarter. Yes, it certainly is a seductive place, but to go to New Orleans and never leave the Quarter is like going to New York, remaining in Greenwich Village, and believing you've seen Manhattan. Katrina has only demonstrated how fragile this place is, so take in more of it, as much as you can. Stroll the lush Garden District or marvel at the surviving oaks in City Park. Ride the streetcar down St. Charles Avenue, once it returns (in the meantime you can take a bus), and gape with envy at the gorgeous homes. Get active and go visit some gators on a swamp tour. And yes, if you like, go and see the ruined neighborhoods; it's the only way any of us can comprehend the extent of the disaster. But if you only leave the Quarter to visit clubs and restaurants, we won't blame you a bit. At least you are here, and so is it.

1 The French Quarter

There's a great deal to the French Quarter—history, architecture, cultural oddities—and to overlook all that in favor of T-shirt shops and the ubiquitous bars is a darn shame. Which is not to say we don't understand, and rather enjoy, the lure of the more playful angle. We just don't want you to end up like some tourists who never even get off Bourbon. (And when you do head there, please remember that you are walking by people's homes. You wouldn't like it if someone did something biologically disgusting on your doorstep. Afford French Quarter dwellers the same courtesy.)

The Quarter was laid out in 1718 by a French royal engineer named Adrien de Pauger, and today it's a great anomaly in contemporary America. Almost all other American cities have torn down or gutted their historic centers, but thanks to a strict preservation policy, and despite the recent adversity (hardly the first time the Quarter was in jeopardy; it was nearly entirely destroyed by fire twice in the 1700s), the area looks almost exactly as it always has and is still the center of town.

Aside from Bourbon Street, you will find the most bustling activity at **Jackson Square,** where musicians (some of whom are as good or better than any you might hear in a Chicago or New York City jazz club for an expensive cover charge), artists, fortunetellers, jugglers, and those peculiar "living statue" performance artists (a step below mime, and that's pretty pathetic) gather to sell their wares or entertain for change. Their numbers will only increase as time passes and many entertainers are able to return home again, or at least, so it is hoped. **Royal Street** is home to numerous pricey antiques shops, with other interesting stores on **Chartres and Decatur streets** and the cross streets between.

The closer you get to **Esplanade Avenue** and toward **Rampart Street,** the more residential the Quarter becomes, and buildings are entirely homes. Walk through these areas, peeping in through any open gate; surprises wait behind them in the form of graceful brick and flagstone-lined courtyards filled with foliage and bubbling fountains.

The Quarter is particularly pedestrian-friendly. The streets are laid out in an almost perfect rectangle, so it's nearly impossible to

New Orleans Attractions

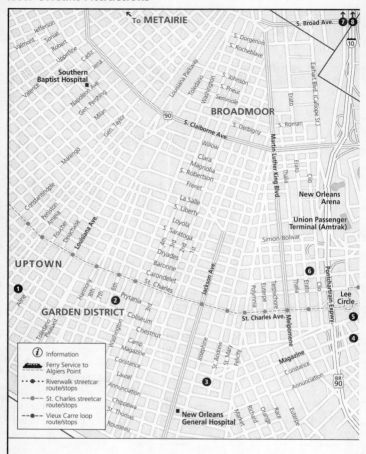

get lost. It's also so well traveled that it is nearly always safe, particularly in the central parts. Again, although the crime rate has fallen significantly since Katrina, and may well likely stay fairly low, as you get toward the fringes (especially near Rampart) and as night falls, you should exercise caution; stay in the more bustling parts and try not to walk alone.

The Historic French Market 🕿🕿 (Kids)   Legend has it that the site of the French Market was originally used by Native Americans as a bartering market. It began to grow into an official market in 1812. From around 1840 to 1870, it was part of Gallatin Street, an impossibly rough area so full of bars, drunken sailors, and criminals of every shape and size that it made Bourbon Street look like Disneyland. Today, it's a mixed bag (and not nearly as colorful as its past). The 24-hour Farmer's Market makes a fun amble as you admire everything from fresh produce to more tourist-oriented items like hot sauces and Cajun and Creole mixes. Snacks like gator on a stick (when was the last time you had that?) will amuse the kids. The Flea Market, just down from the Farmer's Market, is considered a must-shop place, but the reality is that the goods are kind of junky: T-shirts, jewelry, hats, crystals, toys, sunglasses, and that sort of thing. Still, some good deals can be had.

On Decatur St., toward Esplanade Ave. from Jackson Sq. Daily roughly 9am–6pm (tends to start shutting down about an hour before closing).

St. Louis Cathedral 🕿   The St. Louis Cathedral prides itself on being the oldest continuously active cathedral in the United States. What usually doesn't get mentioned is that it is also one of the ugliest. The outside is all right, but the rather grim interior wouldn't give even a minor European church a run for its money.

Still, its history is impressive and somewhat dramatic. The cathedral formed the center of the original settlement, and it is still the major landmark of the French Quarter. The first post-Katrina Mass, held on October 2, 2005 and presided over by the Archbishop of New Orleans, was a deeply moving affair attended by hundreds of locals. This is the third building to stand on this spot. A hurricane destroyed the first in 1722. On Good Friday 1788, the bells of its replacement were kept silent for religious reasons rather than ringing out the alarm for a fire—which eventually went out of control and burned down more than 850 buildings, including the cathedral itself.

Rebuilt in 1794, the structure was remodeled and enlarged between 1845 and 1851 by J. N. B. de Pouilly. It's of Spanish design with a tower at each end and a higher central tower. The brick used

Audubon Aquarium of the Americas **9**
Beauregard-Keyes House **22**
The Cabildo **14**
The Cornstalk Fence **20**
The 1850 House **17**
Gallier House Museum **21**
Germaine Wells
  Mardi Gras Museum **5**
Hermann-Grima House **4**
The Historic French Market **24**
Historic New Orleans Collection **7**
Madame John's Legacy **18**
Musée Conti Wax Museum **3**
Napoleon House **11**

New Orleans Historic
  Voodoo Museum **10, 19**
New Orleans Historical Pharmacy
  Museum **12**
Old Absinthe House **6**
Old Ursuline Convent **23**
The Old U.S. Mint **25**
Our Lady of Guadeloupe Chapel–
  International Shrine of St. Jude **2**
The Presbytère **16**
St. Louis Cathedral **15**
St. Louis Cemetery No. 1 **1**
Spring Fiesta Historic House **13**
Williams Research Center **8**

in its construction was taken from the original town cemetery and was covered with stucco to protect the mortar from dampness. It's worth going in to catch one of the free docent tours; the knowledgeable guides are full of fun facts about the windows and murals and how the building nearly collapsed once from water table sinkage. Be sure to look at the slope of the floor; clever architectural design somehow keeps the building upright even as it continues to sink.

615 Pere Antoine Alley. ✆ **504/525-9585.** Fax 504/525-9583. www.stlouis cathedral.org. Free admission. Mon–Sat 9am–5pm; Sun 2–5pm. Free tours run continuously, pending docent availability.

HISTORIC BUILDINGS

Beauregard-Keyes House ✦ This "raised cottage," with its Doric columns and handsome twin staircases, was built as a residence by a wealthy New Orleans auctioneer, Joseph Le Carpentier, in 1826. Confederate general P. G. T. Beauregard lived in the house with several members of his family for 18 months between 1865 and 1867, and from 1944 until 1970 it was the residence of Frances Parkinson Keyes (pronounced *Cause*), who wrote many novels about the region. Mrs. Keyes left her home to a foundation, and the house, rear buildings, and garden are open to the public. The gift shop has a wide selection of her novels.

1113 Chartres St., at Ursulines St. ✆ **504/523-7257**. Fax 504/523-7257. Admission $5 adults; $4 seniors, students, and AAA members; $2 children ages 6–13; free for children under 6. Mon–Sat 10am–3pm. Tours on the hour. Closed Sun and holidays.

Old Absinthe House

The Old Absinthe House was built in 1806 by two Spaniards and is still owned by their descendants (who live in Spain and have nothing to do with running the place). The building now houses the Old Absinthe House bar and two restaurants, Tony Moran's and Pasta e Vino. The drink for which the building and bar were named is now outlawed in this country (it caused blindness and madness). But you can sip a legal libation in the business-card-covered bar and feel at one with the famous types who came before you, listed on a plaque outside: William Makepeace Thackeray, Oscar Wilde, Sarah Bernhardt, and Walt Whitman. Andrew Jackson and the Lafitte brothers plotted their desperate defense of New Orleans here in 1815.

The house was a speak-easy during Prohibition, and when federal officers closed it in 1924, the interior was mysteriously stripped of its antique fixtures—including the long marble-topped bar and the old water dripper that was used to infuse water into the absinthe. Just as mysteriously, they all reappeared down the street at a corner establishment called, oddly enough, the Old Absinthe House Bar (400 Bourbon St.). The latter closed, and a neon-bedecked daiquiri shack opened in its stead. Needless to say, the fixtures are nowhere in sight—though rumor has it some original fixtures have turned up in the restaurant housed in the back of this bar!

240 Bourbon St., between Iberville and Bienville sts. ✆ **504/523-3181**. www.old absinthehouse.com. Free admission. Daily from 9am (closing time varies—call for information).

Old Ursuline Convent ⭐⭐

Forget tales of America being founded by brawny, brave, tough guys in buckskin and beards. The real pioneers—at least, in Louisiana—were well-educated French women clad in 40 pounds of black wool robes. That's right; you don't know tough until you know the Ursuline nuns, and this city would have been a very different place without them.

The Sisters of Ursula came to the mudhole that was New Orleans in 1727 after enduring a journey that several times nearly saw them lost at sea or to pirates or disease. Once in town, they provided the first decent medical care (saving countless lives) and later founded the first local school and orphanage for girls. They also helped raise girls shipped over from France as marriage material for local men, teaching the girls homemaking of the most exacting sort.

The convent dates from 1752 (the Sisters moved uptown in 1824, where they remain to this day), and it is the oldest building in the Mississippi River Valley and the only surviving building from the French Colonial period in the United States. Unfortunately, docents' histories ramble all over the place, rarely painting the full, thrilling picture of these extraordinary ladies to whom the city owes so much.

1110 Chartres St., at Ursulines St. © 504/529-3040. Admission $5 adults, $4 seniors, $3 students, free for children under 8. Tours Tues–Fri 10am–3pm on the hour (closed for lunch at noon); Sat–Sun 11:15am, 1pm, and 2pm.

Our Lady of Guadaloupe Chapel—International Shrine of St. Jude ✎

This is known as the "funeral chapel." It was erected (in 1826) conveniently near St. Louis Cemetery No. 1, specifically for funeral services, so as not to spread disease through the Quarter. We like it for three reasons: the catacomb-like devotional chapel with plaques thanking the Virgin Mary for favors granted, the gift shop full of religious medals including a number of obscure saints, and the statue of St. Expedite. He got his name, according to legend, when his crate arrived with no identification other than the word *expedite* stamped on the outside. Now he's the saint you pray to when you want things in a hurry. (We are not making this up.) Expedite has his cults in France and Spain and is also popular among the voodoo folks. He's just inside the door on the right.

411 N. Rampart St., at Conti St. Parish office. © 504/525-1551. www.saintjude shrine.com.

MUSEUMS

In addition to the destinations listed here, you might be interested in the **Germaine Wells Mardi Gras Museum** at 813 Bienville St., on the second floor of Arnaud's restaurant (© **504/523-5433;** fax 504/581-7908), where you'll find a private collection of Mardi Gras costumes and ball gowns dating from around 1910 to 1960. Admission is free, and the museum is open during restaurant hours.

The Cabildo 🐊🐊🐊 Constructed from 1795 to 1799 as the Spanish government seat in New Orleans, The Cabildo was the site of the signing of the Louisiana Purchase transfer. It was severely damaged by fire in 1988 and closed for 5 years for reconstruction, which included total restoration of the roof by French artisans using 600-year-old timber-framing techniques. It is now the center of the Louisiana State Museum's facilities in the French Quarter, and only sustained some window and shutter damage from the storm. It's located right on Jackson Square and is quite worth your time.

A multiroom exhibition informatively, entertainingly, and exhaustively traces the history of Louisiana from exploration through Reconstruction from a multicultural perspective. It covers all aspects of life, not just the obvious discussions of slavery and the battle for statehood. Topics include antebellum music, mourning and burial customs (a big deal when much of your population is succumbing to yellow fever), and immigrants and how they fared here. Throughout are fabulous artifacts, including Napoleon's death mask.

701 Chartres St. ⓒ **800/568-6968** or 504/568-6968. Fax 504/568-4995. Admission $5 adults, $4 students and seniors, free for children under 13. Tues–Sun 9am–5pm.

Gallier House Museum 🐊 James Gallier, Jr., designed and built the Gallier House Museum as his residence in 1857. Anne Rice fans will want to at least walk by—this is the house she was thinking of when she described Louis and Lestat's New Orleans residence in *Interview with the Vampire*. Gallier and his father were leading New Orleans architects—they designed the old French Opera House, the original St. Charles Exchange Hotel, Municipality Hall (now Gallier Hall), and the Pontalba Buildings. This carefully restored town house contains an early working bathroom, a passive ventilation system, and furnishings of the period. Leaders of local ghost tours swear that Gallier haunts the place. Look for seasonal special programs.

1118 and 1132 Royal St., between Governor Nicholls and Ursuline sts. ⓒ **504/525-5661.** www.hgghh.org. Admission $6 adults; $5 seniors, students, AAA members, and children ages 8–18; free for children under 8. Mon–Fri 10am–4pm. Tours offered Mon–Fri at 10am, 11am, noon, 2pm, and 3pm.

Hermann-Grima House 🐊 The 1831 Hermann-Grima House is a symmetrical Federal-style building (perhaps the first in the Quarter) that's very different from its French surroundings. The knowledgeable docents who give the regular tours make this a satisfactory stop at any time, but keep an eye out for the frequent special tours. At Halloween, for example, the house is draped in typical

1800s mourning, and the docents explain mourning customs. The tour of the house, which has been meticulously restored, is one of the city's more historically accurate offerings.

820 St. Louis St. ① 504/525-5661. www.hgghh.org. Admission $6 adults; $5 seniors, students, AAA members, and children ages 8–18; free for children under 8. Mon–Fri 10am–4pm. Tours offered Mon–Fri at 10am, 11am, noon, 2pm, and 3pm.

The Historic New Orleans Collection—Museum/Research Center 🌟🌟   The Historic New Orleans Collection's museum of local and regional history is almost hidden away within a complex of historic French Quarter buildings. The oldest, constructed in the late 18th century, was one of the few structures to escape the disastrous fire of 1794. These buildings were owned by the collection's founders, Gen. and Mrs. L. Kemper Williams. There are excellent tours of the Louisiana history galleries, which feature expertly preserved and displayed art, maps, and original documents like the transfer papers for the Louisiana Purchase of 1803. The collection is owned and managed by a private foundation, not a governmental organization, and therefore offers more historical perspective and artifacts than boosterism.

If you want to see another grandly restored French Quarter building, visit the **Williams Research Center,** 410 Chartres St. (① **504/ 598-7171**), which houses and displays the bulk of the collection's many thousands of items. Admission is free.

533 Royal St., between St. Louis and Toulouse sts. ① 504/523-4662. Fax 504/598-7108. www.hnoc.org. Free admission, tours $4. Tues–Sat 10am–4:30pm; tours Tues–Sat 10am, 11am, 2pm, and 3pm. Closed major holidays and Mardi Gras.

Musée Conti Wax Museum 🌟 (Kids)   You might wonder about the advisability of a wax museum in a place as hot as New Orleans, but the Musée Conti is pretty neat—and downright spooky in spots. A large section is devoted to a sketch of Louisiana legends (Andrew Jackson, Napoleon, Jean Lafitte, Marie Laveau, Huey Long, a Mardi Gras Indian, Louis Armstrong, and Pete Fountain) and historical episodes. The descriptions, especially of the historical scenes, are surprisingly informative and witty.

917 Conti St. ① 504/525-2605. www.historyofneworleans.com. Admission $6.75 adults, $6.25 seniors (over 62), $5.75 children ages 4–17, free for children under 4. Mon–Sat 10am–5pm; Closed Mardi Gras and Christmas.

New Orleans Historic Voodoo Museum 🌟   Some of the hardcore voodoo practitioners in town might scoff at the Voodoo Museum, and perhaps rightly so. It is largely designed for tourists, but it is also probably the best opportunity for tourists to get acquainted with the history and culture of voodoo. Don't expect high-quality, comprehensive exhibits—the place is dark, dusty, and musty. There are occult objects from all over the globe plus some articles that allegedly belonged to the legendary Marie Laveau. Unless someone on staff talks you through it—which they will, if you ask—you might come away with more confusion than facts. Still, it's an adequate introduction—and who wouldn't want to bring home a voodoo doll from here? There is generally a voodoo priestess on-site, giving readings and making personal gris-gris bags. Again, it's voodoo for tourists, but for most tourists, it's probably the right amount. (Don't confuse this place with the Marie Laveau House of Voodoo on Bourbon St.)

The museum can arrange psychic readings and visits to voodoo rituals if you want to delve deeper into the subject.

724 Dumaine St., at Bourbon St. ⓒ 504/680-0128. www.voodoomuseum.com. Admission $7 adults; $5.50 students, seniors, and military; $4.50 high school students; $3.50 grade school students, free for children under 5. Daily 10am–6pm.

New Orleans Pharmacy Museum ⓡ Founded in 1950, the New Orleans Pharmacy Museum is just what the name implies. In 1823, the first licensed pharmacist in the United States, Louis J. Dufilho, Jr., opened an apothecary shop here. The Creole-style town house doubled as his home, and he cultivated the herbs he needed for his medicines in the interior courtyard. Inside you'll find old apothecary bottles, voodoo potions, pill tile, and suppository molds.

514 Chartres St., at St. Louis St. ⓒ 504/565-8027. www.pharmacymuseum.org/main.htm. Admission $2 adults, $1 seniors and students, free for children under 12. Tues–Sun 10am–5pm.

2 Outside the French Quarter

UPTOWN & THE GARDEN DISTRICT

If you can see just one thing outside the French Quarter, make it the Garden District. It has no significant historic buildings or important museums. It's simply beautiful. In some ways, even more so than the Quarter, this is New Orleans. Authors as diverse as Truman Capote and Anne Rice have been enchanted by its spell. Gorgeous homes of superb design stand quietly amid lush foliage, elegant but ever so slightly (or more) decayed. You can see why this is the setting for so many novels. Though a little battered around the edges post-Katrina, its beauty remains.

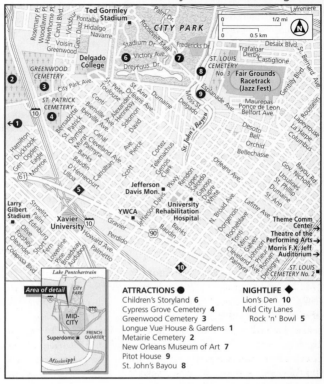

ATTRACTIONS ●
Children's Storyland **6**
Cypress Grove Cemetery **4**
Greenwood Cemetery **3**
Longue Vue House & Gardens **1**
Metairie Cemetery **2**
New Orleans Museum of Art **7**
Pitot House **9**
St. John's Bayou **8**

NIGHTLIFE ◆
Lion's Den **10**
Mid City Lanes
    Rock 'n' Bowl **5**

TROLLING ST. JOHN'S BAYOU & LAKE PONTCHARTRAIN ✸✸✸

St. John's Bayou is a body of water that originally extended from the outskirts of New Orleans to Lake Pontchartrain, and it's one of the most important reasons New Orleans is where it is today. Jean Baptiste Le Moyne, Sieur de Bienville, was commissioned to establish a settlement in Louisiana that would both make money and protect French holdings in the New World from British expansion. Bienville chose the spot where New Orleans now sits because he recognized the strategic importance of "back-door" access to the Gulf of Mexico provided by the bayou's linkage to the lake. Boats could enter the lake from the Gulf and then follow the bayou until they were within easy portage distance of the mouth of the Mississippi River. Area Native American tribes had used this route for years.

The early path from the city to the bayou is today's Bayou Road, an extension of Governor Nicholls Street in the French Quarter. Modern-day Gentilly Boulevard, which crosses the bayou, was another Native American trail.

New Orleans grew and prospered, and the bayou became a suburb as planters moved out along its shores. In the early 1800s, a canal was dug to connect the waterway with the city, reaching a basin at the edge of Congo Square. The basin became a popular recreation area with fine restaurants and dance halls (as well as meeting places for voodoo practitioners). Gradually, New Orleans reached beyond the French Quarter and enveloped the whole area.

The canal is gone, filled in long ago, and the bayou is a meek re-creation of itself, though it did overflow its banks during the post-Katrina flooding. It is no longer navigable (even if it were, bridges were built too low to permit the passage of boats of any size), but residents still prize their waterfront sites, and rowboats and sailboats make use of the bayou's surface. It's one of the prettiest areas of New Orleans, full of the old houses (most of which survived the flooding) tourists love to marvel at but without the hustle, bustle, and confusion of more high-profile locations. A walk along the banks and through the nearby neighborhoods is one of our favorite things to do on a nice afternoon.

GETTING THERE   The simplest way to reach St. John's Bayou from the French Quarter is to drive straight out Esplanade Avenue about 20 blocks. Right before you reach the bayou, you'll pass **St. Louis Cemetery No. 3** (just past Leda St.). It's the final resting place of many prominent New Orleanians, among them Thomy Lafon, the black philanthropist who bought the old Orleans Ballroom as an orphanage for African-American children and put an end to its infamous "quadroon balls." Just past the cemetery, turn left onto Moss Street, which runs along the banks of St. John's Bayou. If you want to see an example of an 18th-century West Indies–style plantation house, stop at the Pitot House, 1440 Moss St. (more about Pitot House later in this chapter).

To continue, drive along Wisner Boulevard, on the opposite bank of St. John's Bayou from Moss Street, and you'll pass some of New Orleans's grandest modern homes—a sharp contrast to those on Moss Street. At this point, you can take a Katrina-damage tour through the flooded neighborhood of Gentilly, all the way to Lake Pontchartrain. Stay on Wisner to Robert E. Lee Boulevard, turn right, drive to Elysian Fields Avenue, and then turn left. That's the University of New Orleans campus on your left, which didn't have as much flooding as some of the other major campuses in the city (such as Dillard), though it did have a great deal of wind damage, and underground electrical systems took on water. Classes have resumed and the campus is coming back to life. At any point, you can take a street off to the left or the right if you wish to go through the neighborhoods in more detail, though by the time you read this, there may be less to see, depending on what sort of plans have been made for reconstruction. Regardless, please remember these are neighborhoods, and not sights, and treat whatever you see, even if it's abandoned desolation, with respect.

Turn left onto the broad concrete highway, Lake Shore Drive. It runs for 5½ miles along the lake, and normally in the summer, the parkway alongside its seawall is swarming with swimmers and picnickers. On the other side are more luxurious, modern residences. Thanks to higher ground, these and other houses nearby did not flood, though they did sustain incredible wind damage. Further, the road buckled, and, at this writing, part of the lake wall is gone. About 2 miles down the road to the west is the fishing-oriented Bucktown neighborhood, which was totally devastated by the 17th St. Canal breech, including the marina, where expensive yachts were piled on top of each other by the power of the storm. Commercial fishing fleets (terribly hard hit by the storm) of some kind have been working out of Bucktown since the late 1800s (some local families have been living and working here just about that long) but that seems to be coming to an end; engineers need to reclaim the area for a temporary floodgate for the canal, work that may be completed as early as June 2006. Fishermen, some of whom have been working this area for decades, will need to move elsewhere, and this also means the likely end of the beloved Sid-Mar's restaurant.

Lake Pontchartrain itself is some 40 miles long and 25 miles wide. Native Americans once lived along both sides, and it was a major waterway long before white people were seen in this hemisphere. You can drive across it over the 23¾-mile Greater New Orleans Causeway, the longest bridge in the world. Oddly, it was not damaged by the storm, and has reopened.

When you cross the mouth of St. John's Bayou, you'll be where **the old Spanish Fort** was built in 1770. Its remains are now nestled amid modern homes. Look for the **Mardi Gras fountain** on your left. If you time your visit to coincide with sundown, you'll see the fountain beautifully lit in the Mardi Gras colors of purple (for justice), green (for faith), and gold (for power).

WHERE THE BODIES AREN'T BURIED 🐊🐊🐊

Along with Spanish moss and lacy iron balconies, the cities of the dead are part of the indelible landscape of New Orleans. Their ghostly and inscrutable presence enthralls visitors, who are used to traditional methods of burial—in the ground or in mausoleums.

Why above ground? Well, it rains in New Orleans. A lot. And then it floods. Soon after the city was settled, it became apparent that Uncle Etienne had an unpleasant habit of bobbing back to the surface (doubtless no longer looking his best). Add to that cholera and yellow fever epidemics, which helped increase not only the number of bodies, but also the possibility of infection. Given that the cemetery of the time was in the Vieux Carré, it's all pretty disgusting to think about.

So in 1789, the city opened St. Louis No. 1, right outside the city walls on what is now Rampart Street. The "condo crypt" look—the dead are placed in vaults that look like miniature buildings—was inspired to a certain extent by the famous Père Lachaise cemetery in Paris. Crypts were laid out haphazardly in St. Louis No. 1, which quickly filled up even as the city outgrew the Vieux Carré and expanded around the cemetery. Other cemeteries followed. They have designated lanes, making for a more orderly appearance. The rows of tombs look like nothing so much as a city—a city where the dead inhabitants peer over the shoulders of the living.

For many years, New Orleans cemeteries were in shambles. Crypts lay open, exposing their pitiful contents—if they weren't robbed of them—bricks lay everywhere, marble tablets were shattered, and visitors might even trip over stray bones. Thanks to local civic efforts, several of the worst eyesores have been cleaned up, though some remain in deplorable shape. Concerns were high over the fate of the cemeteries during the flooding, but the houses of the dead held firm. Some tombs were damaged, and most bear flood waterlines like many other buildings, but by and large, "The system worked," as one New Orleans cemetery expert marveled.

THREE CEMETERIES YOU SHOULD SEE WITH A TOUR

For more information on tour companies, see "Organized Tours," later in this chapter.

Lafayette No. 1   Right across the street from Commander's Palace restaurant, this is the lush uptown cemetery. Once in horrible condition, it's been beautifully restored. Anne Rice's Mayfair witches have their family tomb here.
1427 Sixth St.

Tips **Safety First**

In the past, visitors have been warned against going to the cemeteries alone and urged to go with a scheduled tour group (see "Organized Tours" later in this chapter). Thanks to their location and layout—some are in dicey neighborhoods, and the crypts obscure threats to your safety—some cemeteries could be quite risky, making visitors prime pickings for muggers and so forth. Other cemeteries, those with better security and in better neighborhoods, not to mention with layouts that permit driving, weren't such a risk. Ironically, two of the most hazardous, St. Louis No. 1 and Lafayette No. 1, were often so full of tour groups that you could actually go there without one and be fairly safe. As we've said, the crime rate in New Orleans has dropped considerably, and may well stay that way, so it's likely the cemeteries no longer pose such a risk. A good tour is fun and informative, so why not take the precaution?

If you're going to make a day of the cemeteries, you should also think about renting a car. You won't be driving through horrendous downtown traffic, you can visit tombs at your own pace, and you'll feel safer.

St. Louis No. 1   This is the oldest extant cemetery (1789) and the most iconic. Here lie Marie Laveau, Bernard Marigny, and assorted other New Orleans characters. Louis the vampire from Anne Rice's *Vampire Chronicles* even has his (empty) tomb here. The acid-dropping scene from *Easy Rider* was shot here.

Basin St., between Conti and St. Louis sts.

St. Louis No. 2   Established in 1823, the city's next-oldest cemetery, unfortunately, is in such a terrible neighborhood (next to the so-called Storyville Projects) that regular cemetery tours don't usually bother with it. If there is a tour running when you are in town, go—it's worth it. Marie Laveau II, some Storyville characters, and others lie within its three blocks.

Note: As of this writing, there is no regular tour of St. Louis No. 2, which is absolutely unsafe. Do not go there, even in a large group, without an official tour.

N. Claiborne Ave., between Iberville and St. Louis sts.

SOME CEMETERIES YOU COULD SEE ON YOUR OWN

But if you do, please exercise caution. Take a cab (albeit expensive) to and from or consider renting a car for the day. Most of these cemeteries (such as St. Louis No. 3 and Metairie) have offices that can sometimes provide maps; if they run out, they will give you directions to any grave location you like. All have sort-of-regular hours—figure from 9am to 4pm as a safe bet.

Cypress Grove and Greenwood Cemeteries   Located across the street from each other, both were founded in the mid-1800s by the Firemen's Charitable and Benevolent Association. Each has some highly original tombs; keep your eyes open for the ones made entirely of iron. These two cemeteries are an easy bus ride up Canal Street from the Quarter.

120 City Park Ave. and 5242 Canal Blvd. By car, take Esplanade north to City Park Ave., turn left until it becomes Metairie Ave.

Metairie Cemetery   Don't be fooled by the slightly more modern look—some of the most amazing tombs in New Orleans are here. Not to be missed is the pyramid-and-Sphinx Brunswig mausoleum and the "ruined castle" Egan family tomb, not to mention the former resting place of Storyville madam Josie Arlington.

5100 Pontchartrain Blvd. ⟨𝒞⟩ **504/486-6331.** By car, take Esplanade north to City Park Ave., turn left until it becomes Metairie Ave.

St. Louis No. 3   Conveniently located next to the Fair Grounds Race Course (home of the Jazz Fest), St. Louis No. 3 was built on top of a former graveyard for lepers. Storyville photographer E. J. Bellocq lies here. The Esplanade Avenue bus will take you there.

3421 Esplanade Ave.

BUILDINGS WITH A HISTORY (& ONE WITH BULK)

Degas House ⟨⚵⟩   Legendary French Impressionist Edgar Degas felt very tender toward New Orleans; his mother and grandmother were born here, and he spent several months in 1872 and 1873 visiting his brother at this house. It was a trip that resulted in a number of paintings, and this is the only residence or studio associated with Degas anywhere in the world that is open to the public. One of his paintings showed the garden of the house behind his brother's. His brother liked that view, too; he later ran off with the wife of the judge who lived there. His wife and children later took back her maiden name, Musson. The Musson home, as it is formally known, was erected in 1854 and has since been sliced in two and redone in an Italianate manner. Both buildings have been restored and are open to the public. Both also house a very nice (though fairly humble) B&B setup.

2306 Esplanade Ave., north of the Quarter, before you reach N. Broad Ave. © 504/
821-5009. www.degashouse.com. $10 donation requested. Daily 10am–3pm by
advance appointment only.

Gallier Hall   This impressive Greek Revival building was the inspiration of James Gallier, Sr. Erected between 1845 and 1853, it served as City Hall for just over a century and has been the site of many important events in the city's history. Several important figures lay in state in Gallier Hall, including Jefferson Davis and General Beauregard. More than 5,000 mourners came to Gallier Hall on July 14, 2001, to pay their respects to the flamboyant R&B legend Ernie K-Doe, who was laid out in a white costume and a silver crown and delivered to his final resting place in a big, brassy jazz procession.

545 St. Charles Ave. Not usually open to the public.

Jackson Barracks and Military Museum ℱ   On an extension of Rampart Street downriver from the French Quarter is this series of fine old brick buildings with white columns. They were built in 1834 and 1835 for troops who were stationed at the river forts. Some say Andrew Jackson, who never quite trusted New Orleans Creoles, planned the barracks to be as secure against attack from the city as from outside forces. The barracks now serve as headquarters for the Louisiana National Guard, and there's an extensive military museum in the old powder magazine. Call before you go to confirm that the barracks and museum are open.

6400 St. Claude Ave. © 504/278-8242. Fax 504/278-8614. Free admission. Call
for operating hours.

Pitot House ℱ   The Pitot House is a typical West Indies–style plantation home, restored and furnished with early-19th-century Louisiana and American antiques. Dating from 1799, it originally stood where the nearby modern Catholic school is. In 1810, it became the home of James Pitot, the first mayor of incorporated New Orleans (he served from 1804–05). Tours are usually given by a most knowledgeable docent and are surprisingly interesting and informative.

1440 Moss St., near Esplanade Ave. © 504/482-0312. Fax 504/482-0363. www.
pitothouse.org/pitot.htm. Admission $5 adults, $4 seniors and students, $2 children
under 12, parties of 10 or more $3 each. Call for operating hours.

The Superdome ℱ   Completed in 1975 (at a cost of around $180 million), The Superdome is a landmark civic structure that the world will never look at the same again. When it was proposed as a shelter during Katrina, that suggestion was intended as the last resort for those who simply had no other evacuation choice. As such, adequate plans were not in place, and when tens of thousands of refugees came or were brought there, within 24 hours it had turned into hell on earth. Along with the Convention Center, it became a symbol of suffering, neglect, and despair, as people were trapped without sufficient food, water, medical care, or, it seemed, hope.

It's hard to imagine enjoying a football game there again, but at press time, considerable effort was going into restoring the place in time for the generally hapless Saints team's 2006–07 season. Here are its stats: it's a 27-story windowless building with a seating capacity of 76,000 and a computerized climate-control system that uses more than 9,000 tons of equipment. It's one of the largest buildings in the world in diameter (680 ft.), and its grounds cover some 13 acres. Inside, no posts obstruct the spectator's view of sporting events, be they football, baseball, or basketball, while movable partitions and seats allow the building to be configured for almost any event. Most people think of The Superdome as a sports center only (the Super Bowl was held here again in 2002), but this flying saucer of a building plays host to conventions, balls, as well as big theatrical and musical productions.

1500 block of Poydras St., near Rampart St. ℂ **504/587-3808**. www.superdome. com.

MUSEUMS & GALLERIES

Confederate Memorial Museum 🏵🏵   Not far from the French
Quarter, the Confederate Museum was established in 1891 and currently houses the second-largest collection of Confederate memorabilia in the country. It opened so soon after the end of the war that many of the donated items are in excellent condition. Among these are 125 battle flags, 50 Confederate uniforms, guns, swords, photographs, and oil paintings. You'll see personal effects of Confederate general P. G. T. Beauregard and Confederate president Jefferson Davis (including his evening clothes), and part of Robert E. Lee's silver camp service. It's somewhat cluttered and not that well laid out—for the most part, only buffs will find much of interest here, though they can have remarkable temporary exhibitions like a most moving one on Jefferson Davis's youngest daughter, Winnie.

929 Camp St., at St. Joseph's. ℂ **504/523-4522**. www.confederatemuseum.com. Admission $5 adults, $4 students and seniors, $2 children under 12. Thurs–Sat 10am–4pm.

Contemporary Arts Center ✿✿ Redesigned in the early 1990s to much critical applause, the Contemporary Arts Center is a main anchor of the city's young arts district (once the city's old Warehouse District, it's now home to a handful of leading local galleries). Over the past 2 decades, the center has consistently exhibited influential and groundbreaking work by regional, national, and international artists in various mediums.

900 Camp St. ℂ **504/528-3805.** Fax 504/528-3828. www.cacno.org. Gallery admission $5 adults, $3 seniors and students, free for members and kids 15 and under, free to all on Thurs. Performance and event tickets $3–$25. Tues–Sun 11am–5pm.

National D-Day Museum ✿✿✿ Opened on D-day, June 6, 2000, this is the creation of the late best-selling author (and *Saving Private Ryan* consultant) Stephen Ambrose, and it is the only museum of its kind in the country. It tells the story of all 19 U.S. amphibious operations worldwide on that fateful day of June 6, 1944. A rich collection of artifacts (including some British Spitfire airplanes) coupled with top-of-the-line educational materials makes this new museum one of the highlights of New Orleans.

A panorama allows visitors to see just what it was like on those notorious beaches. There is also a copy of Eisenhower's contingency speech, in which he planned to apologize to the country for the failure of D-day—thankfully, it was a speech that was never needed.

945 Magazine St., in the Historic Warehouse District. ℂ **504/527-6012.** www. ddaymuseum.org. Admission $14 adults, $8 seniors, $6 children ages 5–17, free for children under 5. Tues–Sat 9am–5pm. Open until 7pm on Thursdays. Closed holidays.

New Orleans Museum of Art ✿✿ Often called NOMA, this museum is located in an idyllic section of City Park. The front portion of the museum is the original large, imposing neoclassical building ("sufficiently modified to give a subtropical appearance," said the architect Samuel Marx); the rear portion is a striking contrast of curves and contemporary styles.

The museum opened in 1911 after a gift to the City Park Commission from Isaac Delgado, a sugar broker and Jamaican immigrant. During the hurricane, in a great show of dedication to the place, security staff and their families stayed in the museum, leaving only when the National Guard forced them to evacuate. Today, it houses a 40,000-piece collection including pre-Columbian and Native American ethnographic art; 16th- through 20th-century European paintings; Early American art; Asian art; and one of the six largest decorative glass collections in the United States.

The changing exhibits frequently have regional resonance, such as the one devoted to religious art and objects collected from local churches. The museum recently opened the **Besthoff Sculpture Garden** 𝒢𝒢𝒢 , 5 acres of gardens, grass, and walkways that spotlight 50 modern sculptures by artists such as Henry Moore, Gaston Lachaise, Elizabeth Frink, George Segal, and others. The garden, which lost only one piece to the storm (the artist has already repaired it) has quickly become a New Orleans cultural highlight and is open Thursday to Sunday 10am to 5pm, with free admission.

1 Collins Diboll Circle, at City Park and Esplanade. ℂ 504/488-2631. Fax 504/488-6662. www.noma.org. Admission $8 adults, $7 seniors (over 64), $4 children 3–17, free to Louisiana residents. Fri–Sun 10am–4:30pm. Closed most major holidays.

The Ogden Museum of Southern Art 𝒢𝒢   A significant addition to the New Orleans cultural scene, this may well be the premier collection of Southern art in the United States. We say "may be" because even though the building is dazzling, it is built around an atrium that takes up a great deal of space that could be devoted to art. It does make for a dramatic interior (nothing compared to the Guggenheim's spiral, of course), but the fear is that certain exhibits may get short shrift and the breadth and range of Southern artistry may be limited to outsider folk artists or photographers who specialize in old bluesmen (two of our favorite genres, we must admit). But we must admit that the facility is wonderful, the artists are impressive, and the graphics are well designed. Ultimately, it's worth a stop.

925 Camp St. ℂ 504/539-9600. www.ogdenmuseum.org. Admission $10 adults, $8 seniors and students, $5 children 5–17. Tues–Sun 9:30am–5:30pm; Thurs 9:30am–8:30pm with live music.

FLOATING ACROSS THE RIVER TO ALGIERS POINT

Algiers, annexed by New Orleans in 1870, stretches along the western side of the Mississippi River and is easily accessible via the free ferry that runs from the base of Canal Street. *Take note:* The ferry is one of New Orleans's best-kept secrets. It's a great way to get out onto the river and see the skyline. With such easy access (a ferry leaves every 15–20 min.), who knows why the Point hasn't been better assimilated into the larger city, but it hasn't. Though it's only about a quarter-mile across the river from the French Quarter, it still has the feel of an undisturbed turn-of-the-20th-century suburb.

The last ferry returns at around 11:15pm, but be sure to check the schedule before you set out, just in case. While you're over there, you might want to stop in at . . .

Blaine Kern's Mardi Gras World *(Kids)*   Few cities can boast a thriving float-making industry. New Orleans can, and no float maker thrives more than Blaine Kern, who makes more than three-quarters of the floats used by the various krewes every Carnival season. Blaine Kern's Mardi Gras World offers tours of its collection of float sculptures and its studios, where you can see floats being made year-round. (Likely with new thrilling details about working overtime to get floats ready for Mardi Gras 2006, and tales of damaged floats.) Visitors see sculptors at work, doing everything from making small "sketches" of the figures to creating and painting the enormous sculptures that adorn Mardi Gras floats each year. You can even try on some heavily bejeweled and dazzling costumes (definitely bring your camera!).

223 Newton St., Algiers Point. © **800/362-8213** or 504/361-7821. www.mardigras world.com. Admission $15 adults, $11 seniors (over 62), $7.25 children 3–12, free for children under 3. Daily 9:30am–4:30pm. Closed Mardi Gras, Easter, Thanksgiving, Christmas. Cross the river on the Canal St. Ferry and take the free shuttle from the dock (it meets every ferry).

3 Parks & Gardens

PARKS

One of the many unsettling details following weeks of Katrina flooding was how normally verdant New Orleans had turned to shades of gray and brown. The vegetation itself had drowned. Regular rainfall is gradually restoring New Orleans' lushness, but parks and gardens all took a beating from high winds, from battered plants to fallen trees. There is something particularly painful about the loss of the latter, especially centuries-old oaks. With enough funds and TLC, all but the most badly damaged buildings can be repaired, but a massive old oak cannot be replaced in our lifetime. Look for most of the following to be perhaps a bit less substantial, foliage-wise, than they might have been in previous years, though with some nurturing, they should all come back.

Audubon Park   Across from Loyola and Tulane universities, Audubon Park and the adjacent Audubon Zoo (see "A Day at the Zoo," below) sprawl over 340 acres, extending from St. Charles Avenue all the way to the Mississippi River. This tract once belonged to city founder Jean-Baptiste Le Moyne. The city purchased it in 1871 and used much of the land for the World's Industrial and Cotton Centennial Exposition in 1884 and 1885. Despite having the (then) largest building in the world as its main exhibition hall (33 acres under one roof), the exposition was such a financial disaster that everything except the Horticultural Hall had to be sold off—and that hall fell victim to a hurricane a little later. After that, serious work to make this into a park began. Although John James Audubon lived only briefly in New Orleans, the city honored him by naming both the park and the zoo after him. The park was briefly used as a campground for the National Guard after Katrina, but was soon restored post-hurricane to its recreational purposes.

The huge trees with black bark are live oaks; some go back to plantation days, and more than 200 additional ones were recently planted here, though any number of young and old oaks did not survive Hurricane Katrina. Still, there is a gratifyingly large number left, which is good, because with the exception of the trees, it's not the most visually interesting park in the world—it's just pretty and a nice place to be.

Without question, the most utilized feature of the park is the 1¾-mile paved traffic-free road that loops around the lagoon and golf course. Along the track are 18 exercise stations; tennis courts and horseback riding facilities can be found elsewhere in the park. Check out the pavilion on the riverbank for one of the most pleasant views of the Mississippi you'll find. The **Audubon Zoo** is toward the back of the park, across Magazine Street.

6500 Magazine St., between Broadway and Exposition Blvd. ✆ 504/581-4629. www.auduboninstitute.org. Daily 6am–10pm.

City Park ✸✸✸ Once part of the Louis Allard plantation, City Park has been here a long time and has seen it all—including that favorite pastime among 18th-century New Orleans gentry: dueling. At the entrance, you'll see a statue of General P. G. T. Beauregard, whose order to fire on Fort Sumter opened the Civil War and who New Orleanians fondly refer to as "the Great Creole." The extensive, beautifully landscaped grounds got walloped pretty hard during the storm and subsequent flooding, much more so than Audubon Park, thanks to the latter's Uptown (where it did not flood) location. It may be a bit before the Park fully springs back, which would be a shame, since it's a significant civic location, holding botanical gardens and a conservatory, four golf courses, picnic areas, a restaurant, lagoons for boating and fishing, tennis courts, a bandstand, two miniature trains, and Children's Storyland, an amusement area with a carousel ride for children. At Christmastime, the mighty oaks (too many were casualties of the storm), already dripping with Spanish moss, are strung with lights—quite a magical sight (and one of the first signs of post-Katrina recovery, when the lights returned, albeit in somewhat smaller quantity, for Christmas 2005). During Halloween, there is usually a fabulous haunted house. You'll also find the **New Orleans Museum of Art,** at Collins Diboll Circle, in a building that is itself a work of art (see "Museums & Galleries," earlier in this section). The park's main office is in the casino building.

1 Palm Dr. ℭ **504/482-4888.** (Temporary phone number ℭ **225/342-4933**). www.neworleanscitypark.com. Daily 6am–7pm.

GARDENS

Longue Vue House & Gardens 🌀🌀   The Longue Vue mansion is a unique expression of Greek Revival architecture set on an 8-acre estate. It was constructed from 1939 to 1942 for Edgar Stern, who had interests in cotton, minerals, timber, and real estate and who was also a noted philanthropist. Longue Vue House & Gardens is listed on the National Register of Historic Places and is accredited by the American Association of Museums. Styled in the manner of an English country house, the mansion was designed to foster a close rapport between indoors and outdoors, with vistas of formal terraces and pastoral woods. Leaks caused some (though not as much as initially feared) damage to the collections, while flooding destroyed the electrical system. At this writing, only a couple of buildings were open on a limited basis, though plans were for further openings as soon as possible. The enchanting gardens, some parts of which were inspired by those of Generalife, the former summerhouse of the sultans in Granada, Spain, took a pounding from the storm and flooding, and will need extensive restoration. From a gardening standpoint, this is both depressing and exciting; years and years of hard work are gone, but then again, the possibilities for the future are many.

7 Bamboo Rd., New Orleans, near Metairie. ℭ **504/488-5488.** (Phone not working at this time.) www.longuevue.com. Check website for operating hours and admission prices.

A DAY AT THE ZOO

Audubon Zoo 🌀🌀🌀 *Kids*   It's been more than 20 years since the Audubon Zoo underwent a total renovation that turned it from one of the worst zoos in the country into one of the best. The result is a place of justifiable civic pride as well as a terrific destination for visitors with children. What's more, nearly perfectly planned and executed hurricane preparation meant the zoo virtually sailed through the catastrophe, with almost zero animal loss.

Here, in a setting of subtropical plants, waterfalls, and lagoons, some 1,800 animals (including rare and endangered species) live in natural habitats rather than cages. Don't miss the replica of a Louisiana swamp (complete with a rare white gator, plus a whole Katrina themed exhibit, with duct-taped fridges and other wry satirical touches) or the new "Butterflies in Flight" exhibit, where more than 1,000 butterflies live among lush, colorful vegetation.

6500 Magazine St. ⓒ 504/581-4629. www.auduboninstitute.org. Admission $12 adults, $9 seniors (over 64), $7 children 2–12. As of March 1, 2006, hours are Wed–Sun 10am–4pm. Call for updates in operating hours. Last ticket sold 1 hr. before closing. Closed holidays.

4 Especially for Kids

The following destinations are particularly well suited for younger children.

Children's Storyland 🎈🎈 (Kids)   We hope the needed post-Katrina renovations go quickly for this beloved playground, which so delights the under-8 set (*Child* magazine rated it one of the 10 best in the country), restoring the decor, inspired by children's stories and rhymes, to its full sweetness.

Also in City Park, and thus also closed in order to renovate is the **Carousel Gardens.** Once it's reopened, kids and adults will again enjoy the carousel, two Ferris wheels (one big, one small), bumper cars, some miniature trains, a ladybug shaped roller coaster and other rides. Delighting local families since 1906, the carousel is one of only 100 all-wood merry-go-rounds in the country, and the only one in the state.

City Park at Victory Ave. ⓒ **504/483-9381.** (Temporary phone number ⓒ **225/342-4933**). Admission $2 adults and children ages 2 and up, free for children under 2; $10 buys unlimited rides. Sat–Sun 11am–4:30pm. Call for updates in operating hours.

Louisiana Children's Museum 🎈🎈🎈 (Kids)   This popular interactive museum is really a playground in disguise that will keep kids occupied for a good couple of hours. Along with changing exhibits, the museum offers an art shop with regularly scheduled projects, a mini grocery store, a chance to be a "star anchor" at a simulated television studio, and activities exploring music, fitness, water, and life itself. If you belong to your local science museum, check your membership card for entry privileges.

420 Julia St., at Tchoupitoulas St. ⓒ **504/523-1357.** Fax 504/529-3666. www.lcm. org. Admission $7. Tues–Sat 9:30am–4:30pm, Sun noon–4:30pm; summer Mon–Sat 9:30am–4:30pm. Call for updates in operating hours.

5 Organized Tours

IN THE FRENCH QUARTER

Historic New Orleans Tours ⋆⋆⋆ (𝒞 504/947-2120; www.tour neworleans.com) is the place to go for authenticity. Tour guides are carefully chosen for their combination of knowledge and entertaining manner. The daily French Quarter tours are the best straightforward, nonspecialized walking tours of this neighborhood, $12 adults. They also offer a Voodoo tour and a Haunted tour, $15 adults; and a Garden District tour, $15 adults. A recent addition is a Music tour Saturday and Sunday for $15.

The Bienville Foundation ⋆⋆⋆, run by Roberts Batson (𝒞 504/945-6789; nolabienville@aol.com), offers a stage show (based on Batson's popular Scandal Tour) called "Amazing Place, This New Orleans" at Trew Brew Theatre, and a highly popular and recommended Gay Heritage Tour. The tours last roughly 2½ hours and generally cost $20 per person. Visa and MasterCard are accepted. Times and departure locations change seasonally, so call or e-mail to find out what's happening when.

Kenneth Holdrich, a professor of American literature at the University of New Orleans, runs **Heritage Literary Tours** ⋆⋆⋆, 732 Frenchmen St. (𝒞 504/949-9805). In addition to a general tour about the considerable literary legacy of the French Quarter, some tours, arranged in advance, can be designed around a specific author, such as the Tennessee Williams tour. The narratives are full of facts both literary and historical, are loaded with anecdotes, and are often downright humorous. Group tour rates are available ($20 for adults), and tours are "scheduled for your convenience."

BEYOND THE FRENCH QUARTER

Author Robert Florence (who has written two excellent books on New Orleans cemeteries) loves his work, and his **Historic New Orleans Tours** ⋆⋆⋆ (𝒞 504/947-2120) are full of meticulously researched facts and more than a few good stories. (More than ever post-Katrina, needless to say.) A very thorough tour of the Garden District and Lafayette Cemetery (a section of town not many of the other companies go into) leaves daily at 11am and 1:45pm from the Garden District Book Shop (in the Rink, corner of Washington Ave. and Prytania St.). Rates are $14 adults, $12 students and seniors, free for children under 12.

The local office for **Gray Line Tours** ⋆⋆ (𝒞 800/535-7786 or 504/569-1401), like all businesses around town, took a hard hit, between severely reduced staff (most of whom, including the head of the local company, lost their homes), and, of course, being a business that involves sightseeing. Consequently, they took the controversial move of adding **"Katrina Disaster Tours"** to their menu. Initially the locals thought the tours seemed like exploitation, but upon reflection, a majority agreed: These sights need to be seen, so that this disaster, and its victims, are not forgotten. And, as we have said, the only way to really understand the scope of this catastrophe is to see it for yourself. Certainly, the company has gone to great lengths to operate these tours with respect. Guides are locals, with their own storm stories to tell, tourists are not allowed to exit the vans while in the damaged neighborhoods, a portion of the ticket price goes to Katrina relief (and passengers can choose which organization, out of a selection, their money will go to), and petitions to various government officials are sent around for voluntary signatures.

Tours by Isabelle ✾ (✆ **504/391-3544;** www.toursbyisabelle. com) offers eight different tours for small groups in air-conditioned passenger vans. Price and departure times vary. For $58 you can join Isabelle's afternoon Combo Tour, which begins at 1pm and adds Longue Vue House & Gardens to a tour of the French Quarter, St. Louis Cemetery No. 3, Bayou St. John, the shores of Lake Pontchartrain, and the uptown and downtown neighborhoods. Many more tours are available, including, at this writing, a controversial Katrina disaster tour; contact them for more information.

SWAMP TOURS

Swamp tours can be a hoot, particularly if you get a guide who calls alligators to your boat for a little snack of chicken (please keep your hands inside the boat—they tend to look a lot like chicken to a gator). On all of the following tours you're likely to see alligators, bald eagles, waterfowl, egrets, owls, herons, ospreys, feral hogs, otters, beavers, frogs, turtles, raccoons, deer, and nutria (maybe even a black bear or a mink)—and a morning spent floating on the bayou can be mighty pleasant. Most tours last approximately 2 hours.

Among the companies we recommend are **Lil Cajun Swamp Tours** ✾ (✆ **800/725-3213** or 504/689-3213; www.lilcajun swamptours.com), **Honey Island Swamp Tours** ✾✾ (✆ **985/641-1769;** www.honeyislandswamp.com), and **Westwego Swamp Adventures** ✾✾ (✆ **800/633-0503;** www.westwegoswamp adventures.com).

MYSTICAL & MYSTERIOUS TOURS

While most of the ghost tours are a bunch of hooey hokum, we are pleased that there is one we can send you to with a clear conscience: **Historic New Orleans Tours** ☆☆☆ (© 504/947-2120) offers a Cemetery and Voodoo Tour, the only one that is fact- and not sensation-based, though it is no less entertaining for it. They also use tour revenue for much-needed tomb restoration, including several highly visible and worthy projects like the Musicians tomb in St. Louis No.1. The trip goes through St. Louis Cemetery No. 1, Congo Square, and an active voodoo temple. It leaves Monday through Saturday at 10am and 1pm and Sunday at 10am only, from the courtyard at 334-B Royal St. Rates are $15 for adults, $13 for students and seniors, and free for children under 12. They also offer a nighttime haunted tour, perhaps the only one in town where well-researched guides offer genuine thrills and chills. It leaves at 7:30pm from 508 Toulouse St.

BOAT TOURS

For those interested in doing the Mark Twain thing, a number of operators offer riverboat cruises; some cruises have specific destinations like the zoo or Chalmette, while others just cruise the river and harbor without stopping. Docks are at the foot of Toulouse and Canal streets, and there's ample parking. Call for reservations, which are required for all these tours, and to confirm prices and schedules. Among the boats are the steamboat *Natchez* and the stern-wheeler *John James Audubon,* 2 Canal St., Suite 2500 (© 800/233-BOAT or 504/586-8777; www.steamboatnatchez.com), a fun way to reach the Audubon Zoo; and the paddle-wheeler *Creole Queen,* Riverwalk Dock (© 800/445-4109 or 504/529-4567; www.neworleanspaddle wheels.com), which departs from the Poydras Street Wharf.

6 Gambling

After years of political and legal wrangling—much of which is still an ongoing source of fun in the daily paper—**Harrah's Casino** opened. "Oh, goody" we said, along with other even more sarcastic things. Then again, post-Katrina, the Harrah's company was financially generous to all of their hurricane-affected casino employees and has been similarly generous with Katrina relief benefits. So what the hey; come here and spend your money, if you like. You will find something exactly like a Vegas casino (100,000 sq. ft. of nearly 3,000 slot machines and 120 tables plus buffet and twice-nightly live "Mardi Gras parade" shows), which is mighty shocking to the system and also a bit peculiar because like many a Vegas casino, it is Mardi Gras/New Orleans–themed—but exactly like a Vegas casino interpretation of same, which means it's almost exactly *not* like the real thing. Under normal New Orleans circumstances, we can't understand anyone coming here (and listen, we're fond of Vegas, so we're not anti-casino in general). But right now, anything that generates tax money is okay by us. It can be found on Canal Street at the river (© **504/533-6000**).

7 Planning to Reopen

THE FRENCH QUARTER

Aquarium of the Americas 🐟🐟🐟 *Kids*   The world-class Audubon Institute's Aquarium of the Americas was one of the saddest of so many terrible Katrina stories. The facility had superb hurricane contingency plans, not to mention engineering that one only wishes was shared by the levee system, and consequently both building and fishy residents came through the initial storm beautifully. But as the days following the evacuation stretched out, generators failed, and most of its 10,000 fish died, breaking the hearts of not only the staff who worked so hard to keep their charges healthy and alive, but just about anyone who had ever visited this lovely place. Survivors include the popular otter pair, the penguins, the leafy and weedy sea dragons, and Midas, the 250-pound sea turtle.

We sincerely hope that the aquarium is soon reopened and restored to its deserved international status. When it is, it will once again be highly entertaining and painlessly educational, with beautifully constructed exhibits, and a deserved stop on your trip.

1 Canal St., at the river. © **800/774-7394** or 504/581-4629. www.auduboninstitute. org.

The 1850 House 🐟   James Gallier, Sr., and his son designed the historic Pontalba Buildings for the Baroness Micaela Almonester de Pontalba. The rows of town houses on either side of Jackson Square were the largest private buildings in the country at the time. Legend has it that the Baroness, miffed that her friend Andrew Jackson wouldn't tip his hat to her, had his statue erected in the square, permanently doffing his chapeau toward her apartment on the top floor of the Upper Pontalba. It's probably not true, but we never stand in the way of a good story.

Plans to reopen are uncertain due to state budget restrictions incurred as a result of Hurricane Katrina.

523 St. Ann St., Lower Pontalba Building, Jackson Sq. ℭ **800/568-6968** or 504/568-6968. Fax 504/568-4995. http://lsm.crt.state.la.us/1850ex.htm.

The Old U.S. Mint 🕷🕷 🄚🄸🄳🄼 The Old U.S. Mint, a Louisiana

State Museum complex, houses exhibits on New Orleans jazz and the city's Carnival celebrations. The first exhibit contains a collection of pictures, musical instruments, and other artifacts connected with jazz greats—Louis Armstrong's first trumpet is here. It tells of the development of the jazz tradition and New Orleans's place in that history. Across the hall is a stunning array of Carnival mementos, and there is usually one temporary exhibit on a special theme, such as the 2005 exhibit devoted to the history of beverages (no, not just booze, but a lot of that, to be sure) in New Orleans.

Unfortunately, the Mint was damaged during Katrina and is under extensive renovation. No reopening date is set at this writing. 400 Esplanade Ave., at N. Peters St. (enter on Esplanade Ave. or Barracks St.). ℭ **800/568-6968** or 504/568-6968. Fax 504/568-4995.

Madame John's Legacy 🕷 Madame John's Legacy, the second-

oldest building in the Mississippi Valley (after the Ursuline Convent) and a rare example of Creole architecture, miraculously survived the 1794 fire. Built around 1788 on the foundations of an earlier home destroyed in the fire of that year, the house has had a number of owners and renters, but none of them were named John. Or even Madame. It acquired its moniker courtesy of author George Washington Cable, who used the house as a setting for his short story "Tite Poulette." The protagonist was a quadroon named Madame John after her lover, who willed this house to her.

Madame John's Legacy is closed as of this writing. The reopening is uncertain due to budgetary constraints following Hurricane Katrina. Please call when visiting for updated information. 632 Dumaine St. ℭ **504/568-6968**.

The Presbytère 🕷🕷🕷 The Presbytère was planned as housing

for the clergy but was never used for that purpose. Currently, it's part of the Louisiana State Museum, which has just turned the entire building into a smashing Mardi Gras museum. Five major themes (History, Masking, Parades, Balls, and the Courir du Mardi Gras) trace the history of this high-profile but frankly little-understood (outside of New Orleans) annual event. The exhibits are stunning and the attention to detail is startling, with everything from elaborate Mardi Gras Indian costumes to Rex Queen jewelry from the turn of the 20th century.

Regrettably, The Presbytère remains closed at press time. Plans are to reopen, but no firm date has been set. Please call before your visit for updated information.

751 Chartres St., Jackson Sq. ℂ **800/568-6968** or 504/568-6968. Fax 504/568-4995.

8 The Top Nearby Plantations

As we urge you to spend money—er, help stimulate the local economy—don't forget about the plantations. Their business is no longer agricultural, but touristic, and though suffering little to no storm damage, post-Katrina times aren't easy, with numbers of daily visitors cut in half or more. Both of the following are an easy partial-day trip from the city (they are less than an hour's drive away), and make a nice contrast in terms of architectural style and presentational approach.

Laura: A Creole Plantation 🐊🐊🐊 *Tips*   If you see only one plantation, make it this one. Laura is the very model of a modern plantation—that is, when you figure that today's crop is tourism, not sugar cane or indigo. And it's all thanks to the vision of developer and general manager Norman Marmillion, who was determined to make this property rise above the average antebellum mansion. The hoopskirted tours found elsewhere are banished in favor of a comprehensive view of daily life on an 18th- and 19th-century plantation, a cultural history of Louisiana's Creole population, and a dramatic, entertaining, in-depth look at one extended Creole family.

This is a classic Creole house, simple on the outside but with real magic within. Unlike many other plantation homes, much is known about this house and the family that lived here, thanks to extensive records, particularly the detailed memoirs of Laura Locoul.

Sadly, a huge fire hit the plantation on August 8, 2004. Employees worked hard and saved many artifacts, and a significant portion of the original house survived. Tours continued the very next morning, and renovation plans have moved along nicely, as the house is gradually being restored to its original 1805 contours. (The ongoing process has been filmed for a History Channel special, and can be followed on their website.) Perhaps, given this, it was only fair that none of the buildings were damaged by hurricanes Katrina or Rita. Basic tours of the main building and the property start every 20 minutes, last about 55 minutes, and are organized around true (albeit spiced-up) stories from the history of the home and its residents. (*Of special note:* The stories that eventually became the beloved Br'er Rabbit were first collected here by a folklorist in the 1870s.)

2247 La. 18, Vacherie, LA 70090. ℂ 888/799-7690 or 225/265-7690. www.laura plantation.com. Admission $10 adults, $5 children 6–17, free for children under 6. Daily 9:30am–5pm. Last tour begins at 4pm. Closed major holidays.

Oak Alley Plantation ⚜⚜⚜   Also not suffering any hurricane damage, this is precisely what comes to mind when most people think "plantation." A splendid white house, its porch lined with giant columns, approached by a magnificent drive lined with stately oak trees—yep, it's all here. Consequently, this is the most famous (and probably most photographed) plantation house in Louisiana. (Parts of *Interview with the Vampire* and *Primary Colors* were shot here.) It's also the slickest operation, with a large parking lot, an expensive lunch buffet (bring your own picnic), hoopskirted guides, and golf carts traversing the blacktopped lanes around the property.

The house was built in 1839 by Jacques Telesphore Roman III and was named Bon Séjour—but if you walk out to the levee and look back at the quarter-mile avenue of 300-year-old live oaks (which fortunately survived the hurricanes), you'll see why steamboat passengers dubbed it "Oak Alley." Roman was so enamored of the trees that he planned his house to have exactly as many columns—28 in all. Oak Alley lay disintegrating until 1914, when Mr. and Mrs. Jefferson Hardin of New Orleans bought it. In 1925, it passed to Mr. and Mrs. Andrew Stewart, whose loving restoration won it National Historic Landmark designation.

Overnight accommodations are available in five really nice century-old Creole cottages (complete with sitting rooms, porches, and air-conditioning). Rates are $115 to $165 and include breakfast but not a tour. The overpriced restaurant is open for breakfast and lunch daily from 9am to 3pm. A new cafe and ice-cream parlor is open from 8am to 5:30pm.

3645 La. 18 (60 miles from New Orleans), Vacherie, LA 70090. ℂ 800/44-ALLEY or 225/265-2151. www.oakalleyplantation.com. Admission $10 adults, $5 students, $3 children 6–12, free for children under 6. Nov–Feb daily 9am–5pm; Mar–Oct daily 9am–5:30pm. Closed part of New Year's Day, Thanksgiving, and Christmas.

9 A Side Trip to Cajun Country

Its official name is Acadiana, and it consists of a rough triangle of Louisiana made up of 22 parishes (counties), from St. Landry Parish at the top of the triangle to the Gulf of Mexico at its base. Lafayette is its "capital," and it's dotted with such towns as St. Martinville, Abbeville, and Eunice. You won't find its boundaries on any map, nor the name "Acadiana" stamped across it. But those 22 parishes are Cajun country, and its history and culture are unique in America.

Contact the **Lafayette Convention & Visitors Commission,** P.O. Box 52066, Lafayette, LA 70505 (© **800/346-1958** in the U.S., 800/543-5340 in Canada, or 337/232-3737; www.lafayette travel.com). The office is open weekdays from 8:30am to 5pm and weekends from 9am to 5pm.

EUNICE

Founded in 1894 by C. C. Duson, who named the town for his wife, Eunice is a prairie town, not as picturesque as, say, Opelousas or Washington. Some of the most significant Cajun cultural happenings come out of this friendly town, however, including the Saturday morning jam sessions at the Savoy Music Center, the Liberty Theater's live radio broadcasts, and the Acadian Cultural Center.

Liberty Theater ☆☆☆ *(Moments)* This classic 1927 theater has been lovingly restored and turned into a showcase for Cajun music. There's live music most nights, but Saturday attracts the big crowds for the "Rendezvous des Cajuns" radio show. From 6 to 8pm, Cajun historian and folklorist Barry Ancelet hosts a live program, simulcast on local radio, that features Cajun and zydeco bands. Oh, and it's all in French. Locals and tourists alike pack the seats and aisles, with dancing on the sloped floor by the stage. Don't understand what's being said? As Barry points out, turn to your neighbors—they will be happy to translate. This is the right way (actually, *the* way) to begin your Saturday night of music in Cajun country.

2nd and Park. © **337/457-7389** www.eunice-la.com. Admission $5 adults, $3 children, free for children under 6.

Prairie Acadian Cultural Center ☆☆☆ *(Finds)* A terrific small museum, the Acadian Cultural Center is devoted to Cajun life and culture. Exhibits explain everything from the history of the Cajuns to how they worked, played, and got married. The graphics are lively and very readable, and most of the items on display were acquired from local families who have owned them for generations. The center has a collection of videos about Cajun life and will show any and all in the small theater (just ask). Anything by Les Blanc is a good choice, but you might also check out "Anything I Can Catch," a documentary about the nearly lost art of hand-fishing (you need to see someone catch a giant catfish with his bare hands).

250 W. Park. © **337/457-8490.** www.lsue.edu/acadgate/lafitte.htm. Free admission; donations accepted. Tues–Fri 8am–5pm; Sat 8am–6pm. Closed Christmas.

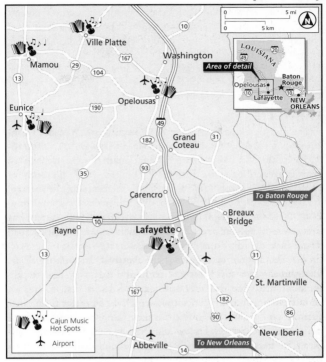

Savoy Music Center ⊛⊛⊛   On weekdays, this is a working music store with instruments, accessories, and a small but essential selection of Cajun and zydeco CDs and tapes. In the back is the workshop where musician Marc Savoy lovingly crafts his Acadian accordions—not just fine musical instruments but works of art— amid cabinets bearing his observations and aphorisms. On most Saturday mornings, though, this nondescript Kelly-green building on the outskirts of Eunice is the spiritual center of Cajun music. Keeping alive a tradition that dates from way before electricity, Marc and his wife, Ann, host a jam session where you can watch the tunes being passed down from generation to generation. Here the older musicians are given their due respect, with septuagenarians and octogenarians such as Aldus Roger often leading the sessions while players as young as preteens glean all they can—if they can keep up. Meanwhile, nonmusical guests munch on hunks of boudin sausage and sip beer while listening or socializing. All comers are welcome. But don't come empty-handed—a pound of boudin or a six-pack of something is appropriate. And if you play guitar, fiddle, accordion, or triangle, bring one along and join in. Don't try to show off. Simply follow along with the locals, or you're sure to get a cold shoulder.

Hwy. 190 E. (3 miles east of Eunice). © **337/457-9563**. www.savoymusiccenter. com. Tues–Fri 9am–5pm; Sat 9am–noon.

LAFAYETTE

Make your first stop the **Lafayette Convention & Visitors Commission Center,** 1400 NW Evangeline Thruway (© **800/346-1958** in the U.S., 800/543-5340 in Canada, or 337/232-3808; www.lafayettetravel.com). Turn off I-10 at Exit 103A, go south for about a mile, and you'll find the office in the center of the median. It's open weekdays from 8:30am to 5pm and weekends from 9am to 5pm. Near the intersection of Willow Street and the thruway, the attractive offices are in Cajun-style homes set on landscaped grounds that hold a pond and benches.

We also highly recommend the **Festival International de Louisiane** ⋒, a 6-day music and art festival that many find to be a good alternative to the increasingly crowded Jazz Fest. There's an interesting lineup each year, with an emphasis on music from other French-speaking lands. The festival takes place in the center of town with streets blocked off. It's low-key and a manageable size, and best of all, it's free! The festival is held at the end of April; call or write the Festival International de Louisiane, 735 Jefferson St., Lafayette, LA 70501 (© **337/232-8086;** www.festivalinternational.com).

SEEING THE SIGHTS

You shouldn't leave the area without exploring its bayous and swamps. Gliding through misty bayous dotted with gnarled cypress trees that drip Spanish moss, seeing native water creatures and birds in their natural habitat, and learning how Cajuns harvest their beloved crawfish is an experience not to be missed. To arrange a voyage, contact Terry Angelle at **Angelle's Atchafalaya Basin Swamp Tours,** Whiskey River Landing, P.O. Box 111, Cecilla, LA 70521 (© **337/228-8567;** www.angelleswhiskeyriver.com). His tour gives you nearly 2 hours in the third-largest swamp in the United States with Cajun guides who travel the mysterious waterways as easily as you and I walk city streets. The fares are $12 for adults, $10 for seniors, and $6 for children under 12.

Vermilionville ⋒⋒   This reconstruction of a Cajun-Creole settlement from the 1765-to-1890 era sits on the banks of the brooding

Bayou Vermilion, adjacent to the airport on U.S. 90. While it may sound like a "Cajunland" theme park, it's actually quite a valid operation. Hundreds of skilled artisans labored to restore original Cajun homes and to reconstruct others that were typical of such a village. (It *must* be authentic; one Cajun we know refuses to go, not because he dislikes the place or finds it offensive but because "I already *live* in Vermilionville!")

300 Fisher Rd., off Surrey St. ℂ **866/99-BAYOU** or 337/233-4077. www.vermilion ville.org. Admission $8 adults, $6.50 seniors, $5 students, free for children under 6. Tues–Sun 10am–4pm. Closed New Year's Eve, New Year's Day, Martin Luther King, Jr., Day, Thanksgiving, Christmas Eve, and Christmas. Take I-10 to exit 103A. Take Evangeline Thruway south to Surrey St. and then follow the signs.

ACCOMMODATIONS

Aaah! T'Frere's Bed & Breakfast 𝕮𝕮𝕮
Everything about this place cracks us up, from the name (it's so they're first in any alphabetical listing) to the evening "T'Juleps" to the cheerful owners themselves, Pat and Maugie Pastor—the latter would be adorable even if she didn't daily preside over breakfast in red silk pajamas (she and Pat used to operate restaurants, and after years in chef's whites, she wanted as radical a change as possible). Oh, wait, did we mention the goofily named breakfasts? Daily extravaganzas, easily the best around, like the "Ooh-La-La, Mardi Gras" breakfast—eggs in white sauce on ham-topped biscuits, cheese and garlic grits, tomato grille, and chocolate muffins? The rooms (and grounds) are gorgeous, though the ones in the Garconniere in the back are a bit more Country Plain than Victorian Fancy. Look, they've been in business for years, they know how to do this right; just stay here, okay?

1905 Verot School Rd., Lafayette, LA 70508. ℂ **800/984-9347**. Fax 337/984-9347. www.tfreres.com. 8 units, all with private bathroom. $120 double; extra person $30. Rates include full breakfast. AE, DC, DISC, MC, V. **Amenities:** Welcome drinks and hors d'oeuvres. *In room:* A/C, TV, dataport, coffeemaker, terry-cloth robes.

DINING

Prejean's 𝕮𝕮 CAJUN
From the outside, Prejean's looks pretty much the way it always has, an unpretentious family restaurant with live Cajun music every night. But inside, chef James Graham has turned Prejean's from a fried seafood emporium to one of Acadiana's finest restaurants, showcasing the best ingredients and styles Cajun cuisine has to offer. Dance if there's room—but do whatever's necessary to sample the full range of excellent Cajun fare. Seafood is the specialty, with large menu sections devoted to fish, shrimp, oysters, crawfish, and crab dishes, and a few alligator dishes.

3480 I-49 N. ℂ **337/896-3247.** Fax 337/896-3278. www.prejeans.com. Reservations for 8 or more. Children's menu $3.50–$8.95; main courses $15–$26. AE, DC, DISC, MC, V. Sun–Thurs 7am–10pm; Fri–Sat 7am–11pm. Take I-10 to exit 103B and then I-49 north to exit 2/Gloria Switch.

Randol's Restaurant and Cajun Dance Hall ⚜ CAJUN

In addition to better-than-average Cajun food, Randol's offers a good-size, popular dance floor where dancers are likely to be locals enjoying their own *fais-do-do*. A house specialty is the seafood platter, which includes a cup of seafood gumbo, fried shrimp, oysters, catfish, stuffed crab, crawfish étouffée, bread, and coleslaw.

2320 Kaliste Saloom Rd. ℂ **800/YO-CAJUN** or 337/981-7080. www.randols.com. Reservations accepted only for parties of 20 or more. Main courses $7.95–$18. MC, V. Sun–Thurs 5–10pm; Fri–Sat 5–11pm. Closed major holidays. From New Orleans, take I-10 west to exit 103A. Follow Evangeline Thruway to Pinhook Rd., turn right, and follow Pinhook to Kaliste Saloom Rd. (on the right). Randol's will be on your right.

VILLE PLATTE ⚜

If you want to take some Cajun music with you, you have a good reason to detour to the town of Ville Platte.

Floyd's Record Shop ⚜⚜

Floyd Soileau is in some ways the unofficial mayor of Acadiana. But he's meant much more to the region as one of the key entrepreneurs of bayou music. Long before Cajun and zydeco were known outside the region, he was recording and releasing the music, selling records by mail order and at this store. This is a must-stop locale with a fine selection of Floyd's releases by such artists as D. L. Menard (the Cajun Hank Williams) and Clifton Chenier (the King of Zydeco).

434 E. Main St. ℂ **800/738-8668** or 337/363-2185. Fax 337/363-5622. www.floydsrecords.com. DISC, MC, V. Mon–Sat 8:30am–4:30pm.

DINING

The Pig Stand ⚜⚜ PIG

A local institution, The Pig Stand is a little dump of a local hangout that serves divine barbecued chicken and other Southern specialties for cheap prices. It's a treat—don't miss it. And it's just down the street from Floyd's in case you worked up an appetite buying music.

318 E. Main St. ℂ **337/363-2883.** Main courses $12 and under. AE, DISC, MC, V. Tues–Thurs 7am–9pm; Fri–Sat 7am–10pm; Sun 7am–2pm.

6

Shopping

Shopping in New Orleans is a highly evolved leisure activity with a shop for every strategy and a fix for every shopaholic—and every budget. The range is as good as it gets—many a clever person has come to New Orleans just to open up a quaint boutique filled with strange items gathered from all parts of the globe or produced by local, somewhat twisted, folk artists. And what's a better thing to do to help stimulate a struggling economy than throwing money at it?

Having said that, nearly every store is, at press time, undergoing varying levels of post-Katrina difficulty, either problems with sufficient staff, or difficulties stocking merchandise thanks to postal or shipping issues. In many cases, those problems may have abated by the time you go, but be aware that operating hours (and in some extreme cases, the very fate of the store itself) may still be affected, so call ahead to be sure.

1 Major Hunting Grounds

CANAL PLACE   At the foot of Canal Street (365 Canal St.) where it reaches the Mississippi River, this sophisticated shopping center holds more than 50 shops, many of them branches of the world's most elegant retailers: Brooks Brothers, Bally, Saks Fifth Avenue, Gucci, Williams-Sonoma, and Jaeger. Open Monday through Wednesday from 10am to 6pm, Thursday from 10am to 8pm, Friday and Saturday from 10am to 7pm, and Sunday from noon to 6pm.

THE FRENCH MARKET   Shops in the Market begin on Decatur Street across from Jackson Square; offerings include candy, cookware, fashion, crafts, toys, New Orleans memorabilia, and candles. It's open from 10am to 6pm (and the Farmer's Market Café du Monde is open 24 hr.). Quite honestly, you'll find a lot of junk, but there are some good buys mixed in.

JACKSON BREWERY   Just across from Jackson Square at 600–620 Decatur St., the old brewery building has been transformed into a jumble of shops, cafes, restaurants, and entertainment. Many shops in the Brewery close at 5:30 or 6pm, before the

Brewery itself. Open Sunday through Thursday from 10am to 9pm, Friday and Saturday from 10am to 10pm.

JULIA STREET   From Camp Street down to the river on Julia Street, you'll find many of the city's best contemporary art galleries. Of course, some of the works are a bit pricey, but there are good deals to be had if you're collecting and fine art to be seen if you're not. You'll find many of them listed below.

MAGAZINE STREET   This is the Garden District's premier shopping street. More than 140 shops (some of which are listed below) line the street in 19th-century brick storefronts and quaint cottagelike buildings. Among the offerings are antiques, art galleries, boutiques, crafts, and dolls. If you're so inclined, you could shop all the way from Washington Street to Audubon Park. The most likely section goes, roughly, from the 3500 to 4200 blocks (from about Aline St. to Milan St., with the odd block or so of nothing). Pick up a copy of *Visit Magazine Street: For a Shopper's Dream,* a free guide and map to most of the stores on 6 miles of Magazine, available all along the street.

NEW ORLEANS CENTRE   New Orleans's newest shopping center, at 1400 Poydras St., features a glass atrium and includes upscale stores like Lord & Taylor and Macy's. There are three levels of specialty shops and restaurants. Open Monday through Saturday from 10am to 8pm and Sunday from noon to 6pm.

RIVERBEND   To reach this district (in the Carrollton area), ride the St. Charles Avenue streetcar (or the free bus temporarily replacing it) to stop 44 and then walk down Maple Street 1 block to Dublin Park, the site of an old public market that was once lined with open stalls. Nowadays, renovated shops inhabit the old general store, a produce warehouse made of bargeboard, and the town surveyor's raised-cottage home.

RIVERWALK MARKETPLACE *(Kids*   A mall is a mall is a mall, unless it has picture windows offering a Mississippi panorama. Even though you almost certainly have a mall at home, this is worth visiting. Besides, if you need T-shirts instead of sweaters or vice versa, this is the closest Gap to the Quarter. Note that the best river views are in the section of the mall closest to the Convention Center. Other than a branch of Café du Monde, it's the usual mall suspects. 1 Poydras St. Open Monday through Thursday from 10am to 9pm, Friday and Saturday from 10am to 10pm, and Sunday from 12:30 to 5:30pm.

2 Shopping A to Z

ANTIQUES

Audubon Antiques ✿   Audubon has everything from collectible curios to authentic antique treasures at reasonable prices. There are two floors of goods, so be prepared to lose yourself. 2025 Magazine St. ✆ 504/581-5704. Mon–Sat 10:30am–5pm; Sun call first.

Bush Antiques ✿✿✿   This wonderful treasure-trove features impressive European religious art and objects and a beautiful array of beds—sadly, the latter are out of most of our price ranges, but boy, are they fantastic. An extra treat is the collection of folk art on the rear patio. 2109–2111 Magazine St. ✆ 504/581-3518. Fax 504/581-6889. www.bushantiques.com. Mon–Sat 11am–4pm.

Harris Antiques ✿✿✿   Harris features 18th- and 19th-century European fine art and antiques, jewelry, grandfather clocks, and Oriental rugs. The collection of tall-case clocks is one of the most impressive in the country. The company is a long-standing family-run business; the firm has helped many younger collectors make some of their initial purchases. 237 Royal St. ✆ 504/523-1605. www.harrisantiques. com. Mon–Sat 10am–5pm

Ida Manheim Antiques   At this gallery you'll find an enormous collection of Continental, English, and Oriental furnishings along with porcelains, jade, silver, and fine paintings, and sometimes attitude to match. The store is also the agent for Boehm Birds. 409 Royal St. ✆ 888/627-5969 or 504/620-4114. www.idamanheimantiques.com. Mon–Sat 9am–5pm.

Jack Sutton Antiques ✿   In some ways, the Suttons are to jewelry and antiques what the Brennans are to food: one family, different businesses. Of the number of Suttons around New Orleans, this one, our favorite, specializes in jewelry and objects. The selection of estate jewelry ("estate" meaning "older than yesterday but less than 100 years") is often better than that at other antiques stores—the author's engagement ring came from here—but due to the ebb and flow of the estate business, you can never be sure what may be offered. The store has a room devoted to "men's gift items" such as antique gambling, cigar, and drinking paraphernalia. 315 Royal St. ✆ 504/522-0555. Mon–Sat 10am–5pm.

Keil's Antiques ✿✿✿   Kiel's, established in 1899 and currently run by the fourth generation of the founding family, has a considerable collection of 18th- and 19th-century French and English furniture, chandeliers, jewelry, and decorative items. 325 Royal St. ℭ 504/522-4552. www.keilsantiques.com. Mon–Sat 9am–5pm.

Lucullus ℛℛℛ   An unusual shop, Lucullus has a wonderful collection of culinary antiques as well as 17th-, 18th-, and 19th-century furnishings to "complement the grand pursuits of cooking, dining, and imbibing." 610 Chartres St. ℭ 504/528-9620. Mon–Sat 9:30am–5pm. Closed on Mon during the summer.

Miss Edna's Antiques ℛ   Miss Edna's carries eclectic antiques—furniture, specialty items, curios—and paintings, with a focus on 19th-century works. Miss Edna recently moved a few feet up Magazine, doubling her inventory and expanding her art collection. 2035 Magazine St. ℭ 504/524-1897. Mon–Sat 10am–5pm.

Rothschild's Antiques ℛ   Rothschild's is a fourth-generation furniture merchandiser. Some of the most interesting things you'll find here are antique and custom-made jewelry (the store is also a full-service jeweler). There's a fine selection of antique silver, marble mantels, porcelains, and English and French furnishings. Rothschild's devotes tens of thousands of square feet to displaying and warehousing antiques. 321 Royal St. ℭ 504/523-5816 or 504/523-2281. www.rothschildsantiques.com. Mon–Sat 9:30am–5pm; Sun by appointment.

Sigle's Antiques & Metalcraft ℛ   If you've fallen in love with the lacy ironwork that drips from French Quarter balconies, this is the place to pick out some pieces to take home. Sigle's has also converted some of the ironwork into useful household items. 935 Royal St. ℭ 504/522-7647. Mon–Sat 10am–noon and 1–4:30pm.

Whisnant Galleries ℛ   The quantity and variety of merchandise in this shop is mind-boggling. You'll find all sorts of unusual and unique antique collectibles including items from Ethiopia, Russia, Greece, South America, Morocco, and other parts of North Africa and the Middle East. 222 Chartres St. ℭ 504/524-9766. www.whisnant galleries.com. Mon–Sat 9:30am–5:30pm; Sun 10am–5pm.

ART GALLERIES

With one major exception, galleries in New Orleans follow the landscape of antiques shops: **Royal and Magazine streets.**

Ariodante   A contemporary craft gallery, Ariodante features handcrafted furniture, glass, ceramics, jewelry, and decorative accessories by nationally acclaimed artists. Rotating shows offer a detailed look at works by various artists. 535 Julia St. ℭ 504/524-3233. Thurs–Sat 11am–5pm. Call for additional hours.

Arthur Roger Gallery 🐸🐸   Arthur Roger sets the pace for the city's fine-art galleries. Since opening in New Orleans 20 years ago, Roger has played a major role in developing the art community and in tying it to the art world in New York. Time and again, he has taken chances—moving early into the Warehouse District and briefly opening a second gallery in New York—and he continues to do so, scheduling shows that range from strongly regional work to the far-flung. The gallery represents many artists including Francis Pavy, Ida Kohlmeyer, Douglas Bourgeois, Paul Lucas, Clyde Connell, Willie Birch, Gene Koss, and George Dureau. 730 Tchoupitoulas. 🕾 504/524-9393. www.arthurrogergallery.com. Tues–Sat 11am–6pm.

Bergen Putman Gallery   Bergen Putman Gallery has the city's largest selection of posters and limited-edition graphics on such subjects as Mardi Gras, jazz, and the city itself and by such artists as Erté, Icart, Nagel, Maimon, and Tarkay. Bergen also features a large collection of works by sought-after African-American artists. The service by Margarita and her staff is friendly and extremely personable. 730 Royal St. 🕾 504/523-7882. www.bergenputmangallery.com. Daily 9am–9pm.

Berta's and Mina's Antiquities 🐸🐸   In years past, Antiquities was just another place that bought and sold antiques and second-hand furniture and art. That all ended on the day in 1993 that Nilo Lanzas (Berta's husband and Mina's dad) began painting. Now you can barely see the furniture in the shop for all the new art. Dubbed "folk art" or "outsider art," Lanzas's works are colorful scenes from life in New Orleans or his native Latin America, stories out of the Bible, or images sprung from his imagination. His paintings are on wood with titles or commentaries painted on the frames. Don't be surprised to find Lanzas quietly painting away near the counter—he paints 10 to 12 hours a day. 4138 Magazine St. 🕾 504/895-6201. Mon–Sat 10am–6pm; Sun noon–6pm.

Bryant Galleries   This gallery represents renowned artists Ed Dwight, Fritzner Lamour, and Leonardo Nierman as well as other American, European, and Haitian artists. The varied work on display here may include jazz bronzes, glasswork, and graphics. The staff is very friendly and helpful. 316 Royal St. 🕾 800/844-1994 or 504/525-5584. www.bryantgalleries.com. Sun–Wed 10am–6pm; Thurs–Sat 10am–9pm.

Cole Pratt Gallery, Ltd. 🐸   This gallery showcases the work of Southern artists whose creations include abstract and realist paintings, sculptures, and ceramics. The art is of the highest quality and the prices are surprisingly reasonable. 3800 Magazine St. ⓒ **504/891-6789**. www.coleprattgallery.com. Tues–Sat 10am–5pm.

The Davis Galleries 🏵🏵🏵   One of two world-class galleries in New Orleans (the other being A Gallery for Fine Photography; see below), this may be the best place in the world for Central and West African traditional art. The owner makes regular trips to Africa for collecting. Works on display might include sculpture, costuming, basketry, textiles, weapons, and/or jewelry. 904 Louisiana Ave. ⓒ **504/895-5206**. By appointment only.

Diane Genre Oriental Art and Antiques 🏵🏵   If all of the 18th- and 19th-century European antiques in the stores along Royal are starting to look the same, it's time to step into Diane Genre's shop. By comparison, the atmosphere in here seems as delicate as one of the ancient East Asian porcelains on display. Get an eyeful of furniture, 18th-century Japanese woodblock prints, and a world-class collection of Chinese and Japanese textiles. There are also scrolls, screens, engravings, and lacquers. 431 Royal St. ⓒ **504/595-8945**. Fax 504/899-8651. www.dianegenreorientalart.com. By appointment only.

Galerie Royale 🏵🏵   This gallery's collection is built around the works of William Tolliver, an African-American artist from Mississippi whose untimely death at the age of 48 in 2000 received national coverage. Despite a lack of formal training, he quickly became an internationally recognized contemporary Impressionist painter. (He was chosen to create the official poster for the 1996 Summer Olympics.) At Galerie Royale you can find a selection of Tolliver's museum-quality pieces as well as work by other artists including Salvador Dalí, Bonny Stanglmaier, and Verna Hart. 3648 Magazine St. ⓒ **504/894-1588**. www.galerieroyale.com. Wed–Sun 11am–4pm, or by appointment.

A Gallery for Fine Photography 🏵🏵🏵   It would be a mistake to skip this incredibly well stocked photography gallery. Even if you aren't in the market, it's worth looking around. Owner Joshua Mann Pailet (a photographer) calls this "the only museum in the world that's for sale." It really is like a museum of photography, with just about every period and style represented and frequent shows of contemporary artists. The staff is more than happy to show you some of the many photos in the files. The gallery emphasizes New Orleans and Southern history and contemporary culture (you can buy Ernest Bellocq's legendary Storyville photos) as well as black culture and music. There is something in just about every price range as well as a terrific collection of photography books if that better fits your budget. 241 Chartres St. *C* **504/568-1313**. www.agallery.com. Tues–Sat 10am–5pm.

Hanson King Gallery   Hanson King Gallery shows paintings, sculptures, and limited-edition prints by contemporary artists such as Peter Max, Frederick Hart, Pradzynski, Anoro, Thysell, Deckbar, Zjawinska, Erickson, LeRoy Neiman, Richard MacDonald, and Behrens. 523 Royal St. *C* **504/556-8240**. www.hansonking.com. Mon–Sat 10am–5pm; Sun 11am–5pm.

Kurt E. Schon, Ltd. *G̃G̃*   Here you'll find the country's largest inventory of 19th-century European paintings. Works include French and British Impressionist and post-Impressionist paintings as well as art from the Royal Academy and the French Salon. Serious collectors can make appointment visits. 510 St. Louis St. *C* **504/ 524-5462**. www.kurteschonltd.com. Mon–Fri 9am–4pm; Sat 9am–3pm.

LeMieux Galleries *G̃*   LeMieux represents contemporary artists and craftspeople from Louisiana and the Gulf Coast. They include Leslie Staub, Dr. Bob, Charles Barbier, Pat Bernard, Mary Lee Eggart, Leslie Elliottsmith, Joann Greenberg, David Lambert, Shirley Rabe Masinter, Evelyn Menge, Dennis Perrin, Kathleen Sidwell, and Kate Trepagnier. 332 Julia St. *C* **504/522-5988**. www.lemieux galleries.com. Mon–Sat 10am–6pm.

Marguerite Oestreicher Fine Arts   Like the other Julia Street galleries, this one concentrates on contemporary painting, sculpture, and photography. It also consistently shows work by emerging artists. The gallery's recent shows have included works by Drew Galloway and Raine Bedsole. 720 Julia St. *C* **504/581-9253**. Tues–Sat 10am–5pm and by appointment.

New Orleans GlassWorks and Printmaking Studio *G̃G̃G̃*   This institution serves multiple purposes. Here, within 20,000 square feet of studio space, are a 550-pound tank of hot molten glass and a pre–Civil War press. Established glasswork artists and master printmakers display their work in the on-site gallery and teach classes in glassblowing, kiln-fired glass, hand-engraved printmaking, papermaking, and bookbinding. Absolutely unique to the area, the place is worth a visit during gallery hours. Daily glassblowing and fusing demonstrations are open for viewing. 727 Magazine St. *C* **504/ 529-7277**. www.neworleansglassworks.com. Mon–Sat 10am–5pm. Closed Sat June–Aug.

Peligro ✹✹✹   A bit out of the way but worth checking out, Peligro is one of the best folk-art galleries in the city, with an emphasis on primitive and outsider art (but also work from Latin American countries). The owners have a terrific eye for up-and-coming artists. At times they have smaller items that make for marvelous, original gifts. 305 Decatur St. ✆ **504/581-1706.** Wed, Fri, Sat 10:30am–6pm; Sun noon–6pm.

Shadyside Pottery ✹   If you want to see a master potter at work, Shadyside Pottery is an excellent place to stop. Charlie Bohn, who apprenticed in Japan, can be seen at his wheel all day Tuesday through Friday and until midafternoon on Saturday. He specializes in the Japanese tradition of raku, a type of pottery that has a "cracked" look. In addition to his own work, Bohn carries some glass pieces and a selection of Japanese kites by Mitsuyoshi Kawamoto. 3823 Magazine St. ✆ **504/897-1710.** Mon–Sat 10am–5pm.

BATH & BEAUTY PRODUCTS

Hové ✹✹✹   Founded in 1931, Hové is the oldest perfumery in the city. It features all-natural scents (except the musk, which is synthetic), and the selection is almost overwhelming. Strips with various options, for both men and women, are laid out to help you. They have some original creations ("Kiss in the Dark") and some very Southern smells, such as vetiver and tea olive. This is the place to establish your signature scent. 824 Royal St. ✆ **504/525-7827.** www. hoveparfumeur.com. Mon–Sat 10am–5pm.

BOOKS

Literary enthusiasts will find many destinations in New Orleans. **Maple Street Book Shop,** 7523 Maple St. (✆ **504/866-4916**), is an uptown mecca for bookworms; the **Maple Street Children's Book Shop** is next door at 7529 Maple St. (✆ **504/861-2105**); and **Beaucoup Books** is at 3951 Magazine St. (✆ **504/895-2663**).

Beckham's Bookshop ✹   Beckham's has two entire floors of old editions, rare secondhand books, and thousands of classical LPs that will tie up your whole afternoon or morning if you don't tear yourself away. The owners also operate **Librairie Bookshop,** 823 Chartres St. (✆ **504/525-4837**), which has a sizable collection of secondhand books. 228 Decatur St. ✆ **504/522-9875.** Daily 10am–5pm.

Crescent City Books ✹   Two floors of dusty treasures (the emphasis is on history, social history, literary criticism, philosophy, and art) and a staff that ranges from nonchalant to quite sweet and

helpful. 204 Chartres St. ⓒ **800/546-4013** or 504/524-4997.www.crescentcity
books.com. Daily 10am–7pm.

FAB, Faubourg Marigny Art & Books 𝒸
This well-stocked gay
and lesbian bookstore also carries some local titles. It has a used section, CDs, posters, cards, and gifts (all with a more or less gay or lesbian slant) and holds regular readings and signings. The staff makes
this a fine resource center—you can call them for local gay and lesbian info. 600 Frenchmen St. ⓒ **504/947-3700.** Mon–Fri 10am–8pm; Sat–Sun
10am–6pm.

Faulkner House Books 𝒸𝒸𝒸
This shop is on a lot of walking
tours of the French Quarter because it's where Nobel prize–winner
William Faulkner lived while he was writing his early works *Mos-
quitoes* and *Soldiers' Pay.* Those who step inside instead of just snap-
ping a photo and walking on will find something remarkable:
possibly the best selection per square foot of any bookstore in the
whole wide world, with every bit of shelf space occupied by a book
that's both highly collectible and of literary value. The shop holds a
large collection of Faulkner first editions and rare and first-edition
classics by many other authors. Taking up one room and a hallway,
Faulkner House feels like a portion of somebody's private home—
which it is—but the selection of books here is almost magical. 624
Pirates Alley. ⓒ **504/524-2940.** Daily 10am–6pm.

Garden District Book Shop 𝒸𝒸𝒸
Owner Britton Trice has
stocked his medium-size shop with just about every regional book
you can think of; if you want a New Orleans or Louisiana-specific
book, no matter what the exact focus (interiors, exteriors, food, Creoles, you name it), you should be able to find it here. This is also
where Anne Rice does book signings whenever she has a new release.
They usually have autographed copies of her books plus fancy special editions of Rice titles that they publish themselves and a large
selection of signed books by local and non-local authors. 2727 Prytania St. (in the Rink). ⓒ **504/895-2266.** Fax 504/895-0111. Mon–Sat 10am–6pm;
Sun 10am–4pm.

Kaboom 𝒸𝒸
On the edge of the Quarter, Kaboom is a bit off the
beaten path, but bibliophiles should make the trek. This is a reader's
bookstore, thanks to an owner whose knowledge of literature is
almost scary. The stock (used books only) tends to lean heavily on
fiction, but there is little you won't find here. 915 Barracks St. ⓒ **504/
529-5780.** kaboombooks@bellsouth.net. Daily 11am–6pm.

Octavia Books ⚓ We do love our independent bookstores, and although this may be a bit far uptown, a sweet, tiny patio, complete with waterfall, is the customer's reward—what better way to linger over a purchase from stock that is chosen with obvious literary care? Book signings and other literary events are common. 513 Octavia St. (at Laurel St.). © **504/899-7323.** www.octaviabooks.com. Mon–Sat 10am–6pm; Sun noon–5pm.

CANDIES & PRALINES

Aunt Sally's Praline Shop ⚓ At Aunt Sally's, you can watch skilled workers perform the 150-year-old process of cooking the original Creole pecan pralines right before your eyes. You'll know they're fresh. The large store also has a broad selection of regional cookbooks, Creole and Cajun foods, folk and souvenir dolls, and local memorabilia. In addition, Aunt Sally's has a collection of zydeco, Cajun, R&B, and jazz CDs and cassettes. They'll ship any purchase. In the French Market, 810 Decatur St. © **800/642-7257** or 504/524-3373. www.auntsallys.com. Daily 8am–8pm.

Laura's Candies ⚓ Laura's is said to be the city's oldest candy store, established in 1913. It has fabulous pralines, but it also has rich, delectable golf ball–size truffles—our personal favorite indulgence, although they've gotten a bit pricey as of late. 331 Chartres St. © **504/525-3880.** www.laurascandies.com. Daily 10:30am–5pm.

Leah's Candy Kitchen ⚓⚓ After you've tried all of the city's Creole candy shops, you might very well come to the conclusion that Leah's tops the list. Everything here, from the candy fillings to the chocolate-covered pecan brittle, is made from scratch by second- and third-generation members of Leah Johnson's praline-cookin' family. 714 St. Louis St. © **888/523-5324** or 504/523-5662. www.leahspralines. com. Daily 10am–6pm.

COSTUMES & MASKS

Costumery is big business in New Orleans, and not just in the days before Lent. In this city, you never know *when* you're going to want or need a costume. A number of shops in New Orleans specialize in props for Mardi Gras, Halloween, and other occasions. ***Here's a tip:*** New Orleanians often sell their costumes back to these shops after Ash Wednesday, and you can sometimes pick up a one-time-worn outfit at a small fraction of its original cost.

Little Shop of Fantasy In the Little Shop of Fantasy, owners Laura and Anne Guccione sell the work of a number of local artists and more than 20 mask makers. Mike creates the feathered masks, Jill does the velvet hats and costumes, and Laura and Anne produce homemade toiletries. Some of the masks and hats are just fun and fanciful, but there are many fashionable ones as well. There are lots of clever voodoo items here, too, plus unusual toys and novelties. 515 St. Louis. ⓒ **504/945-2435.** www.littleshopoffantasy.com. Most days 11am–6pm.

Uptown Costume & Dance Company 𝕲 The walls of this small store are covered with spooky monster masks, goofy arrow-through-the-head-type tricks, hats, wigs, makeup, and all other manner of playfulness. It draws a steady, yearlong stream of loyal customers: kids going to parties, dancers, clowns, actors, and so forth. Conventioneers come here for rental disguises. At Mardi Gras, though, things really get cooking. The shop designs party uniforms for a number of Mardi Gras krewe members. Owner Cheryll Berlier also creates a limited number of wacky Mardi Gras tuxedo jackets, which get gobbled up quickly. 4326 Magazine St. ⓒ **504/895-7969.** Mon–Fri 10am–6pm; Sat 10am–5pm.

FASHION & VINTAGE CLOTHING

Fleur de Paris and Fleur de Paris Millinery 𝕲★𝕲★𝕲★ Remember when a woman was simply not dressed unless she wore a hat? Help bring back those times by patronizing this shop, which makes hand blocked, stylishly trimmed hats. Think you aren't a hat person? The experts here can take one look at any head and face, and find the right style to fit it. Expensive, but works of art often are. Across the street, 25 years worth of experience shows in the ever-changing collection of vintage gowns. 1920s and 1930s elegance is on display, constantly bringing us to our knees with covetousness. Millinery: 717 Royal St., ⓒ **504/525-1900;** 712 Royal St. ⓒ **504/525-1899.** Daily 10am–6pm.

House of Lounge 𝕲★𝕲★ If you want to be a couch potato, you might as well be a well-dressed one. Or do you want to treat your humble bedroom more like a boudoir? House of Lounge offers all sorts of silky robes and impressive "hostess gowns," plus sexy lingerie (and admittedly, there isn't much difference between the categories). 2044 Magazine St. ⓒ **504/671-8300.** www.houseoflounge.com. Mon–Sat 11am–6pm; Sun noon–5pm.

Trashy Diva 𝕲★𝕲★ Despite the name, there is nothing trashy about the vintage-inspired clothes found here. The heyday of women's garments—in the sense of designs that know how to flatter curves—is present in these floaty and velvety numbers that will please everyone from the hat and gloves-wearing crowds to the inner flappers to the

Goth teens. Dresses can be a bit dear, but there is often a sales rack full of incredible bargains. 2048 Magazine St. Ⓒ **888/818-DIVA** or 504/299-8777. www.trashydiva.com. Mon–Sat 10am–6pm; Sun 1–5pm.

Violet's 𝕮𝕮   This is our greatest temptation among French Quarter shops, given how we feel about romantic, Edwardian, and '20s-inspired clothes in lush velvets and satins. There are some dazzling creations here with appropriate accessories (jewelry, hats, scarves) as well. They also have a Violet's Two at 507 St. Ann St. (Ⓒ **504/588-9894**). 808 Chartres St. Ⓒ **504/569-0088**. Fax 504/569-0089. Mon–Sat 11am–6pm; Sun 11am–5pm.

Yvonne LaFleur—New Orleans 𝕮   Yvonne LaFleur, a confessed incurable romantic, is the creator of beautifully feminine original designs. Her custom millinery, silk dresses, evening gowns, lingerie, and sportswear are surprisingly affordable, and all are enhanced by her signature perfume. Her store is in the Riverbend district. 8131 Hampson St. Ⓒ **504/866-9666**. www.yvonnelafleur.com. Mon–Wed and Fri–Sat 10am–6pm; Thurs 10am–8pm.

GIFTS

Mardi Gras Madness & Accent Annex 𝕮𝕮𝕮   Need some Mardi Gras beads, masks, and other accouterments? This is one of the biggest suppliers of such things, and it has just about everything you need to properly celebrate Mardi Gras or stock up for that party you want to throw back home. String some green, gold, and purple beads around your neck, and everyone will know where you've been. Note the reasonably priced bags of used beads. Riverwalk. Ⓒ **504/568-9000**. www.accentannex.com. Mon–Sat 10am–9pm; Sun 11am–7pm.

Shop of the Two Sisters 𝕮   This shop has upscale "girly" items such as throw pillows, lamps, sconces, accessories, unique accent pieces (with an emphasis on florals and fruits), and upholstery. Here you'll find consumerism at its most beautiful, but be prepared to pay for it. 1800 Magazine St. Ⓒ **504/525-2747**. www.shopofthetwosisters.com. By appointment only.

Simon of New Orleans 𝕮𝕮   Folk artist Simon, whose brightly painted signs are seen throughout New Orleans in homes and businesses, will paint-to-order your own personal sign and ship it to you. This gallery and shop is shared with Simon's wife, Maria, who has particularly good taste in primitive furniture, antiques, and hodge-podgery. 2126 Magazine St. Ⓒ **504/561-0088**. Thurs–Sat 11am–5pm.

Three Dog Bakery   An increasingly high-profile chain offering dog treats that mimic the sugary-chocolatey delights humans love, but dogs can't eat. Here they are made dog-friendly and are a big hit with guilt-ridden travelers who left Fido and Rover at home. 827 Royal St. © **504/525-2253.** Fax 504/525-2252. www.threedog.com. Daily 10am–6pm.

MUSIC
Louisiana Music Factory ✵✵✵   This popular store carries a large selection of regional music—including Cajun, zydeco, R&B, jazz, blues, and gospel—plus books, posters, and T-shirts. It also has frequent live music and beer bashes—shop while you bop! 210 Decatur St. © **504/586-1094.** www.louisianamusicfactory.com. Sat 10am–7pm; Sun 11am–7pm.

7

New Orleans After Dark

New Orleans is one of the most beautiful cities in the United States—yes, still—but we won't mind if you never see a bit of it, provided, however, that the omission is because you are spending the daylight hours recovering from the equally extraordinary nightlife.

This is a city of music and rhythm. It is impossible to imagine New Orleans without a soundtrack of jazz, blues, brass bands, Cajun, and zydeco. Music streams from every doorway, it seems, and barely had Katrina passed by than people were dancing down the street, celebrating their survival. (After all, this is the town that sends you to your grave with music and then dances back from the cemetery.) You walk down Bourbon, for all its trash and tacky shops, and yet with every step you hear music of all varieties. Maybe none of it is world-class, but that doesn't seem to matter. It's darn infectious.

This is why there is so much concern over the future of neighborhoods such as the Treme and Lower 9th Ward. The roots of New Orleans's precious musical legacy, the soundtrack of generations, are buried deep there. If the many musicians who lost everything do not return, what does that do to the soul of the city?

Still, something will go on. This remains the city of decadence and good times rolling, not to mention really loose liquor laws and drinks in "go" cups (plastic containers you can take with you; many bars and clubs even have walk-up windows for easy refills). And all this increases four-fold at night. We aren't just talking about the open-air frat party that is Bourbon Street some (okay, most) evenings. In fact, we prefer not to talk about that at all.

Most important is that, virtually every night, clubs all over town—but especially in the neighborhoods listed below—offer music that can range from average to extraordinary but is never less than danceable. Cover prices vary, of course, but rarely will you have to pay more than $10—and then only for more high-falutin' places like the House of Blues. When the clubs get too full, no matter; the crowd spills into the street, talking, drinking, and still dancing right there on the sidewalk. Sometimes the action outside is even more fun than inside.

While most clubs in flooded neighborhoods are closed and face an uncertain future, and far too many local musicians remain, at this writing, displaced by the hurricane, a heartening number of Quarter and other clubs were able to reopen and local musicians once again stand proudly on their stages. Their presence is all the more valuable for having been revealed to be so fragile. And yet, it may be a sign of normalcy when we once again begin to take it all for granted.

Club hopping is easy, and some of the better choices will require leaving the Quarter by cab or some other vehicle. Don't worry; most are a cheap cab ride away, if not in walking distance of each other. And only steps away from the Quarter is the scene in the Faubourg Marigny, where at least five clubs are going at once within 3 blocks of each other.

For information on what's happening around town, look for current editions of **Gambit** and **Offbeat,** both distributed for free in most hotels and all record stores. You can also check out *Offbeat* on the Internet (www.nola.com; once you get to the NOLA home page, go to the music and entertainment section). Other sources include the **Times-Picayune**'s daily entertainment calendar and Friday's **"Lagniappe"** section of the newspaper. **WWOZ** (90.7 FM), the city's excellent public radio station, which should be nonstop on your hotel room radio, broadcasts the local music schedule several times throughout the day.

Note: Aside from the venues listed in the section "Will They Reopen?" all venues listed below are open for business, despite some of their telephone numbers being out of service.

1 Jazz & Blues Clubs

THE FRENCH QUARTER & THE FAUBOURG MARIGNY

Donna's ✸✸✸   A corner bar at the very northern edge of the Quarter, Donna's is one of the top spots for great local music, including the revival of the brass band experience and a variety of jazz and blues traditions. A recent makeover, with a better-placed stage and table and chairs, has made it even more appealing. But the main asset may be Donna herself, monitoring the door to make sure you don't bring in drinks from outside and making sure you do order something inside. She's been one of the true boosters of new generations of New Orleans music (she's managed both the hip-hop-edged brass band Soul Rebels and the new-funk ensemble Galactic) and has helped promote awareness of veteran brass bands

New Orleans Nightlife

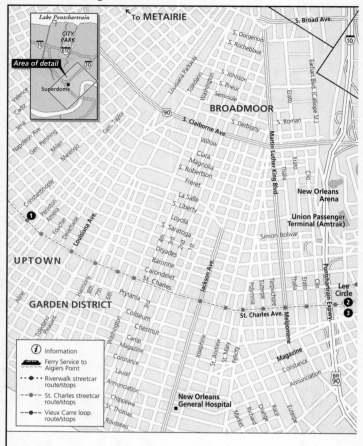

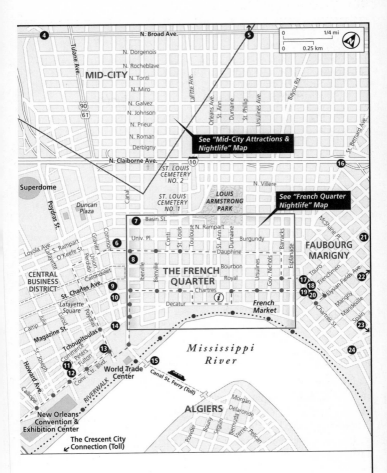

like Treme and Olympia. As with most real New Orleans hangouts, atmosphere is minimal, but spirits (liquid and otherwise) are high. The cover charge for performances is usually no more than the cost of a good mixed drink. Well worth a stop on an evening of club hopping. *Note:* Donna's is in a transitional neighborhood, so be careful entering and leaving. 800 N. Rampart St. ℰ **504/596-6914**. www. donnasbarandgrill.com. Closed Tues–Wed. Cover varies.

The Famous Door John Wehner no longer owns the club, so it's up to you to see how famous it still is. Open since 1934, The Famous Door is the oldest music club on Bourbon Street. Many local jazz, pop, and rock musicians have passed through here. One of them, Harry Connick, Jr., played his first gigs here at the age of 13. So far, it seems the club is similar to its old identity, but that may have changed by the time you read this. 339 Bourbon St. ℰ **504/598-4334**. Occasional (but rare) cover.

Fritzel's European Jazz Pub ℱ You might walk right past this small establishment, but that would be a big mistake because the 1831 building brings some of the city's best musicians to play on its tiny stage. In addition to the regular weekend program of late-night jazz (Fri–Sat from 10:30pm; Sun from 10pm), there are frequent jam sessions in the wee hours during the week when performers end their stints elsewhere and gather to play "Musicians' Music." The full bar also stocks a variety of schnapps (served ice-cold) and German beers. 733 Bourbon St. ℰ **504/561-0432**. 1-drink minimum per set.

Maison Bourbon Despite its location and the sign saying the building is DEDICATED TO THE PRESERVATION OF JAZZ (which seems a clear attempt to confuse tourists into thinking this is the legendary Preservation Hall), Maison Bourbon is not a tourist trap. The music is very authentic, and often superb, jazz. Stepping into the brick-lined room, or even just peering in from the street, takes you away from the mayhem outside. From about midafternoon until the wee hours, Dixieland and traditional jazz hold forth, often at loud and lively volume. Players have included Wallace Davenport, Steve Slocum, and Tommy Yetta. Patrons must be at least 21 years old. 641 Bourbon St. ℰ **504/522-8818**. 1-drink minimum.

Palm Court Jazz Cafe ℱℱ This is one of the most stylish jazz haunts in the Quarter. Run by dedicated jazz enthusiasts, it's an elegant setting in which to catch top-notch jazz groups Wednesday through Sunday. The music varies nightly but is generally traditional or classic jazz. If you collect jazz records, peek at the records

French Quarter Nightlife

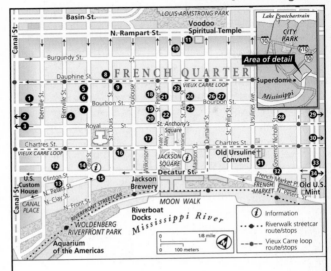

for sale in a back alcove, many of which are issued on the owner's own well-regarded traditional jazz record label. *Tip:* You might want to make reservations—it's that kind of place. 1204 Decatur St. © 504/ 525-0200. www.palmcourtjazzcafe.com. Wed–Sun 7–11pm. Cover $5 per person at tables; no cover at bar.

Preservation Hall ⚜⚜⚜ The gray, bombed-out building that looks as if it was erected just shortly after the dawn of time doesn't seem like much, but it's a mecca for traditional jazz fans and an essential spot for any visitor. It doesn't get any more authentic than this.

With no seats and constant crowds, you won't be able to see much, but you won't care because you will be having too cheerfully sweaty a time. Even if you don't consider yourself interested in jazz, there is a seriously good time to be had here, and you very probably will come away with a new appreciation for the music. Patrons start lining up at 6:15pm—the doors open at 8pm, so the trick to avoid the line is to get there either just as the doors open or later in the evening. The band plays until midnight, and the first audience usually empties out around 10pm.

A 30-year-old sign on the wall gives prices for requests, but the prices are out-of-date. As the doorwoman said, "If we still took $5 for 'Saints Go Marchin' In,' they'd be playing it all night." (One night, some big spenders tossed seven $100 bills for seven rounds of "Saints.") Try about $10, and for other requests, "just offer something."

Thanks to the casual atmosphere, not to mention cheap cover, Preservation Hall is one of the few nightspots where it's appropriate to take kids. Early in the evening, you'll notice a number of local families doing just that.

Note: At this writing, Preservation Hall is open on a limited basis. Check the website or call when making plans. 726 St. Peter St. © 888/ 946-JAZZ or 504/522-2841. www.preservationhall.com. Cover $8.

Snug Harbor ⚜⚜ If your idea of jazz extends beyond Dixieland and if you prefer a concert-type setting over a messy nightclub, get your hands on Snug Harbor's monthly schedule. On the fringes of the French Quarter, Snug Harbor is the city's premier showcase for contemporary jazz, with a few blues and R&B combos thrown in for good measure. Here, jazz is presented as it should be: part entertainment, part art, and often, part intellectual stimulation. This is the surest place to find Ellis Marsalis (patriarch of the Marsalis dynasty) and Charmaine Neville. Not only does Snug offer good music, but the two-level seating provides universally good viewing of the bandstand. *Be warned:* Waiting for a show usually means hanging in the crowded, low-ceilinged bar, where personal space is at a minimum. 626 Frenchmen St. ℂ **504/949-0696.** www.snugjazz.com. Cover $12–$20, depending on performer.

ELSEWHERE AROUND THE CITY

Vaughn's Lounge   Tucked deep in the Bywater section of New Orleans, Vaughn's Lounge is way down home. It's in a residential neighborhood and feels almost as though you're in someone's house. The long bar takes up so much room that people almost fall over the band at the end of the room. Thursday—Kermit Ruffins' night—is the night to go to Vaughn's. Go early and get some of the barbecue Kermit is usually cooking up before a show—he tends to bring his grill along with him wherever he is playing. Or you might catch a Mardi Gras Indian practice. Be sure to call ahead to see if there will be live music on a given night, and be sure to take a taxi. 4229 Dauphine St. ℂ **504/947-5562.** Cover varies.

2 Cajun & Zydeco Joints

Mid City Lanes Rock 'n' Bowl ⭐⭐⭐   Anything we've said about tourist traps and inauthentic experiences does not apply here. It does not get any more authentic than a club set in the middle of a bowling alley, which is itself set in the middle of a strip mall. Actually, as a bowling alley, Mid City bowling is nothing to write home about unless you like lanes that slope. But as a club, it's one of the finest experiences in New Orleans. Certainly it's the best place for zydeco, particularly on the nights devoted to Zydeco Wars. It also features top New Orleans rock and R&B groups. On good nights (though we do wonder if Mid City has any that aren't), the dance floor is crowded beyond belief, the noise level is ridiculous, the humidity level is 300%, and you won't want to leave. You might even bowl a few frames.

Having said all of that, the ground floors of the aforementioned strip mall flooded badly post-Katrina, and while the hope is that whatever work is needed does not affect Rock n' Bowl, you should probably call in advance to make sure the status quo remains. 4133 S. Carrollton Ave. ℂ **504/482-3133.** www.rockandbowl.com. Bowling: daytime and evening $15 per hour; show admission $5–$10.

Mulate's ⭐   A branch of the original (out in Cajun Country) and a not-unlikely place to find authentic, and decent, Cajun bands.

The stage and dance area are relatively spacious, and the food isn't bad. 201 Julia St., at Convention Center Blvd. ✆ **800/854-9149** or 504/522-1492. www.mulates.com.

3 Rhythm, Rock & the Rest of the Music Scene

Most clubs in New Orleans feature an eclectic lineup that reflects the town's music scene; the ReBirth Brass Band, for example, attracts as many rock fans as it does brass band fans. Consequently, the bulk of the club scene escapes categorization (and, of course, booking policies are often subject to change)—even the local papers refer to club lineups as "mixed bags." Check listings night by night. Some places are generally good fun on their own regardless of who is playing; any night at the **Maple Leaf** is going to be a good one, while wandering from spot to spot in the Frenchmen section is a well-spent evening. Really, in New Orleans, you can't go too wrong going just about anywhere simply to hang out. And in the process, you might be exposed to a new, wonderful genre of music or an incredible band.

THE FRENCH QUARTER & THE FAUBOURG MARIGNY

Blue Nile ✿ Having sustained a huge amount of damage to their building, this fine little club has managed to rig the place up so that they can have acts downstairs before closing again for necessary massive renovations. Look for weekend gigs and watch for a grand reopening in October 2006 or so. For the few weeks it's open, and especially when it comes back this club should be a part of your Frenchmen Street hopping, as they book a variety of acts, everything from rock to jazz to world, plus regular salsa dancing nights, and Latin jazz, both local (look for Kermit Ruffins and Henry Butler) and out of town. 532 Frenchmen St. ✆ **504/948-2583.** Cover varies.

Cafe Brasil ✿ Day (when it is a great place to get a cup of coffee) or night (when it delivers danceable music), Cafe Brasil is the center of the increasingly lively and popular Frenchmen section of the Faubourg Marigny. It features Latin or Caribbean music, R&B, or jazz almost every night, and chances are whatever is playing will be infectious. Anticipate a hip and trendy, though still casual, crowd and be prepared to act cool. The decent-size dance floor fills up quickly, and the crowd spills into the street to see and be seen. 2100 Chartres St. ✆ **504/949-0851** (temporarily disconnected). Cover varies according to performer.

Checkpoint Charlie's   Somewhere between a biker bar and a college hangout, the dark Checkpoint Charlie's only *seems* intimidating—an effect that's helped by the hard rock sounds usually blaring from the stage. It's easy to overlook straight rock with all the other New Orleans sounds around, but this would be the place to start trying to find it. R&B and blues sneak into the mix as well. A full bar, food, and pool tables help soften the ambience for the easily intimidated, and it's open 24 hours, making it a less touristy place for a quick drink during the day. Plus, there's a coin laundry, so a dusty traveler can clean up while enjoying the music. And right across the street is a fire station known for its hunky firemen, who on sultry nights sit outside and admire the views. Admire them right back. 501 Esplanade Ave. ☎ **504/949-7012** (temporarily disconnected).

House of Blues ☎   New Orleans was a natural place for this franchise to set up shop, but its presence in the French Quarter seems rather unnatural. With all the great, funky music clubs in town, why build one with ersatz "authenticity" that wouldn't be out of place in Disneyland? And while it's noble that they've patronized many deserving Southern "primitive" artists, whose colorful works line the walls, there's a certain Hearst Castle grab-bag element to that, too, which diminishes the value and cultural context of the works.

That isn't to say the facility is without its qualities. The music room has adequate sightlines and good sound, and the chain's financial muscle assures first-rate bookings, from the Neville Brothers to Los Lobos. But patronizing this club rather than the real thing, like Tipitina's (which lost considerable business after the HoB opened), is akin to eating at McDonald's rather than Mother's. Having said all of that, a smaller room, the **House of Blues Parish,** features both local and national acts, and on any given day, probably offers more (for a cheaper price) than the big room. 225 Decatur St. ☎ **504/310-4999.** www.hob.com. Cover varies.

The Spotted Cat Cocktail Lounge ☎☎☎   Right now, this is our favorite live-music venue in New Orleans, but that's because of our particular New Orleans aesthetic bent; we are partial to tiny, sometimes candle-specked rooms where the band plays without much (if any) amplification, and what they play is usually fresh takes on classic big-band jazz. This is *the* place on Frenchmen to go for late-night canoodling or an otherwise intimate evening, with chocolate martinis and local acts playing nightly. Traditional jazz is regularly featured, and on Monday and Friday, you'll find us hanging around the doorway, listening to the New Orleans Jazz Vipers. 623 Frenchmen St. © 504/943-3887 (temporarily disconnected).

ELSEWHERE AROUND THE CITY

Throughout this book, we keep nagging you to leave the Quarter, especially at night. It's not that there aren't worthwhile clubs in the Quarter or at the fringes. It's just that there are so many terrific (and, in some cases, outright better) ones elsewhere. And not only do they feature some of the best music in town, they aren't designed as tourist destinations, so your experience will be that much more legitimate.

Carrollton Station 🐦🐦   A long, narrow space means that folks at the back won't get to see much of what's up onstage, but hey, that puts them closer to the bar, so everyone wins. Way uptown in the Riverbend area, Carrollton Station is a gourmet beer house that, thanks to some renovations to the room and the stage, is a prime folk, acoustic, and local rock venue, if one with lousy sightlines. The crowd is a good mix of college students, music aficionados, and fans of whatever act is appearing on a given night. 8140 Willow St. © 504/865-9190. www.carrolltonstation.com. Cover varies.

The Howlin' Wolf 🐦🐦🐦   This is arguably the premier club in town in terms of the quality and fame of its bookings, especially since an October 2005 move down the block and across the street has put it into an even better space. The move was in the works last summer, and given that the building next to their old one collapsed, the timing worked out in their favor. And with 10,000 square feet (quite a bit more than they used to have), including more bathrooms, a wide but shallow room (which means great sightlines from about anywhere; sightlines are a problem in most New Orleans clubs), a bar that came from Al Capone's hotel in Chicago, and bookings that range from top local acts to national touring rock bands, it's probably the best place right now locally to see a show. In addition to regular bookings, they are currently doing a lot of nonprofit work, allowing anyone who needs the space for benefits to use it free, and have raised a lot of money for various charitable organizations. 907 S. Peters St., in the Warehouse District. © 504/522-WOLF. www.howlin-wolf.com. Cover varies, though some shows are free.

Maple Leaf Bar 🐦🐦🐦   This is what a New Orleans club is all about, and its reputation was only furthered when it became the very first live music venue to reopen, just weeks after Katrina, with an emotional, generator-powered performance by Walter "Wolfman"

Washington. It's medium-size but feels smaller when a crowd is packed in. And by 11pm on most nights, it is, with personal space at times becoming something you can only wistfully remember. But that's no problem. The stage is against the window facing the street, so more often than not, the crowd spills onto the sidewalk and into the street to dance and drink (and escape the heat and sweat, which are prodigious despite a high ceiling). You can hear the music just as well and then dance some more. With a party atmosphere like this, outside is almost more fun than in. A good bar and a rather pretty patio make the Maple Leaf worth hanging out at even if you don't care about the music on a particular night. But if the ReBirth Brass Band is playing do not miss it; go and dance till you drop. 8316 Oak St. ℂ 504/866-9359. Cover varies, depending on day of week and performer.

Republic New Orleans   Taking over the old Howlin' Wolf location (nice space over all; bad sightlines, though), this new combo dance club and live music venue (music provided by the usual local suspects) is currently promoting regular smoke-free concerts, the only such venture in the city. 828 South Peters. ℂ 504/528-8282.

Tipitina's ✹✹✹   Dedicated to the late piano master Professor Longhair, Tip's was long *the* New Orleans club. But due to circumstances both external (increased competition from House of Blues and others as well as the club's capacity being cut in half by city authorities) and internal (locals say the bookings have not been up to snuff for some time), its star has faded considerably. It remains a reliable place for top local bands, though. Bookings range from top indigenous acts (a brass-bands blowout is a perennial highlight of Jazz Fest week) to touring alt-rock and roots acts, both U.S.-based and international. The place is nothing fancy—just four walls, a wraparound balcony, and a stage. Oh, and a couple of bars, of course, including one that serves people milling outside the club, which is as much a part of the atmosphere as what's inside. They also have two other rooms; Tips French Quarter and the Ruins at this point are only being used for special events. 501 Napoleon Ave., Uptown. ℂ 504/895-8477 or 504/897-3943 for concert line. www.tipitinas.com. Cover varies.

4 The Bar Scene

You won't have any trouble finding a place to drink in New Orleans. Heck, thanks to "go" (or *"geaux"*) cups, you won't have to spend a minute without a drink in your hand. (It's legal to have liquor outside as long as it's in a plastic cup. Actually, given the number of people who take advantage of this law, it almost seems illegal *not* to have such a cup in your hand.) Note that many of the clubs listed above are terrific spots to hoist a few (or a dozen), while some of the bars below also provide music—but that is strictly background for their real design. Piano bars, in particular, have begun to pop up; they're everywhere; in addition to the ones listed below, you can find a piano bar in almost every large hotel.

Many bars stay open all the time or have varying hours depending upon the night or the season. If you have your heart set on a particular place, it's always best to call and make sure what their hours will be for that day. Unless noted, none of the places listed below has a cover charge.

THE FRENCH QUARTER & THE FAUBOURG MARIGNY

In addition to the places below, you might consider the clubby bar at **Dickie Brennan's Steakhouse,** once it reopens, at 716 Iberville St. (© **504/522-2467**), a place where manly men go to drink strong drinks, smoke smelly cigars (they have a vast selection for sale), and chat up girlie girls. Or you could enjoy the low-key sophistication found at **Beque's at the Royal Sonesta,** 300 Bourbon St. (© **504/586-0300**), where a jazz trio is usually playing.

The Abbey   Despite the name, this place is more basement rumpus room (walls covered with stickers and old album covers) than Gothic church (well, there are some motley stained-glass windows). But the jukebox plays The Cramps and Iggy Pop, and the clientele is very David Lynchian (maybe still left over from the place's heyday 15 years ago!). Still, you might find this a scary dump rather than a cool dump. 1123 Decatur St. © **504/523-7150** (temporarily disconnected).

Apple Barrel   A small, dusty, wooden-floored watering hole complete with jukebox and darts (of course). You can find refuge here from the hectic Frenchmen scene (catch your breath and have a beer)—or gear up to join in. 609 Frenchmen St. © **504/949-9399.**

The Bombay Club   This posh piano bar features jazz Wednesday through Saturday evenings. It's also a restaurant (the food is not great) and a martini bar—the drink has been a specialty here for years, so don't accuse the club of trying to ride the current martini trend. In fact, the Bombay's martinis are hailed as the best in town. The bar bills itself as casually elegant—a polite way of saying don't wear jeans and shorts. 830 Conti St. © **800/699-7711** or 504/586-0972. www.thebombayclub.com. Tues–Sun.

Carousel Bar & Lounge ✿✿   There is piano music here Tuesdays through Saturdays, but the real attraction is the bar itself—it really is a carousel, and it really does revolve. The music goes on until 2am, and who knows if the carousel ever stops revolving. It's really a great spot to step back in time and have a cocktail. In the Monteleone Hotel, 214 Royale St. ✆ **504/523-3341.**

Feelings Cafe ✿   Here's a funky, low-key neighborhood restaurant and hangout set around a classic New Orleans courtyard, which is where most folks drink. It's authentic in the right ways but is also more cheerful than some of the darker, hole-in-the-wall spots that deserve that adjective. A bit out of the way in the Faubourg Marigny, but everyone who goes comes back raving about it. 2600 Chartres St. ✆ **504/945-2222.** www.feelingscafe.com.

French 75 Bar ✿✿   A beautiful bar space in one of the Quarter's most venerable restaurants, it feels like drinking in New Orleans should, in terms of classy presentation and atmosphere. Any dedicated cocktailian should come by to test the bartenders on their knowledge or to experiment with curious beverages. 813 Bienville St. ✆ **504/523-5433.**

Hard Rock Cafe *(Overrated)*   Gag. This prefab commercial horror is particularly offensive in New Orleans, where there is real music to be had at every turn. It bemuses us to see tourists lined up outside this place when original experiences—as opposed to assembly-line experiences—are just feet away. Better burgers and better beer are to be found elsewhere as well. 418 N. Peters St. ✆ **504/529-5617.** www.hardrock.com.

Kerry Irish Pub ✿   This traditional Irish pub has a variety of beers and other spirits but is most proud of its properly poured pints of Guinness and hard cider. The pub is a good bet for live Irish and "alternative" folk music; it's also a place to throw darts and shoot pool. In case you want one last nightcap on your way back through the Quarter, you should know that Kerry specializes in very-late-night drinking. 331 Decatur St. ✆ **504/286-5862.** www.kerryirishpub.com.

Lafitte's Blacksmith Shop ✿✿✿   It's some steps away from the main action on Bourbon, but you'll know Lafitte's when you see it. Dating from the 1770s, it's the oldest building in the Quarter—possibly in the Mississippi Valley—and it looks it (though we all could have done without that really bad exterior remodel job that made fake what had been authentic exposed brick and plaster). In other towns, this would be a tourist trap. Here, it feels authentic—definitely worth swinging by even if you don't drink. 941 Bourbon St. ✆ 504/522-9377.

Napoleon House Bar & Café ✿✿✿   Set in a landmark building, the Napoleon House is just the place to go to have a quiet drink (as opposed to the very loud drinks found elsewhere in the Quarter) and maybe hatch some schemes. Like Lafitte's (see above), it's dark, dark, dark, with walls you really wish could talk. Also like Lafitte's, it seems too perfect to be real—surely this must be constructed just for the tourists. It's not. Even locals like it here. 500 Chartres St. ✆ 504/524-9752. www.napoleonhouse.com.

New Orleans Grapevine Wine Bar & Bistro ✿✿   Now that *Sideways* has shown us all what a great big metaphor for life wine can be, come sample the possibilities off the staggering list at this quiet little refuge. Take note of their special menu of seasonal tasties and consider making a meal of it, too. 720 Orleans Ave. ✆ 504/523-1930.

Pat O'Brien's   Pat O'Brien's is world famous for the gigantic, rum-based drink with the big-wind name. The formula (according to legend) was stumbled upon by bar owners Charlie Cantrell and George Oechsner while they were experimenting with Caribbean rum during World War II. The drink is served in signature 29-ounce hurricane lamp-style glasses. The bar now offers a 3-gallon Magnum Hurricane that stands taller than many small children. It's served with a handful of straws and takes a group to finish (we profoundly hope)—all of whom must drink standing up. Naturally, the offerings and reputation attract the tourists and college yahoos in droves. Which is not to say that Pat's isn't worth a stop—it's a reliable, rowdy, friendly introduction to New Orleans. Just don't expect to be the only person who thinks so. Fortunately, it's large enough to accommodate nearly everyone—in three different bars, including a large lounge that usually offers entertainment—with the highlight, on non-rainy days at least, being the attractive tropical patio.

There's no minimum and no cover, but if you buy a drink and it comes in a glass, you'll be paying for the glass until you turn it in at the register for a $3 refund. 718 St. Peter St. ✆ 504/525-4823. www.pat obriens.com.

The R Bar and Royal Street Inn ✿✿✿   The R (short for Royal St.) Bar is a little taste of New York's East Village in the Faubourg Marigny. It is a quintessential neighborhood bar in a neighborhood full of artists, wannabe artists, punk rock intellectuals, urban gentrifiers, and well-rounded hipsters. It's a talkers' bar (crowds tend to

gather in layers along the bar) and a haven for strutting, overconfi-
dent pool players. On certain nights, you can get a haircut and a
drink for $10. Sometimes the cuts aren't bad, depending on how
much the gal wielding the scissors has had to drink. The R Bar has
one of the best alternative and art-rock jukeboxes in the city. You'll
see a sign behind the bar for The Royal Street Inn, otherwise known
as the R Bar Inn, a B&B (bed-and-beverage, that is). If you like the
bar, you'll probably love the accommodations, too (p. 57). 1431 Royal
St. ✆ 504/948-7499. www.royalstreetinn.com.

Saturn Bar ✿   Sometimes the victims of Katrina were not obvious, and the crusty curmudgeon owner of this most beloved dive
was one of them. The family says his heart just gave out, and there
is much to be read in that. We aren't sure what this will mean for the
bar or the hipster set who love it, but for now, the family is keeping
it open. If it stays that way (as we hope), come join the genuine
barflies and slumming celebs passed out in the crumbling (and we
mean it) booths, or blending in with the pack-rat collection that
passes as decor. It's hard to decide if the devotion to this place is genuine or comes from a postmodern, ironic appreciation of the
grubby, art-project (we can only hope) interior—it must be seen to
be believed. After all, if it changes now, will we regret ever com-
plaining about it? 3067 St. Claude Ave., in the Faubourg Marigny. ✆ 504/949-
7532 (temporarily disconnected).

ELSEWHERE AROUND THE CITY

In addition to those listed below, hang with the local beautiful people at any of the following: **Loa,** the bar at the International House
hotel, 221 Camp St., in the Central Business District (for more
information on this hotel, see p. 65) is a hip and happening hangout. Hot on its heels for hipness and with a slightly higher energy
level is the bar at **Loft 523,** a gorgeous space that beautifully shows
off the old timbers that hold up this former warehouse; for information on the hotel, see p. 62. **Ray's Over the River,** 2 Canal Place
(in the World Trade Center; ✆ 504/595-8900), doesn't have the
views one would hope from the name, but it might be the number-
one pickup spot in town.

Circle Bar ✿✿   This tiny bar is among the most bohemian-hip in
town, courtesy of the slightly twisted folks behind Snake & Jake's.
Ambience is the key; it's got the ever-popular "elegant decay" look,
from peeling wallpaper to a neon glow from an old K&B drugstore
sign on the ceiling. The jukebox keeps the quirky romantic mood
going, thanks to bewitching, mood-enhancing selections from the

Velvet Underground, Dusty Springfield, and Curtis Mayfield. The clientele is real and real laid-back. Live music includes mostly local acts such as the sarcastically depressed Glyn Styler. Bet you'll see us there. 1032 St. Charles Ave., in the CBD at Lee Circle. ✆ **504/588-2616**. www. circlebar.net.

The Columns ✸✸   Here's a local favorite for drinks on the white-columned porch under spreading oak trees. Why? Well, aside from the Old South setting, beers at happy hour are a measly $2, and mixed drinks are not much more. But stay on the patio, or be engulfed in cigarette smoke in the dark interior bar. 3811 St. Charles Ave., Uptown. ✆ **504/899-9308**.

Kingpin ✸✸   For those who want that *Barfly* experience without the smelly drunks and in the company of other like-minded folks of a certain (20-something) age. Nominally Elvis-themed (though expect bashes on key dates in the timeline of Himself), this absurdly small space is increasingly popular among hipster/rocker/Dave Navarro types, when they can find it, that is. (**Hint:** It's near the Upperline restaurant.) 1307 Lyons St., Uptown. ✆ **504/891-2373**.

Pals Lounge ✸✸   Well-heeled backers (including Rio Hackford, son of director Taylor) have turned this former corner neighborhood joint into a hipster bar, upping the age and economic demographic considerably. Now you have vintage barflies mingling with the neighborhood bohos who come with their dogs or riding their bikes. It's too smoky for some, and it can be hard to find a seat. Then again, manicures are offered on Thursdays, and the place still flies below the tourist radar. It won't stay that way once word gets out that Jude Law and Sean Penn went here to drink while in town shooting *All the King's Men.* 949 N. Rendon St., St. John's Bayou. ✆ **504/488-PALS**.

The Polo Lounge ✸✸   The Windsor Court is, without a doubt, the city's finest hotel (p. 64), and The Polo Lounge is the place to go if you're feeling particularly stylish. Sazeracs and cigars are popular here. Don't expect to find any kids; if you like to seal your deals with a drink, this is likely to be your first choice. In the Windsor Court Hotel, 300 Gravier St., in the CBD. ✆ **504/523-6000**.

Snake & Jake's Christmas Club Lounge ✸✸   Though admittedly off the beaten path, this tiny, friendly dive is the perfect place for those looking for an authentic neighborhood bar. Co-owned by local musician Dave Clements, decorated (sort of) with Christmas lights, and featuring a great jukebox heavy on soul and R&B, this is the kind of place where everybody not only knows your name, they know your dog's name 'cause you can bring the dog, too. There is almost no light at all, so make friends and prepare to be surprised. Naturally, Snake & Jake's can get really hot, crowded, and sweaty— if you're lucky. *Gambit* readers voted Jose, the bartender, the best in the city. 7612 Oak St., Uptown. ℂ 504/861-2802. www.snakeandjakes.com.

5 Gay Nightlife

For more information, check **Ambush,** 828-A Bourbon St. (ℂ **504/ 522-8047;** www.ambushmag.com), a great source for the gay community in New Orleans and for visitors. The magazine's website has a lot of handy-dandy links to other sites of gay interest, including info on local gay bars. Once you're in New Orleans, you can call the office or pick up a copy at Tower Records, 408 N. Peters St., in the French Quarter, or at Lenny's News, 5420 Magazine St., Uptown.

BARS

In addition to those listed below, you might try the **Golden Lantern,** 1239 Royal St. (ℂ 504/529-2860), a nice neighborhood spot where the bartender knows the patrons by name. It's the second-oldest gay bar in town, and one longtime patron said that "it used to look like one half of Noah's Ark—with one of everything, one drag queen, one leather boy, one guy in a suit." If Levi's and leather is your scene, the **Rawhide 2010,** 740 Burgundy St. (ℂ **504/525-8106;** www.rawhide2010.com), is your best bet; during Mardi Gras, it hosts a great gay costume contest that's not to be missed. The rest of the year, it's a hustler bar. Both of these places are in the Quarter, as are the establishments listed below. There is no cover unless noted.

The Bourbon Pub Parade   This is more or less the most centrally located of the gay bars, with many of the other popular gay bars nearby. The downstairs pub offers a video bar (often featuring surprisingly cutting edge, innovative stuff) and is the calmer of the two; it's open 24 hours daily and usually gets most crowded in the hour just before the Parade Disco opens. (*Note:* A $5 cover charge gets you all the draft beer you can drink from 5–9pm.) The Parade Disco is upstairs and features a high-tech dance floor complete with lasers and smoke. Consistently voted by several sources as a top dance club (in all of America), it usually opens around 9pm except on Sunday, when it gets going in the afternoon. 801 Bourbon St. ℂ 504/529-2107. www.bourbonpub.com.

Café Lafitte in Exile It's one of the oldest gay bars in the United States, having been around since 1953. There's a bar downstairs, and upstairs you'll find a pool table and a balcony that overlooks Bourbon Street. The whole shebang is open 24 hours daily. This is a cruise bar, but it doesn't attract a teeny-bopper or twinkie crowd. One of the most popular weekly events is the Sunday evening "Trash Disco," when, you guessed it, they play trashy disco music from the '70s and everyone has a lot of fun. 901 Bourbon St. ℂ 504/522-8397. www.lafittes.com.

The Corner Pocket While the boast that they have the hottest male strippers in town may be perhaps too generous, you can decide for yourself by checking out this bar Thursday through Sunday nights after 10pm. Locals who aren't a bit ashamed of themselves claim the cutest boys can be found on Friday nights, and sigh that the management has the strippers wear the sort of garments that prevent peeking (not that that prevents anyone from trying). The bar itself is none too special (and despite the name, the only draw for the pool table is that players might not be especially clothed), with the average age of the clientele around 70. 940 St. Louis St. ℂ 504/568-9829. www.cornerpocket.net.

CowPokes Looking for a gay country bar? Never let it be said that Frommer's lets you down. This is a particularly nice gay country bar, though it resides in a transitional neighborhood, so do let a cab bring you out for some of the weekly activities, including free line-dance lessons on Tuesdays and Thursdays and karaoke on Wednesdays. 2240 St. Claude. Ave. ℂ 504/947-0505. www.cowpokesno.com.

Good Friends Bar & Queen's Head Pub This bar and pub is very friendly to visitors and often wins the Gay Achievement Award for Best Neighborhood Gay Bar. They describe themselves as "always snappy casual!" The local clientele is happy to offer suggestions about where you might find the type of entertainment you're looking for. Downstairs is a mahogany bar and a pool table. Upstairs is the quiet Queens Head Pub, which was recently decorated in the style of a Victorian English pub. The bar is open 24 hours. 740 Dauphine St. ℂ 504/566-7191. www.goodfriendsbar.com.

LeRoundup LeRoundup attracts the most diverse crowd around. You'll find transsexuals lining up at the bar with drag queens and well-groomed men in khakis and Levi's. Expect encounters with working boys. It's open 24 hours. 819 St. Louis St. ℂ 504/561-8340.

DANCE CLUBS

Oz Oz is the place to see and be seen, with a primarily young crowd (like its across-the-street neighbor, The Bourbon Pub Parade; see above). It was ranked the city's best dance club by *Gambit* magazine, and *Details* magazine named it one of the top 50 clubs in the country. The music is great, there's an incredible laser-light show, and from time to time there are go-go boys atop the bar. Oz hosts frequent theme nights, so call ahead if you're going and want to dress accordingly. 800 Bourbon St. ✆ **504/593-9491.** www.ozneworleans. com. Cover varies; straights pay extra.

6 Will They Reopen?

Lion's Den ✵ A true neighborhood dive, but it's well worth stopping by should Thomas be in residence. If you're lucky, she's even cooking up some red beans and rice. Thomas has only one hit to her credit ("Wish Somebody Would Care"), but she's still a great, sassy live R&B and soul act with a devoted following, who can never get enough of "You Can Have My Husband, But Please Don't Mess with My Man" and other delights.

This beloved location is, at this writing, flooded and closed, but Miss Irma Thomas remains committed to the city, and she surely will be back, though most likely in another location. Call ahead to see. 2655 Gravier St., at N. Broad Ave. in Mid-City. ✆ **504/821-3745.**

Mother-in-Law Lounge ✵ Ernie K-Doe may be gone, but this shrine to his glorious self and funky lounges everywhere lives on, thanks to wife, Antoinette, the keeper of the K-Doe legend and the bar's owner. Named after his biggest hit, a rousing 1961 number-one pop/R&B novelty, this is a true neighborhood dive bar, weird and wonderful, distinguished by the K-Doe memorabilia that lines the walls. Antoinette (a total kick with one heck of a hurricane story to tell) makes perhaps the best gumbo we have ever had, and if you are lucky, she will be serving it when you come by. K-Doe himself, in the form of a startlingly lifelike mannequin, which has become a celebrity of sorts around town, still holds court. You may want to be careful in the neighborhood, but once you're there, be sure to play one of K-Doe's songs on the jukebox and drink a toast to the man who billed himself as "Emperor of the Universe."

The Mother-in-Law Lounge is closed due to damage from flooding, but plans to reopen. Hopefully, it will have done so by the time you read this. 1500 N. Claiborne Ave., northeast of the Quarter. ✆ **504/947-1078.** www.kdoe.com.

Sazerac Bar & Grill ✿   In the posh Fairmont Hotel, the renovated Sazerac Bar is frequented by the city's young professionals and
was featured in the movie *The Pelican Brief.* The African walnut bar
and murals by Paul Ninas complete the upscale atmosphere. Here is
where you should try the famous Sazerac cocktail (a multilayered
combination of rye whiskey, bitters, sugar, herbsaint, and a hint of
lemon oil), not because they make it the best (that award probably
goes to **Bayona,** p. 85) but because you are here. But do tell the bartender to make it from scratch, not from a pre-mix.

The Sazerac Bar plans to reopen at the same time as the Fairmont
New Orleans (p. 77), between September and November 2006. In the
Fairmont Hotel, University Place, in the CBD. 123 Baronne St. ✆ 504/529-7111.
www.fairmont.com.

Index

See also Accommodations and Restaurant indexes below.

Restaurants